STECK-VAUGHN

Math Skills for the Workforce

FRACTIONS

Author

Karen Lassiter
Austin Community College
Austin, Texas

Consultants

Connie Eichhorn
Omaha Public Schools
Omaha, Nebraska

M. Gail Joiner Ward
Swainsboro Technical Institute
Swainsboro, Georgia

STECK-VAUGHN
COMPANY
ELEMENTARY · SECONDARY · ADULT · LIBRARY

About the Author

Dr. Karen Lassiter is currently a mathematics instructor at Austin Community College. She is a former Senior Math Editor for Steck-Vaughn Company, and has done extensive work with standardized test preparation. Dr. Lassiter holds a Ph.D. in Educational Research, Testing, and Instructional Design and a bachelor's degree in mathematics and science education from Florida State University.

About the Consultants

Connie Eichhorn is a supervisor of adult education programs in the Omaha Public Schools. A former mathematics teacher and ABE/GED instructor, she earned an undergraduate degree in math at Iowa State University and is completing a doctoral program in adult education at the University of Nebraska. She conducts workshops on math instruction for teachers of adult basic education.

M. Gail Joiner Ward is presently working at Swainsboro Technical Institute as an adult education instructor. Previously she worked with adult learners in a multimedia lab through the School of Education at Georgia Southern University. She has bachelor's and master's degrees in art and early childhood education from Valdosta State College and Georgia Southern University.

Staff Credits

Executive Editor:	Ellen Northcutt
Assistant Art Director:	Richard Balsam
Design Manager:	Pamela Heaney
Illustration Credits:	Cindy Aarvig, Richard Balsam, Tami Crabb, Kristian Gallagher, David Griffin, Alan Klemp, Mike Krone
Photo Credits:	Cover: Reagan Bradshaw p. 9 © Tony Freeman/PhotoEdit; p. 39 ©Tony Freeman/PhotoEdit; p. 73 © Ellis Herwig/Stock Boston; p. 107 ©Park Street; p. 127 ©Richard Hutchings/Photo Researchers; p. 145 ©Park Street.
Cover Design:	Bazzirk Inc.
Photo Editor:	Margie Foster

ISBN 0-8172-6376-4

Copyright © 1997 Steck-Vaughn Company

Printed in the United States of America.
13 14 15 16 17 18 19 0956 15 14 13 12 11 10
4500238201

Contents

Unit 4

MULTIPLYING FRACTIONS

Unit 5

DIVIDING FRACTIONS

Unit 6

PUTTING YOUR SKILLS TO WORK

TO THE LEARNER

The four books in the Steck-Vaughn series *Math Skills for the Workforce* are *Whole Numbers; Fractions; Decimals and Percents;* and *Measurement, Geometry, and Algebra.* They are written to help you understand and practice arithmetic skills, real-life applications, and problem-solving techniques.

This book contains features which will make it easier for you to work with fractions and to apply them to your daily life.

A Skills Inventory test appears at the beginning and end of the book.
•The first test shows you how much you already know.
•The final test can show you how much you have learned.

Each unit has several Mixed Reviews and a Unit Review.
•The Mixed Reviews give you a chance to practice the skills you have learned.
•The Unit Review helps you decide if you have mastered those skills.

There is also a glossary at the end of the book.
•Turn to the glossary to find the meanings of words that are new to you.
•Use the definitions and examples to help strengthen your understanding of terms used in mathematics.

The book contains answers and explanations for the problems.
•The answers let you check your work.
•The explanations take you through the steps used to solve the problems.

Fractions Skills Inventory

Reduce to lowest terms. If the fraction is in lowest terms, write LT.

1. $\dfrac{4}{8} =$

2. $\dfrac{9}{12} =$

3. $\dfrac{4}{15} =$

4. $\dfrac{10}{30} =$

5. $\dfrac{32}{48} =$

Raise to higher terms with the given denominator.

6. $\dfrac{1}{3} = \dfrac{}{9}$

7. $\dfrac{2}{5} = \dfrac{}{10}$

8. $\dfrac{3}{7} = \dfrac{}{21}$

9. $\dfrac{7}{10} = \dfrac{}{30}$

10. $\dfrac{4}{9} = \dfrac{}{36}$

Change to a whole or mixed number.

11. $\dfrac{4}{3} =$

12. $\dfrac{8}{2} =$

13. $\dfrac{12}{5} =$

14. $\dfrac{3}{1} =$

15. $\dfrac{18}{10} =$

Change to an improper fraction.

16. $5\dfrac{3}{4} =$

17. $2\dfrac{1}{2} =$

18. $4\dfrac{2}{3} =$

19. $7\dfrac{4}{5} =$

20. $9\dfrac{7}{10} =$

Add. Reduce if possible.

21. $\dfrac{1}{5} + \dfrac{2}{5} =$

22. $\dfrac{3}{8} + \dfrac{3}{8} =$

23. $\dfrac{9}{10} + \dfrac{7}{10} =$

24. $\dfrac{3}{7} + \dfrac{2}{7} + \dfrac{2}{7} =$

25. $\begin{array}{r} 4\dfrac{2}{9} \\ + 3\dfrac{3}{9} \\ \hline \end{array}$

26. $\begin{array}{r} 2\dfrac{5}{12} \\ + 7\dfrac{1}{12} \\ \hline \end{array}$

27. $\begin{array}{r} 1\dfrac{5}{6} \\ + 6\dfrac{5}{6} \\ \hline \end{array}$

28. $\begin{array}{r} \dfrac{3}{10} \\ + 9\dfrac{7}{10} \\ \hline \end{array}$

29. $\begin{array}{r} 10\dfrac{11}{15} \\ + 5 \\ \hline \end{array}$

30. $\begin{array}{r} \dfrac{1}{2} \\ + \dfrac{3}{4} \\ \hline \end{array}$

31. $\begin{array}{r} \dfrac{2}{3} \\ + \dfrac{4}{7} \\ \hline \end{array}$

32. $\begin{array}{r} \dfrac{5}{9} \\ + \dfrac{5}{27} \\ \hline \end{array}$

33. $\begin{array}{r} \dfrac{3}{8} \\ + \dfrac{1}{6} \\ \hline \end{array}$

34. $\begin{array}{r} \dfrac{4}{5} \\ + \dfrac{3}{4} \\ \hline \end{array}$

Add. Reduce if possible.

35.

$$2\frac{3}{7}$$
$$+\,1\frac{1}{6}$$

36.

$$5$$
$$+\,8\frac{1}{2}$$

37.

$$9\frac{2}{3}$$
$$+\,6\frac{7}{15}$$

38.

$$10\frac{9}{11}$$
$$+\quad\frac{4}{22}$$

39.

$$4\frac{9}{10}$$
$$+\,2\frac{5}{6}$$

Subtract. Reduce if possible.

40. $\dfrac{4}{5} - \dfrac{2}{5} =$

41. $\dfrac{8}{9} - \dfrac{2}{9} =$

42. $\dfrac{2}{3} - \dfrac{2}{3} =$

43. $\dfrac{7}{8} - \dfrac{3}{8} =$

44.

$$10\frac{7}{11}$$
$$-\,3\frac{5}{11}$$

45.

$$8\frac{9}{10}$$
$$-\quad\frac{7}{10}$$

46.

$$6\frac{5}{6}$$
$$-\,5\frac{1}{6}$$

47.

$$9\frac{11}{12}$$
$$-\quad\frac{3}{12}$$

48.

$$15\frac{17}{25}$$
$$-\quad 8$$

49.

$$1$$
$$-\quad\frac{3}{5}$$

50.

$$4$$
$$-\quad\frac{7}{8}$$

51.

$$7\frac{1}{3}$$
$$-\quad\frac{2}{3}$$

52.

$$9\frac{2}{7}$$
$$-\,8\frac{5}{7}$$

53.

$$1\frac{4}{9}$$
$$-\quad\frac{8}{9}$$

54.

$$\frac{3}{4}$$
$$-\,\frac{1}{2}$$

55.

$$\frac{7}{10}$$
$$-\,\frac{3}{5}$$

56.

$$\frac{7}{8}$$
$$-\,\frac{7}{12}$$

57.

$$\frac{1}{3}$$
$$-\,\frac{1}{4}$$

58.

$$\frac{5}{6}$$
$$-\,\frac{4}{7}$$

59.

$$8\frac{2}{3}$$
$$-\,6\frac{1}{6}$$

60.

$$5\frac{1}{4}$$
$$-\quad\frac{3}{5}$$

61.

$$3\frac{5}{12}$$
$$-\,2\frac{7}{10}$$

62.

$$1\frac{2}{9}$$
$$-\quad\frac{11}{18}$$

Multiply. Reduce if possible.

63.
$\dfrac{1}{2} \times \dfrac{2}{3} =$

64.
$\dfrac{3}{8} \times \dfrac{4}{9} =$

65.
$\dfrac{5}{6} \times \dfrac{3}{4} =$

66.
$\dfrac{2}{3} \times \dfrac{1}{4} \times \dfrac{3}{5} =$

67.
$\dfrac{2}{9} \times 3 =$

68.
$5 \times \dfrac{3}{10} =$

69.
$8\dfrac{1}{2} \times 4 =$

70.
$7 \times 3\dfrac{2}{3} =$

71.
$1\dfrac{5}{9} \times \dfrac{1}{2} =$

72.
$\dfrac{2}{3} \times 2\dfrac{2}{5} =$

73.
$5\dfrac{1}{4} \times 1\dfrac{1}{7} =$

74.
$4\dfrac{1}{6} \times 5\dfrac{4}{10} =$

Divide. Reduce if possible.

75.
$\dfrac{4}{5} \div \dfrac{3}{10} =$

76.
$\dfrac{5}{6} \div \dfrac{1}{6} =$

77.
$\dfrac{2}{3} \div \dfrac{3}{5} =$

78.
$\dfrac{7}{8} \div \dfrac{7}{16} =$

79.
$9 \div \dfrac{1}{3} =$

80.
$4 \div \dfrac{1}{4} =$

81.
$10\dfrac{1}{2} \div \dfrac{2}{6} =$

82.
$5\dfrac{1}{7} \div \dfrac{3}{7} =$

83.
$\dfrac{1}{2} \div 3 =$

84.
$\dfrac{2}{3} \div 7 =$

85.
$2\dfrac{3}{8} \div 4 =$

86.
$9\dfrac{3}{10} \div 3 =$

87.
$12\dfrac{3}{5} \div 7 =$

88.
$3\dfrac{3}{8} \div 1\dfrac{1}{8} =$

89.
$15\dfrac{5}{9} \div 5\dfrac{1}{3} =$

90.
$21\dfrac{2}{3} \div 3\dfrac{1}{2} =$

Below is a list of the problems in this Skills Inventory and the pages on which the skills are taught. If you missed any problems, turn to the pages listed and practice the skills. Then correct the problems you missed in the Skills Inventory.

Problem	Practice Page	Problem	Practice Page	Problem	Practice Page
Unit 1		*Unit 3*		*Unit 4*	
1-5	15-16	40-43	75-77	63-66	109-110, 112-115
6-10	19-20	44-48	78, 80-81	67-70	117-119
11-15	33-34	49-53	86-90	71-74	122-123
16-20	35-36	54-58	93-96	*Unit 5*	
Unit 2		59-62	100-103	75-78	129-130
21-24	41-42, 44-46			79-82	131-134
25-29	49-51			83-87	137-139
30-34	56-59, 63-65			88-90	140
35-39	67-68				

Unit 1 THE MEANING OF FRACTIONS

We use fractions to name a part of something. You may need them to find the total hours you worked, to project sales, or to fix a car.

In this unit, you will learn how to recognize, write, and compare fractions and mixed numbers.

Getting Ready

You should be familiar with the skills on this page and the next before you begin this unit. To check your answers, turn to page 163.

 To add, line up the digits. Then add, beginning with the ones column.

Add.

1.
$$23 + 47 =$$
$$\begin{array}{r} 23 \\ + 47 \\ \hline 70 \end{array}$$

2.
$$19 + 32 =$$

3.
$$153 + 9 =$$

4.
$$78 + 65 =$$

5.
$$314 + 611 =$$

6.
$$236 + 159 =$$

7.
$$97 + 423 =$$

8.
$$808 + 32 =$$

Getting Ready

To subtract a larger number from a smaller number in the same
column, rename by borrowing from the column to the left.

Subtract.

9.
$$35 - 8 =$$

$$\begin{array}{r} 35 \\ -\ 8 \\ \hline 27 \end{array}$$

10.
$$41 - 16 =$$

11.
$$63 - 28 =$$

12.
$$80 - 12 =$$

For review, see pages 66–69 in **Math Skills for the Workforce, Whole Numbers.**

 To multiply a two-digit number by a one-digit number, first
multiply by the ones digit. Carry if necessary. Then multiply
the tens.

Multiply.

13.
$$22 \times 3 =$$

$$\begin{array}{r} 22 \\ \times\ 3 \\ \hline 66 \end{array}$$

14.
$$46 \times 6 =$$

15.
$$61 \times 2 =$$

16.
$$83 \times 5 =$$

For review, see pages 89–90 in **Math Skills for the Workforce, Whole Numbers.**

 To divide, begin with the first place of the number you're dividing
into. Then work to the right. Use these steps: divide, multiply,
subtract, and bring down. If there's a remainder, write *R* and the
amount left over.

Divide.

17.
$$53 \div 4 =$$

$$\begin{array}{r} 13\ \text{R1} \\ 4\overline{)53} \\ -\underline{4} \\ 13 \\ -\underline{12} \\ 1 \end{array}$$

18.
$$38 \div 2 =$$

19.
$$29 \div 5 =$$

20.
$$42 \div 6 =$$

For review, see pages 127–131 in **Math Skills for the Workforce, Whole Numbers.**

Writing Fractions

A fraction names part of a whole or of a group. There are ten pins on a bowling alley. One bowling pin is 1 of 10, or $\frac{1}{10}$ of a group of ten bowling pins. There are twelve months in a year. One month is 1 of 12 or $\frac{1}{12}$ of a year.

Three of the four parts of the square are shaded.

fraction bar → $\dfrac{3}{4}$ ← numerator ← denominator

Use These Steps

Write a fraction for the parts that are shaded.

1. Make a fraction bar. Count the number of equal parts in the whole. This number is the denominator. Write the denominator under the fraction bar.

$\dfrac{}{8}$

2. Count the number of shaded parts. This number is the numerator. Write the numerator over the fraction bar.

$\dfrac{3}{8}$

Write the fraction for each shaded part.

1.

$\dfrac{4}{8}$

2.

3.

4.

5.

6.

7.

8.

Shade each figure to show the fraction.

9.

$\dfrac{3}{4}$

10.

$\dfrac{2}{3}$

11.

$\dfrac{1}{2}$

12.

$\dfrac{3}{5}$

Writing Fractions

You can also write fractions as words.

The circle below is divided into five equal parts. $\frac{1}{5}$ or one fifth of the circle is shaded.

Use the words in the box to help you when you write fractions.

half	third	fourth
fifth	sixth	seventh
eighth	ninth	tenth

Use These Steps

Write in words the fraction for the shaded parts.

1. Count how many equal parts the square is divided into.

   four

2. Count how many parts of the square are shaded.

   two fourths

Write in words the fraction for the shaded parts.

1.

   one half

2.

3.

4.

5.

6.

7.

8.

9.

10.

11.

12.

Writing Fractions

We use fractions in everyday situations such as measuring with a ruler.

There are 12 inches in a foot. What fraction of a foot is 9 inches?

$$\frac{9}{12}$$ ← number of parts
← parts in the whole

Use These Steps

There are 16 ounces in a pound. What fraction of a pound is 7 ounces?

1. Write the parts in the whole as the denominator.

$$\overline{16}$$

2. Write the number of parts given as the numerator.

$$\frac{7}{16}$$

Write a fraction for each of the parts described.

1. There are 12 months in a year. What fraction of a year is 3 months?

   Answer _____ $\frac{3}{12}$ _____

2. There are 36 inches in a yard. What fraction of a yard is 25 inches?

   Answer _____

3. There are 4 cups in a quart. What fraction of a quart is 1 cup?

   Answer _____

4. There are 3 feet in a yard. What fraction of a yard is 2 feet?

   Answer _____

5. There are 10 dimes in a dollar. What fraction of a dollar is 9 dimes?

   Answer _____

6. There are 60 minutes in an hour. What fraction of an hour is 42 minutes?

   Answer _____

7. There are 24 hours in a day. What fraction of a day is 17 hours?

   Answer _____

8. There are 12 eggs in a dozen. What fraction of a dozen is 12 eggs?

   Answer _____

Application

Manny's Pastry Shop sells cake by the slice. Most cakes are in the shape of a circle or a rectangle. On Saturday there were four round cakes and one rectangular cake for sale.

A   B   C   D   E

You can write a fraction for the part of each cake that is unsold or still on the plate (the shaded part). You can also write a fraction for the part of each cake that was sold (the part that isn't shaded). Together these two fractions make up the whole cake.

Example   Find the cake that was cut into 10 pieces, or tenths. Write the fraction that shows how much of the cake is still on the plate.

Cake B is cut into 10 equal parts (tenths). 6 of the 10 parts have been sold. 4 of the 10 parts are still on the plate.

$\frac{4}{10}$ of the cake is still on the plate.

Answer the following questions about the cakes.

1. Find the cake that was cut into fifths. Write the fraction that shows how much cake is left (the shaded part).

   Answer_____

2. Find the cake that was cut into eighths. Write the fraction that shows how much of the cake has been sold (the part that isn't shaded).

   Answer_____

3. Write the fraction that shows how much cake is left of the one that was cut into sixths.

   Answer_____

4. Write the fraction that shows how much cake has been sold of the one that was cut into fourths.

   Answer_____

5. Write the fraction that shows how much cake has been sold of the one that was cut into tenths.

   Answer_____

6. Write the fraction that shows how much is left of the cake that was cut into eighths.

   Answer_____

Reducing Fractions

Reducing a fraction to lowest terms means dividing both the numerator and denominator by the same number. Sometimes you may have to reduce more than once to get the fraction in lowest terms. A fraction is reduced to lowest terms when you can divide both the numerator and denominator only by 1.

$$\frac{6}{18} = \frac{6 \div 2}{18 \div 2} = \frac{3 \div 3}{9 \div 3} = \frac{1}{3} \quad \text{or} \quad \frac{6}{18} = \frac{6 \div 6}{18 \div 6} = \frac{1}{3}$$

Only 1 divides into 1 and 3 evenly. $\frac{1}{3}$ is in lowest terms.

Use These Steps

Reduce $\frac{14}{28}$ to lowest terms.

1. Find a number that divides into 14 and 28 evenly.

$$\frac{14}{28} = \frac{14 \div 2}{28 \div 2} = \frac{7}{14}$$

2. If any number other than 1 goes into 7 and 14 evenly, the number is not in lowest terms. Reduce again.

$$\frac{7}{14} = \frac{7 \div 7}{14 \div 7} = \frac{1}{2}$$

3. See if you can divide both the numerator and the denominator by a number other than 1.

$\frac{1}{2}$ is in lowest terms

Reduce each fraction to lowest terms.

1. $\frac{8}{12} =$

$$\frac{8 \div 2}{12 \div 2} = \frac{4}{6} = \frac{4 \div 2}{6 \div 2} = \frac{2}{3}$$

2. $\frac{9}{21} =$

3. $\frac{14}{20} =$

4. $\frac{18}{24} =$

5. $\frac{25}{40} =$

6. $\frac{24}{30} =$

7. $\frac{36}{48} =$

8. $\frac{20}{24} =$

9. $\frac{12}{16} =$

10. $\frac{36}{40} =$

11. $\frac{8}{10} =$

12. $\frac{12}{18} =$

13. $\frac{7}{21} =$

14. $\frac{10}{12} =$

15. $\frac{8}{16} =$

16. $\frac{15}{25} =$

17. $\frac{24}{48} =$

18. $\frac{13}{39} =$

Reducing Fractions to Lowest Terms

In some fractions, both the numerator and denominator end in zeros. When this happens, you can use a short cut to reduce the fractions. Cross out an equal number of zeros on the top and on the bottom of the fraction.

The fraction that is left may need to be reduced again. When 1 is the only number you can divide the numerator and denominator by, the fraction is reduced to lowest terms.

Use These Steps

Reduce $\frac{20}{400}$ to lowest terms.

1. Cross out the zero on the top and 1 zero on the bottom.

   $$\frac{2\cancel{0}}{40\cancel{0}}$$

2. Reduce the fraction that is left. Find a number that will divide into both 2 and 40 evenly. Try 2.

   $$\frac{2}{40} = \frac{2 \div 2}{40 \div 2} = \frac{1}{20}$$

3. See if you can divide both the numerator and the denominator by a number other than 1.

   $\frac{1}{20}$ is in lowest terms

Reduce each fraction to lowest terms. If the fraction is already in lowest terms, write LT.

1. $\frac{6\cancel{0}}{10\cancel{0}} =$

   $\frac{6}{10} = \frac{6 \div 2}{10 \div 2} = \frac{3}{5}$

2. $\frac{9}{25} =$

3. $\frac{4}{6} =$

4. $\frac{30}{120} =$

5. $\frac{30}{70} =$

6. $\frac{10}{100} =$

7. $\frac{17}{28} =$

8. $\frac{300}{730} =$

9. $\frac{7}{30} =$

10. $\frac{8}{24} =$

11. $\frac{100}{150} =$

12. $\frac{5}{11} =$

13. $\frac{1}{9} =$

14. $\frac{200}{1400} =$

15. $\frac{6}{13} =$

16. $\frac{30}{50} =$

17. Jack's gas tank holds 20 gallons. He put 10 gallons into the tank. What fraction shows how much gas he put into the gas tank?

18. John needs $\frac{6}{8}$ cup carrots to make a carrot cake. What is this amount in lowest terms?

Answer_____

Answer_____

Problem Solving: Using a Circle Graph

A circle graph shows a total amount divided into parts. Each part is a fraction of the total.

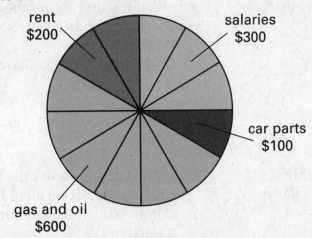

rent $200
salaries $300
car parts $100
gas and oil $600

Expenses for Diaz Garage

The circle graph above shows the expenses paid by Manuel Diaz to operate his garage. He has $1,200 in total expenses.

| **Example** | What fraction of Manuel's expenses is for rent? Reduce the fraction to lowest terms. |

▷ **Step 1.** Write the total expenses, $1,200, as the denominator of a fraction.

$$\overline{1200}$$

▷ **Step 2.** Write the amount paid for rent, $200, as the numerator of the fraction.

$$\frac{200}{1200}$$

▷ **Step 3.** Reduce. Cross out an equal number of zeros on the end of the numerator and the denominator. Reduce again.

$$\frac{20\!\!\!/0\!\!\!/}{120\!\!\!/0\!\!\!/} = \frac{2}{12} = \frac{1}{6}$$

$\frac{1}{6}$ of Manuel's expenses is for rent.

Solve. Reduce to lowest terms.

1. Write the fraction that shows what part of Manuel's expenses is for employees' salaries.

2. What fraction shows the part that Manuel spends on gasoline and oil?

Answer_____

Answer_____

Solve. Reduce to lowest terms.

3. What fraction shows the part that Manuel spends on car parts?

    Answer_____

4. What fraction shows the part that Manuel spends on parts and gas and oil together?
    (Hint: Add the two amounts first. Then write a fraction.)

    Answer_____

5. What fraction shows the part that Manuel spends on rent and salaries together?

    Answer_____

6. What fraction shows the total that Manuel spends on all of his expenses?
    (Hint: Add all the amounts. Then write a fraction.)

    Answer_____

7. Manuel spends a total of $300 on salaries. He pays his mechanic $150. Write the fraction that shows what part of the total salary expense he pays for his mechanic's salary.

    Answer_____

8. Next year Manuel's rent will go up to $250. His total expenses will be $1,250. Write the fraction that shows what part of Manuel's expenses he will have to pay for rent.

    Answer_____

9. **Complete the table below using the circle graph on page 17.**

Expense	Amount	Fraction
rent	$200	$\frac{200}{1200} = \frac{1}{6}$
salaries		
car parts		
gas and oil		

Raising Fractions to Higher Terms

When you change a fraction to an equal fraction with a larger denominator, it is called raising a fraction to higher terms.

To raise a fraction to higher terms, multiply both the numerator and the denominator by the same number.

$$\frac{3}{5} = \frac{3 \times 3}{5 \times 3} = \frac{9}{15}$$

Use These Steps

Raise $\frac{2}{5}$ to higher terms by multiplying the numerator and denominator by 6.

1. Multiply the numerator by 6.

$$\frac{2}{5} = \frac{2 \times 6}{} = \frac{12}{}$$

2. Multiply the denominator by 6.

$$\frac{2}{5} = \frac{2 \times 6}{5 \times 6} = \frac{12}{30}$$

Write equal fractions for each figure.

1.

$$\frac{2}{3} = \frac{4}{6}$$

2.

3.

4.

5.

6.

Multiply the numerator and denominator by 4 to raise each fraction to higher terms.

7. $\frac{2}{5} = \frac{2 \times 4}{5 \times 4} = \frac{8}{20}$

8. $\frac{3}{8} =$

9. $\frac{1}{6} =$

10. $\frac{4}{5} =$

Multiply the numerator and denominator by 5 to raise each fraction to higher terms.

11. $\frac{3}{4} = \frac{3 \times 5}{4 \times 5} = \frac{15}{20}$

12. $\frac{4}{7} =$

13. $\frac{2}{3} =$

14. $\frac{1}{9} =$

Raising Fractions to Higher Terms

You can raise a fraction to higher terms to get a new fraction with a given denominator.

Use These Steps

Raise $\frac{1}{8}$ to higher terms with a denominator of 32.

1. Write the fraction, $\frac{1}{8}$. Write another fraction with the new denominator, 32.

2. To find the number to multiply by, think about the old denominator, 8, and the new denominator, 32. 8 multiplied by what number equals 32?

3. Multiply the numerator, 1, by 4.

$$\frac{1}{8} = \frac{}{32}$$

$$\frac{1}{8} = \frac{}{8 \times 4} = \frac{}{32}$$

$$\frac{1}{8} = \frac{1 \times 4}{8 \times 4} = \frac{4}{32}$$

Write the number used to raise each fraction to higher terms.

1. $\frac{1}{2} = \frac{3}{6}$ ___3___

2. $\frac{3}{4} = \frac{12}{16}$ ___

3. $\frac{7}{8} = \frac{21}{24}$ ___

4. $\frac{5}{9} = \frac{30}{54}$ ___

5. $\frac{6}{10} = \frac{18}{30}$ ___

6. $\frac{12}{15} = \frac{48}{60}$ ___

7. $\frac{2}{9} = \frac{10}{45}$ ___

8. $\frac{5}{12} = \frac{25}{60}$ ___

Raise each fraction to higher terms using the given denominator.

9. $\frac{3}{7} = \frac{\boxed{9}}{21}$

10. $\frac{2}{14} = \frac{\square}{56}$

11. $\frac{15}{25} = \frac{\square}{100}$

12. $\frac{9}{16} = \frac{\square}{48}$

13. $\frac{18}{45} = \frac{\square}{90}$

14. $\frac{24}{30} = \frac{\square}{90}$

15. $\frac{1}{9} = \frac{\square}{54}$

16. $\frac{7}{11} = \frac{\square}{77}$

17. $\frac{14}{28} = \frac{\square}{84}$

18. $\frac{5}{24} = \frac{\square}{96}$

19. $\frac{3}{21} = \frac{\square}{63}$

20. $\frac{8}{12} = \frac{\square}{72}$

21. Kevin read 10 pages of a 25-page marketing report. Beverly read an equal fraction of a 50-page report. How many pages did Beverly read?

22. Carmen input 14 pages of a 30-page technical manual. Scott input an equal fraction of a 60-page manual. How many pages did Scott input?

Answer_____

Answer_____

Application

Ken works in a candy factory. He weighs ingredients on a large scale.
He writes weights as fractions.

Use the information in the box to help answer the questions below.

$$16 \text{ ounces } = 1 \text{ pound}$$
$$2{,}000 \text{ pounds } = 1 \text{ ton}$$

 Ken weighed three drums of sugar.
Together they weighed 1,500 pounds.
What fraction of a ton is this?

$$\frac{15\cancel{0}\cancel{0}}{20\cancel{0}\cancel{0}} = \frac{15}{20} = \frac{3}{4}$$

The drums weigh $\frac{3}{4}$ ton.

Solve. Reduce to lowest terms.

1. Abram put six bags of peanuts on the scale. All together they weighed 1,000 pounds. What fraction of a ton was on the scale?

   Answer_____

2. José weighs the candy after it is made. He packed ten cartons of peanut brittle and put them on the scale. The cartons weighed 700 pounds. What fraction of a ton did the ten cartons of peanut brittle weigh?

   Answer_____

3. Ellen packs boxes of caramels. She has a small scale that measures pounds. Each box of caramels weighs 14 ounces. What fraction of a pound is 14 ounces?

   Answer_____

4. Nora packs boxes of chocolates. Each box weighs 8 ounces. What fraction of a pound is each box?

   Answer_____

5. Keiko prepares the ingredients for each batch of fudge. Each batch requires 100 pounds of sugar. What fraction of a ton is 100 pounds?

   Answer_____

6. Keiko packs the fudge in 12-ounce boxes. What fraction of a pound is each box of fudge?

   Answer_____

Mixed Review

Write the fraction and the word name for the shaded part of each figure.

1.

_____

_____

2.

_____

_____

3.

_____

_____

4.

_____

_____

5. There are 12 inches in a foot. What fraction of a foot is 5 inches?

   Answer_____

6. There are 7 days in a week. What fraction of a week is 2 days?

   Answer_____

7. There are 24 quarts of oil in a full case. What fraction of a case is 13 quarts?

   Answer_____

8. There are 52 weeks in a year. What fraction of a year is 3 weeks?

   Answer_____

Reduce each fraction to lowest terms. If the fraction is in lowest terms, write LT.

9. $\dfrac{15}{25} =$

10. $\dfrac{21}{49} =$

11. $\dfrac{36}{54} =$

12. $\dfrac{81}{90} =$

13. $\dfrac{7}{10} =$

14. $\dfrac{10}{50} =$

15. $\dfrac{20}{40} =$

16. $\dfrac{70}{210} =$

17. $\dfrac{50}{100} =$

18. $\dfrac{200}{1600} =$

Raise each fraction to higher terms using the given denominator.

19. $\dfrac{1}{2} = \dfrac{}{4}$

20. $\dfrac{2}{3} = \dfrac{}{9}$

21. $\dfrac{4}{5} = \dfrac{}{15}$

22. $\dfrac{3}{7} = \dfrac{}{21}$

23. $\dfrac{5}{6} = \dfrac{}{30}$

24. $\dfrac{3}{4} = \dfrac{}{16}$

25. $\dfrac{5}{8} = \dfrac{}{24}$

26. $\dfrac{7}{10} = \dfrac{}{50}$

Comparing Fractions

You can use a number line to compare fractions. The fraction that is farther to the right is the greater fraction.

Remember the symbol $>$ means *greater than.* $\quad \dfrac{1}{2} > \dfrac{1}{4}$

$< $ means *less than.* $\quad \dfrac{5}{8} < \dfrac{7}{8}$

Use These Steps

Compare $\dfrac{5}{8}$ and $\dfrac{1}{2}$.

1. Find the fractions on the number line. Write the fractions.

$\dfrac{5}{8} \quad \dfrac{1}{2}$

2. Decide which fraction is farther to the right on the number line. Write the correct symbol between the fractions.

$\dfrac{5}{8} > \dfrac{1}{2}$

Use the number lines to compare each set of fractions. Write >, <, or =.

1. $\dfrac{3}{8} \boxed{>} \dfrac{2}{10}$

2. $\dfrac{5}{8} \boxed{<} \dfrac{7}{8}$

3. $\dfrac{5}{10} \boxed{=} \dfrac{4}{8}$

4. $\dfrac{3}{8} \ \square \ \dfrac{5}{8}$

5. $\dfrac{3}{4} \ \square \ \dfrac{7}{10}$

6. $\dfrac{4}{10} \ \square \ \dfrac{5}{8}$

7. $\dfrac{1}{8} \ \square \ \dfrac{1}{10}$

8. $\dfrac{3}{8} \ \square \ \dfrac{3}{10}$

9. $\dfrac{1}{2} \ \square \ \dfrac{5}{10}$

10. $\dfrac{7}{10} \ \square \ \dfrac{7}{8}$

11. $\dfrac{9}{10} \ \square \ \dfrac{3}{4}$

12. $\dfrac{1}{4} \ \square \ \dfrac{1}{10}$

Comparing Fractions

Fractions can be compared without using a number line. If the denominators are the same, then compare the numerators.

$$\frac{3}{8} < \frac{5}{8}$$

If the denominators are not the same, you need to first change the fractions to equal fractions with the same denominators.

Use These Steps

Compare $\frac{5}{8}$ and $\frac{3}{4}$.

1. The denominators are not the same. Change $\frac{3}{4}$ to a fraction with 8 as the denominator.

$$\frac{3}{4} = \frac{3 \times 2}{4 \times 2} = \frac{6}{8}$$

2. Compare the numerator of each fraction. 5 is less than 6.

$$\frac{5}{8} < \frac{6}{8}, \text{ so } \frac{5}{8} < \frac{3}{4}$$

Compare each pair of fractions. Write >, <, or =.

1. $\frac{2}{5}$ $\boxed{=}$ $\frac{6}{15}$

   $\frac{2}{5} = \frac{2 \times 3}{5 \times 3} = \frac{6}{15}$

2. $\frac{3}{8}$ $\square$ $\frac{1}{2}$

3. $\frac{2}{4}$ $\square$ $\frac{3}{8}$

4. $\frac{4}{5}$ $\square$ $\frac{2}{10}$

5. $\frac{1}{2}$ $\square$ $\frac{6}{10}$

6. $\frac{4}{9}$ $\square$ $\frac{2}{3}$

7. $\frac{1}{4}$ $\square$ $\frac{4}{12}$

8. $\frac{5}{6}$ $\square$ $\frac{2}{3}$

9. $\frac{1}{4}$ $\square$ $\frac{3}{8}$

10. $\frac{2}{7}$ $\square$ $\frac{5}{14}$

11. $\frac{3}{4}$ $\square$ $\frac{7}{16}$

12. $\frac{4}{7}$ $\square$ $\frac{10}{21}$

13. $\frac{5}{8}$ $\square$ $\frac{13}{16}$

14. $\frac{7}{12}$ $\square$ $\frac{1}{2}$

15. $\frac{2}{5}$ $\square$ $\frac{10}{15}$

16. $\frac{3}{4}$ $\square$ $\frac{16}{20}$

17. $\frac{7}{9}$ $\square$ $\frac{15}{18}$

18. $\frac{3}{10}$ $\square$ $\frac{10}{20}$

19. $\frac{5}{8}$ $\square$ $\frac{15}{24}$

20. $\frac{5}{10}$ $\square$ $\frac{1}{2}$

21. By lunch Pat completed $\frac{2}{3}$ of her work. Lena completed $\frac{5}{9}$ of her work. Who completed more of her work? (Hint: Which fraction is larger?)

22. Barb usually takes $\frac{1}{2}$ hour to process an insurance claim. Today she took $\frac{5}{8}$ hour to process one. Is this more or less than the usual time?

Answer_____

Answer_____

Finding a Common Denominator

To compare some fractions, you will need to change the denominators of both fractions. This is called finding a common denominator. A common denominator is a number that both denominators divide into evenly.

Use These Steps

Compare $\frac{1}{2}$ and $\frac{1}{3}$.

1. Multiply the two denominators to find a common denominator. $2 \times 3 = 6$. The new denominator for both fractions is 6.

$$\frac{1}{2} = \frac{}{2 \times 3} = \frac{}{6}$$

$$\frac{1}{3} = \frac{}{3 \times 2} = \frac{}{6}$$

2. Write each fraction in higher terms with 6 as the denominator.

$$\frac{1}{2} = \frac{1 \times 3}{2 \times 3} = \frac{3}{6}$$

$$\frac{1}{3} = \frac{1 \times 2}{3 \times 2} = \frac{2}{6}$$

3. Compare the numerators of the two new fractions. 3 is more than 2.

$$\frac{3}{6} > \frac{2}{6}, \text{ so } \frac{1}{2} > \frac{1}{3}$$

Compare each set of fractions. Write >, <, or =.

1.
$$\frac{1}{5} \boxed{>} \frac{1}{6}$$

$$\frac{1}{5} = \frac{1 \times 6}{5 \times 6} = \frac{6}{30}$$

$$\frac{1}{6} = \frac{1 \times 5}{6 \times 5} = \frac{5}{30}$$

2.
$$\frac{2}{3} \square \frac{3}{4}$$

3.
$$\frac{1}{2} \square \frac{3}{5}$$

4.
$$\frac{5}{6} \square \frac{4}{7}$$

5.
$$\frac{3}{4} \square \frac{3}{5}$$

6.
$$\frac{4}{5} \square \frac{4}{7}$$

7.
$$\frac{3}{8} \square \frac{2}{3}$$

8.
$$\frac{7}{10} \square \frac{1}{3}$$

9.
$$\frac{1}{2} \square \frac{5}{10}$$

10.
$$\frac{3}{4} \square \frac{9}{10}$$

11.
$$\frac{1}{3} \square \frac{1}{4}$$

12.
$$\frac{2}{4} \square \frac{3}{6}$$

13. Yesterday it rained $\frac{3}{10}$ inch in Orlando. It rained $\frac{3}{4}$ inch in Miami. Which city got more rain?

14. Peterboro received $\frac{3}{4}$ foot of snow on Sunday. Stowe received $\frac{1}{2}$ foot. Which city had more snow?

Answer_____

Answer_____

Whole Numbers, Mixed Numbers, and Fractions

Remember that a fraction shows a part of something. A whole number shows the whole of something. A mixed number shows both a whole and a part.

$\frac{1}{2}$

2

$2\frac{1}{2}$

Use These Steps

Write a mixed number for the shaded parts.

1. Count the number of whole circles that are shaded. Write the whole number.

2. Count the number of parts of the remaining whole circle that are shaded.

2

$2\frac{3}{4}$

Write a whole number or a mixed number for the shaded parts.

1.

$1\frac{1}{2}$

2.

3.

4.

5.

6.

7. A painter used four full gallons of paint and one eighth of another gallon to paint a house. Write a mixed number to show the total amount of paint that he used.

8. When he completed the job, the painter had three whole gallons of blue paint and one half gallon of gray paint left. Write a mixed number to show how many gallons of paint he had left.

Answer_____

Answer_____

Whole Numbers, Mixed Numbers, and Fractions

When you divide whole numbers, the answer may have a remainder. You can write the remainder as the numerator of a fraction. The number you divide by is the denominator. The answer can be written as a mixed number.

$$\begin{array}{r} 4 \\ 3\overline{)14} \\ -12 \\ \hline 2 \end{array} \text{R2} = 4\frac{2}{3} \qquad \begin{array}{r} 5 \\ 6\overline{)33} \\ -30 \\ \hline 3 \end{array} \text{R3} = 5\frac{3}{6} = 5\frac{1}{2}$$

Use These Steps

Write the answer to $10 \div 4$ as a mixed number.

1. Divide.

$$\begin{array}{r} 2 \\ 4\overline{)10} \\ -8 \\ \hline 2 \end{array} \text{R2}$$

2. Write the remainder as a fraction. Write the answer as a mixed number.

$$\begin{array}{r} 2 \\ 4\overline{)10} \\ -8 \\ \hline 2 \end{array} \text{R2} = 2\frac{2}{4}$$

3. Reduce the fraction to lowest terms.

$$2\frac{2}{4} = 2\frac{1}{2}$$

Write each answer as a mixed number. Reduce the fraction if possible.

1.
$$15 \div 6 =$$
$$\begin{array}{r} 2 \\ 6\overline{)15} \\ -12 \\ \hline 3 \end{array} \text{R3} = 2\frac{3}{6} = 2\frac{1}{2}$$

2.
$$9 \div 4 =$$

3.
$$10 \div 7 =$$

4.
$$12 \div 5 =$$

5.
$$20 \div 3 =$$

6.
$$18 \div 8 =$$

7.
$$17 \div 2 =$$

8.
$$22 \div 10 =$$

9.
$$36 \div 14 =$$

10.
$$50 \div 20 =$$

11.
$$72 \div 30 =$$

12.
$$100 \div 15 =$$

Comparing Whole Numbers, Mixed Numbers, and Fractions

To compare whole numbers, mixed numbers, and fractions, first compare the whole numbers. If the whole numbers are the same, then compare the fractions. Make sure that all the fractions have the same denominator.

$$6\frac{1}{2} > 2\frac{3}{4} \qquad 2\frac{3}{4} > 2\frac{1}{4} \qquad 2 < 2\frac{1}{2}$$

Use These Steps

Compare $1\frac{1}{2}$ and $1\frac{2}{5}$.

1. The whole numbers are the same. Find a common denominator for the fractions by multiplying the two denominators. $2 \times 5 = 10$. The new denominator for both fractions is 10.

   $1\frac{1}{2} = 1\frac{}{10}$

   $1\frac{2}{5} = 1\frac{}{10}$

2. Write each fraction in higher terms with 10 as the denominator for each fraction.

   $1\frac{1}{2} = 1\frac{5}{10}$

   $1\frac{2}{5} = 1\frac{4}{10}$

3. Compare the numerators of the two new fractions. 5 is greater than 4.

   $1\frac{5}{10} > 1\frac{4}{10}$,

   so $1\frac{1}{2} > 1\frac{2}{5}$

Compare. Write >, <, or =.

1. $2\frac{3}{8}$ $\boxed{>}$ $2\frac{1}{4}$

   $2\frac{3}{8} = 2\frac{3}{8}$

   $2\frac{1}{4} = 2\frac{2}{8}$

2. $3\frac{1}{3}$ $\square$ $4\frac{1}{8}$

3. $4\frac{1}{5}$ $\square$ $4\frac{2}{10}$

4. $5\frac{3}{4}$ $\square$ $5\frac{7}{8}$

5. $11\frac{1}{2}$ $\square$ $11\frac{1}{10}$

6. 7 $\square$ $7\frac{1}{5}$

7. $\frac{1}{5}$ $\square$ $1\frac{1}{5}$

8. $12\frac{3}{4}$ $\square$ $12\frac{15}{16}$

9. $2\frac{1}{2}$ $\square$ $2\frac{1}{12}$

10. $8\frac{7}{8}$ $\square$ $8\frac{9}{16}$

11. $5\frac{1}{3}$ $\square$ $5\frac{5}{15}$

12. $\frac{9}{10}$ $\square$ $10\frac{1}{10}$

Problem Solving: Using a Ruler

The ruler below is divided into inches and fractions of an inch: halves, fourths, eighths, and sixteenths.

The arrow at A is $\frac{1}{2}$ inch from zero.

The arrow at B is $\frac{7}{8}$ inch from zero.

The arrow at C is $1\frac{1}{4}$ inches from zero.

The arrow at D is $1\frac{11}{16}$ inches from zero.

The arrow at E is 2 inches from zero.

Example   How far from zero is the arrow at F?

▷ **Step 1.**   Find the nearest whole inch mark to the left of the arrow at F.

3

▷ **Step 2.**   Find the fraction of an inch the arrow is pointing to.

$\frac{1}{4}$

▷ **Step 3.**   Write the mixed number.

$3\frac{1}{4}$ inches

Use the ruler above to answer each question.

1. How far from zero is the arrow at G?

    Answer_____

2. How far from zero is the arrow at H?

    Answer_____

3. How far from zero is the arrow at I?

    Answer_____

4. How far from zero is the arrow at J?

    Answer_____

Use the ruler below to answer each question.

5. Find each inch mark on the ruler. Write the number of the inch above the inch mark.
(Hint: Look at the 6-inch mark.)

6. Find 0 on the ruler. Write $\frac{1}{4}$ above the first $\frac{1}{4}$-inch mark to the right of 0.

7. Find the 1-inch mark on the ruler. Write $\frac{1}{2}$ above the first $\frac{1}{2}$-inch mark to the right of the 1-inch mark.

8. Find the 2-inch mark on the ruler. Write $\frac{1}{16}$ above the last $\frac{1}{16}$-inch mark before the 3-inch mark.

9. Find 1 inch on the ruler. Draw an arrow to the mark and label it A.

10. Find $1\frac{3}{8}$ inches on the ruler. Draw an arrow to the mark and label it B.

11. Find $2\frac{3}{16}$ inches on the ruler. Draw an arrow to the mark and label it C.

12. Find $3\frac{1}{4}$ inches on the ruler. Draw an arrow to the mark and label it D.

13. Find $4\frac{1}{2}$ inches on the ruler. Draw an arrow to the mark and label it E.

14. Find $4\frac{3}{4}$ inches on the ruler. Draw an arrow to the mark and label it F.

15. Find $5\frac{9}{16}$ inches on the ruler. Draw an arrow to the mark and label it G.

16. Find $5\frac{7}{8}$ inches on the ruler. Draw an arrow to the mark and label it H.

Reduce the following measurements to lowest terms. If the fraction is in lowest terms, write LT.

17. $3\frac{6}{16}$ inches =

18. $1\frac{2}{4}$ inches =

19. $\frac{6}{8}$ inch =

20. $4\frac{9}{16}$ inches =

21. $5\frac{4}{8}$ inches =

22. $2\frac{4}{16}$ inch =

Improper Fractions

A proper fraction is a fraction with a numerator that is smaller than the denominator.

An improper fraction is a fraction with a numerator equal to or larger than its denominator.

$$\frac{4}{4}$$

$$\frac{9}{4}$$

Use These Steps

Write an improper fraction for the number of pieces of pie remaining.

1. Count the number of equal parts in one pie. Write this number as the denominator.

$$\overline{8}$$

2. Count the total number of remaining (shaded) pieces. Write this number as the numerator.

$$\frac{19}{8}$$

Write an improper fraction for the shaded part of each group of figures.

1.

$$\frac{8}{4}$$

2.

3.

4.

5.

6.

7.

8.

9.

31

Recognizing Proper Fractions, Improper Fractions, Whole Numbers, and Mixed Numbers

A proper fraction has a numerator that is smaller than the denominator.

$$\frac{2}{3} \qquad \frac{3}{7}$$

An improper fraction has a numerator that is equal to or larger than the denominator.

$$\frac{8}{8} \qquad \frac{21}{6}$$

A whole number has no fraction part.

$$2 \qquad 15$$

A mixed number has a whole number and a fraction part.

$$3\frac{1}{2} \qquad 12\frac{2}{7}$$

Write P (proper fraction), I (improper fraction), W (whole number), or M (mixed number) on the line next to each problem.

1. $3\frac{1}{8}$ **M**   2. $\frac{2}{5}$ _____   3. $\frac{9}{1}$ _____   4. $\frac{10}{4}$ _____   5. $2\frac{1}{2}$ _____

6. 19 _____   7. $\frac{35}{6}$ _____   8. $\frac{3}{3}$ _____   9. 11 _____   10. $\frac{30}{30}$ _____

11. $\frac{5}{10}$ _____   12. $\frac{2}{45}$ _____   13. $8\frac{7}{8}$ _____   14. $\frac{61}{7}$ _____   15. 27 _____

16. $2\frac{4}{8}$ _____   17. $11\frac{1}{4}$ _____   18. $\frac{12}{3}$ _____   19. $\frac{13}{13}$ _____   20. $\frac{23}{4}$ _____

21. An average container of pesticide holds 8 quarts. Walter used 8 quarts from one container and 3 quarts from another on the grass in front of the museum. Write the amount he used as an improper fraction.

22. Write the amount that Walter used as a mixed number.

Answer _____

Answer _____

Changing Improper Fractions to Whole or Mixed Numbers

You may need to change an improper fraction to a whole or mixed number. To change an improper fraction, divide the numerator by the denominator.

Use These Steps

Change $\frac{13}{6}$ to a mixed number.

1. Set up a division problem.

$6\overline{)13}$

2. Divide.

$$\begin{array}{r} 2 \text{ R1} \\ 6\overline{)13} \\ -12 \\ \hline 1 \end{array}$$

3. Write the remainder as a fraction.

$2\frac{1}{6}$

Write an improper fraction and a whole or mixed number for each group of figures.

1.

$\frac{17}{6} = 2\frac{5}{6}$

2.

3.

4.

5.

6.

Change each improper fraction to a whole or mixed number.

7. $\frac{9}{4} = 2\frac{1}{4}$

$$\begin{array}{r} 2 \text{ R1} \\ 4\overline{)9} \\ -8 \\ \hline 1 \end{array}$$

8. $\frac{13}{9} =$

9. $\frac{4}{2} =$

10. $\frac{8}{5} =$

11. eighteen sixths $= \frac{18}{6} = 3$

$$\begin{array}{r} 3 \\ 6\overline{)18} \end{array}$$

12. thirteen eighths =

13. twenty ninths =

14. sixteen sevenths =

Changing Improper Fractions to Whole or Mixed Numbers

Sometimes when you are changing an improper fraction to a mixed number, the remainder will be a fraction that needs to be reduced.

Use These Steps

Change $\frac{21}{6}$ to a mixed number.

1. Set up a division problem. Divide the numerator, 21, by the denominator, 6.

$$6\overline{)21}$$

2. Divide. Write the remainder as a fraction.

$$6\overline{)21} \quad \underset{-18}{\phantom{6\overline{)21}}} \quad \overset{3\ R3}{} = 3\frac{3}{6}$$

$$\begin{array}{r} 3\ R3 = 3\frac{3}{6} \\ 6\overline{)21} \\ -18 \\ \hline 3 \end{array}$$

3. Reduce the fraction by dividing the numerator and the denominator by the same number, 3.

$$3\frac{3}{6} = 3\frac{1}{2}$$

Write each fraction as a whole or mixed number. Reduce fractions if possible.

1. $\frac{31}{6} =$

$$\begin{array}{r} 5\ R1 = 5\frac{1}{6} \\ 6\overline{)31} \\ -30 \\ \hline 1 \end{array}$$

2. $\frac{6}{3} =$

3. $\frac{45}{9} =$

4. $\frac{67}{8} =$

5. $\frac{12}{5} =$

6. $\frac{34}{18} = 1\frac{8}{9}$

7. $\frac{55}{9} = 6\frac{1}{9}$

8. $\frac{28}{3} = 9\frac{1}{3}$

9. $\frac{100}{45} = 2\frac{2}{9}$

10. $\frac{18}{5} = 3\frac{3}{5}$

11. $\frac{50}{10} =$

12. $\frac{38}{15} =$

13. $\frac{76}{30} =$

14. $\frac{42}{7} =$

15. $\frac{64}{9} =$

16. $\frac{81}{11} =$

17. $\frac{70}{3} =$

18. $\frac{32}{8} =$

19. $\frac{21}{4} =$

20. $\frac{8}{7} =$

21. Barry's Bakery cuts the pies it sells into 6 pieces each. The bakery sold 26 pieces of pie on Friday. How many pies did the bakery sell?

22. Carroll's Creamery uses 42 eggs to make ice cream. If there are 12 eggs in a dozen, how many dozen eggs are used?

Answer_____

Answer_____

34

Unit *2* ADDING FRACTIONS

Addition problems with fractions usually ask you to figure out a total amount or a sum. You may have needed to add fractions when using a ruler, doing repairs, or figuring out the number of hours that you worked in a week.

In this unit you will apply your understanding of fractions. You will learn how to add fractions, how to solve word problems using fractions, and how to reduce to lowest terms.

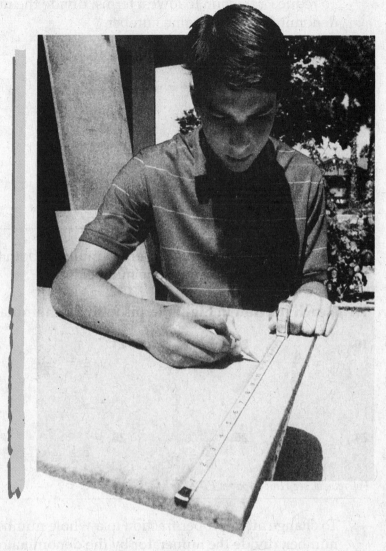

Getting Ready

You should be familiar with the skills on this page and the next before you begin this unit. To check your answers, turn to page 170.

 To compare fractions, make sure that the denominators are the same. Then compare the numerators.

Compare the fractions. Write <, >, or =.

1. $\frac{1}{3}$ $\boxed{<}$ $\frac{2}{3}$
2. $\frac{7}{10}$ $\square$ $\frac{3}{5}$
3. $\frac{9}{12}$ $\square$ $\frac{5}{6}$
4. $\frac{2}{3}$ $\square$ $\frac{3}{4}$

5. $\frac{2}{9}$ $\square$ $\frac{1}{3}$
6. $\frac{3}{8}$ $\square$ $\frac{6}{16}$
7. $\frac{8}{11}$ $\square$ $\frac{5}{11}$
8. $\frac{1}{2}$ $\square$ $\frac{2}{3}$

For review, see Unit 1, pages 23–25. **39** ◆

To reduce a fraction to lowest terms, divide the numerator and the denominator by the same number.

Write each fraction in lowest terms.

9.
$$\frac{8}{12} = \frac{2}{3}$$

10.
$$\frac{15}{20} =$$

11.
$$\frac{18}{36} =$$

12.
$$3\frac{21}{28} =$$

13.
$$1\frac{18}{27} =$$

14.
$$\frac{4}{6} =$$

15.
$$\frac{8}{10} =$$

16.
$$4\frac{14}{28} =$$

17.
$$5\frac{2}{4} =$$

18.
$$10\frac{9}{12} =$$

For review, see Unit 1, pages 15–16.

 To raise a fraction to higher terms, multiply both the numerator and the denominator by the same number.

Write each fraction in higher terms with a denominator of 12.

19.
$$\frac{2}{3} = \frac{8}{12}$$

20.
$$\frac{3}{4} = \frac{}{12}$$

21.
$$\frac{1}{2} = \frac{}{12}$$

22.
$$2\frac{5}{6} = 2\frac{}{12}$$

23.
$$5\frac{1}{4} = 5\frac{}{12}$$

24.
$$\frac{5}{6} = \frac{}{12}$$

25.
$$\frac{1}{3} = \frac{}{12}$$

26.
$$9\frac{1}{2} = 9\frac{}{12}$$

27.
$$3\frac{4}{6} = 3\frac{}{12}$$

28.
$$1\frac{2}{3} = 1\frac{}{12}$$

For review, see Unit 1, pages 19–20.

 To change an improper fraction to a whole number or a mixed number, divide the numerator by the denominator. Write any remainder as a fraction.

Change each improper fraction to a whole number or a mixed number. Reduce if possible.

29.
$$\frac{11}{5} =$$

$$\begin{array}{r} 2\frac{1}{5} \\ 5\overline{)11} \\ -10 \\ \hline 1 \end{array}$$

30.
$$\frac{20}{3} =$$

31.
$$\frac{49}{9} =$$

32.
$$\frac{30}{10} =$$

33.
$$\frac{25}{5} =$$

34.
$$\frac{7}{2} =$$

35.
$$\frac{8}{5} =$$

36.
$$\frac{12}{6} =$$

37.
$$\frac{20}{8} =$$

38.
$$\frac{15}{12} =$$

For review, see Unit 1, pages 33–34.

Adding Fractions with the Same Denominator

To add fractions with the same denominator, add only the numerators. Keep the same denominator.

$$\frac{2}{6} + \frac{3}{6} = \frac{5}{6}$$

Use These Steps

Add $\frac{2}{8} + \frac{1}{8}$

1. The denominators are the same. Write the denominator under the fraction bar.

$$\frac{2}{8} + \frac{1}{8} = \frac{}{8}$$

2. Add only the numerators. 2 + 1 = 3. Write the sum over the denominator.

$$\frac{2}{8} + \frac{1}{8} = \frac{3}{8}$$

Add the fractions and shade in the figures to show the sum.

1.

$$\frac{1}{3} + \frac{1}{3} = \frac{2}{3}$$

2.

$$\frac{1}{4} + \frac{2}{4} =$$

3.

$$\frac{2}{5} + \frac{2}{5} =$$

4.

$$\frac{1}{6} + \frac{4}{6} =$$

Shade in the figures to show the fractions. Add the fractions. Then shade in the final figure to show the sum.

5.

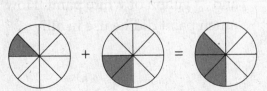

$$\frac{1}{8} + \frac{2}{8} = \frac{3}{8}$$

6.

$$\frac{2}{9} + \frac{5}{9} =$$

Adding Fractions with the Same Denominator

You can add fractions that are lined up vertically as well as horizontally. Remember, when adding fractions with the same denominator, add only the numerators.

Use These Steps

Add
$$\frac{1}{5}$$
$$+\frac{3}{5}$$

1. The denominators are the same. Write the denominator under the fraction bar.

$$\frac{1}{5}$$
$$+\frac{3}{5}$$
$$\overline{5}$$

2. Add only the numerators. $1 + 3 = 4$. Write the sum over the denominator.

$$\frac{1}{5}$$
$$+\frac{3}{5}$$
$$\frac{4}{5}$$

Add.

1.
$$\frac{3}{6}$$
$$+\frac{2}{6}$$
$$\frac{5}{6}$$

2.
$$\frac{6}{12}$$
$$+\frac{1}{12}$$

3.
$$\frac{3}{15}$$
$$+\frac{10}{15}$$

4.
$$\frac{7}{20}$$
$$+\frac{4}{20}$$

5.
$$\frac{5}{10}$$
$$+\frac{4}{10}$$

6.
$$\frac{6}{14}$$
$$\frac{3}{14}$$
$$+\frac{4}{14}$$
$$\frac{13}{14}$$

7.
$$\frac{10}{35}$$
$$\frac{15}{35}$$
$$+\frac{6}{35}$$

8.
$$\frac{7}{40}$$
$$\frac{3}{40}$$
$$+\frac{11}{40}$$

9.
$$\frac{18}{50}$$
$$\frac{8}{50}$$
$$+\frac{5}{50}$$

10.
$$\frac{3}{100}$$
$$\frac{10}{100}$$
$$+\frac{20}{100}$$

11. $\frac{6}{25} + \frac{7}{25} + \frac{1}{25} =$

12. $\frac{1}{9} + \frac{4}{9} + \frac{2}{9} =$

13. $\frac{2}{7} + \frac{1}{7} + \frac{2}{7} =$

14. Before lunch Jenny finished $\frac{2}{5}$ of her work. After lunch she finished another $\frac{2}{5}$. What part of her work did Jenny finish all together?

15. Roberto mixed $\frac{2}{8}$ gallon of blue paint and $\frac{3}{8}$ gallon of white paint. How much paint did he use in all?

Answer_____

Answer_____

Application

Felix works at a health club as a trainer. He keeps track of the time each member of the club works on each piece of exercise equipment. On Saturday he worked with Ann, Petra, and Otis. The chart shows how much time each person spent on each different piece of equipment. The time is kept in $\frac{1}{4}$ hours.

Member	Exercise Bike	Treadmill	Rowing Machine
Ann	$\frac{2}{4}$	$\frac{1}{4}$	$\frac{1}{4}$
Petra	$\frac{1}{4}$	$\frac{1}{4}$	0
Otis	$\frac{3}{4}$	$\frac{2}{4}$	$\frac{1}{4}$

Example How much time did Petra spend on the exercise bike and the treadmill on Saturday?

Petra spent $\frac{1}{4}$ hour on the exercise bike and $\frac{1}{4}$ hour on the treadmill.

$$\frac{1}{4} + \frac{1}{4} = \frac{2}{4} = \frac{1}{2}$$

Petra spent $\frac{1}{2}$ hour on the two pieces of equipment.

Use the chart above to answer the following questions. Change improper fractions to whole or mixed numbers. Reduce if possible.

1. How much time all together did Ann, Petra, and Otis spend on the rowing machine on Saturday?

   Answer_____

2. How much time did Ann spend on all three pieces of equipment?

   Answer_____

3. How much total time did Otis spend on the three pieces of equipment?

   Answer_____

4. How much time in all did Otis and Ann spend on the treadmill?

   Answer_____

Adding and Reducing Fractions

When adding fractions, you may get an answer that can be reduced.
Always reduce answers to lowest terms.

Use These Steps

Add $\frac{1}{8} + \frac{3}{8}$

1. The denominators are the same. Write the denominator under the fraction bar.

$$\frac{1}{8} + \frac{3}{8} = \frac{}{8}$$

2. Add the numerators.

$$\frac{1}{8} + \frac{3}{8} = \frac{4}{8}$$

3. Reduce to lowest terms.

$$\frac{4}{8} = \frac{4 \div 4}{8 \div 4} = \frac{1}{2}$$

Add. Reduce to lowest terms.

1. $\frac{1}{4} + \frac{1}{4} = \frac{2}{4} = \frac{2 \div 2}{4 \div 2} = \frac{1}{2}$

2. $\frac{3}{6} + \frac{1}{6} =$

3. $\frac{6}{10} + \frac{2}{10} =$

4. $\frac{7}{12} + \frac{1}{12} =$

5. $\frac{4}{15} + \frac{6}{15} =$

6. $\frac{9}{45} + \frac{18}{45} =$

7. $\frac{1}{9} + \frac{1}{9} + \frac{4}{9} =$

8. $\frac{1}{16} + \frac{2}{16} + \frac{1}{16} =$

9. $\frac{22}{44} + \frac{11}{44} + \frac{1}{44} =$

10. $\frac{9}{16}$
$+ \frac{5}{16}$

11. $\frac{8}{20}$
$+ \frac{10}{20}$

12. $\frac{7}{18}$
$+ \frac{7}{18}$

13. $\frac{8}{24}$
$+ \frac{12}{24}$

14. $\frac{3}{21}$
$+ \frac{4}{21}$

15. $\frac{12}{30}$
$\frac{5}{30}$
$+ \frac{3}{30}$

16. $\frac{15}{36}$
$\frac{11}{36}$
$+ \frac{4}{36}$

17. $\frac{12}{25}$
$\frac{3}{25}$
$+ \frac{5}{25}$

18. $\frac{16}{64}$
$\frac{20}{64}$
$+ \frac{12}{64}$

19. $\frac{20}{50}$
$\frac{10}{50}$
$+ \frac{5}{50}$

20. Luis drove his bus $\frac{2}{10}$ mile from the depot to Ed's Gas Station, and $\frac{6}{10}$ mile from the gas station to his first stop. How far is it from the bus depot to Luis' first stop?

21. Julia, a dressmaker, is sewing two ribbons side by side. One is $\frac{2}{16}$ inch wide. The other is $\frac{6}{16}$ inch wide. How wide are they all together?

Answer _____

Answer _____

Adding Fractions and Changing to Whole Numbers

Sometimes the answer to an addition problem is an improper fraction that can be changed to a whole number.

Use These Steps

Add $\frac{4}{9} + \frac{5}{9}$

1. The denominators are the same. Write the denominator under the fraction bar.

$$\frac{4}{9} + \frac{5}{9} = \frac{}{9}$$

2. Add the numerators.

$$\frac{4}{9} + \frac{5}{9} = \frac{9}{9}$$

3. The answer is an improper fraction. Divide the numerator by the denominator to get a whole number.

$$\frac{9}{9} = 9\overline{)9}\,^{1} = 1$$

Add. Change each sum to a whole number.

1. $\frac{2}{3} + \frac{1}{3} = \frac{3}{3}$

$\frac{3}{3} = 3\overline{)3}\,^{1} = 1$

2. $\frac{5}{6} + \frac{1}{6} =$

3. $\frac{5}{8} + \frac{3}{8} =$

4. $\frac{1}{4} + \frac{3}{4} =$

5. $\frac{12}{5} + \frac{3}{5} = \frac{15}{5}$

$\frac{15}{5} = 5\overline{)15}\,^{3} = 3$

6. $\frac{6}{4} + \frac{2}{4} =$

7. $\frac{4}{3} + \frac{5}{3} =$

8. $\frac{7}{10} + \frac{13}{10} =$

9. $\frac{4}{3} + \frac{1}{3} + \frac{1}{3} =$

10. $\frac{7}{4} + \frac{2}{4} + \frac{3}{4} =$

11. $\frac{25}{15} + \frac{15}{15} + \frac{5}{15} =$

12. $\begin{array}{r}\frac{3}{8}\\[4pt]+\frac{5}{8}\\\hline\end{array}$

13. $\begin{array}{r}\frac{7}{9}\\[4pt]+\frac{20}{9}\\\hline\end{array}$

14. $\begin{array}{r}\frac{12}{8}\\[4pt]+\frac{20}{8}\\\hline\end{array}$

15. $\begin{array}{r}\frac{2}{15}\\[4pt]+\frac{13}{15}\\\hline\end{array}$

16. $\begin{array}{r}\frac{5}{2}\\[4pt]+\frac{5}{2}\\\hline\end{array}$

17. Casey welded three lengths of pipe together: two that were $\frac{9}{12}$ foot long and one that was $\frac{6}{12}$ foot long. How long is the new pipe?

18. It rained three days last week in Centerville. On Monday it rained $\frac{2}{10}$ inch. On Wednesday $\frac{1}{10}$ inch rain fell. It rained $\frac{7}{10}$ inch on Friday. What was the total rainfall last week?

Answer _____

Answer _____

Adding Fractions and Changing to Mixed Numbers

Sometimes the answer to an addition problem is an improper fraction that can be changed to a mixed number.

Use These Steps

Add $\dfrac{3}{4} + \dfrac{3}{4}$

1. The denominators are the same. Add the numerators.

2. The answer is an improper fraction. Divide the numerator by the denominator to get a mixed number. Write the remainder as a fraction.

3. Reduce the fraction to lowest terms.

$$\frac{3}{4} + \frac{3}{4} = \frac{6}{4}$$

$$\begin{array}{r} 1\frac{2}{4} \\ 4\overline{)6} \\ -4 \\ \hline 2 \end{array}$$

$$1\frac{2}{4} = 1\frac{2 \div 2}{4 \div 2} = 1\frac{1}{2}$$

Add. Change each sum to a mixed number. Reduce if possible.

1.
$$\frac{4}{6} + \frac{4}{6} = \frac{8}{6}$$
$$\frac{8}{6} = 1\frac{2}{6} = 1\frac{1}{3}$$

2.
$$\frac{6}{4} + \frac{8}{4} =$$

3.
$$\frac{13}{10} + \frac{1}{10} =$$

4.
$$\frac{8}{9} + \frac{7}{9} =$$

5.
$$\frac{4}{5} + \frac{3}{5} + \frac{4}{5} = \frac{11}{5}$$
$$\frac{11}{5} = 2\frac{1}{5}$$

6.
$$\frac{11}{3} + \frac{1}{3} + \frac{1}{3} =$$

7.
$$\frac{4}{9} + \frac{5}{9} + \frac{8}{9} =$$

8.
$$\begin{array}{r} \frac{3}{4} \\ +\frac{7}{4} \\ \hline \end{array}$$

9.
$$\begin{array}{r} \frac{9}{15} \\ \frac{11}{15} \\ +\frac{3}{15} \\ \hline \end{array}$$

10.
$$\begin{array}{r} \frac{16}{20} \\ +\frac{7}{20} \\ \hline \end{array}$$

11.
$$\begin{array}{r} \frac{15}{35} \\ \frac{25}{35} \\ +\frac{10}{35} \\ \hline \end{array}$$

12.
$$\begin{array}{r} \frac{33}{50} \\ +\frac{27}{50} \\ \hline \end{array}$$

13. Anita rode her bike in the park for $\dfrac{3}{4}$ hour. Then she ate lunch for $\dfrac{3}{4}$ hour. How much time did she spend in the park?

14. On Fortune Highway, it is $\dfrac{8}{10}$ mile from Adams Street to Bailey Street. The distance from Bailey Street to Carter Street is $\dfrac{9}{10}$ mile. How far is it from Adams Street to Carter Street?

Answer _____

Answer _____

Mixed Review

Reduce each fraction to lowest terms. If it is in lowest terms, write LT.

1. $\dfrac{7}{14} =$

2. $\dfrac{9}{3} =$

3. $4\dfrac{4}{12} =$

4. $\dfrac{5}{20} =$

5. $\dfrac{15}{4} =$

6. $\dfrac{25}{2} =$

7. $3\dfrac{9}{36} =$

8. $\dfrac{6}{6} =$

9. $\dfrac{3}{21} =$

10. $15\dfrac{2}{7} =$

Add. Change any improper fractions to whole or mixed numbers. Reduce fractions to lowest terms.

11. $\dfrac{5}{7} + \dfrac{6}{7} =$

12. $\dfrac{4}{11} + \dfrac{15}{11} =$

13. $\dfrac{13}{15} + \dfrac{5}{15} =$

14. $\dfrac{5}{6} + \dfrac{2}{6} =$

15. $\dfrac{1}{5} + \dfrac{1}{5} =$

16. $\dfrac{7}{10} + \dfrac{2}{10} =$

17. $\dfrac{14}{25} + \dfrac{8}{25} =$

18. $\dfrac{55}{100} + \dfrac{12}{100} + \dfrac{4}{100} =$

19. $\dfrac{2}{10} + \dfrac{6}{10} =$

20. $\dfrac{1}{9} + \dfrac{5}{9} =$

21. $\dfrac{12}{30} + \dfrac{13}{30} =$

22. $\dfrac{3}{15} + \dfrac{7}{15} + \dfrac{2}{15} =$

23. $\dfrac{25}{100} + \dfrac{75}{100} =$

24. $\dfrac{5}{15} + \dfrac{25}{15} =$

25. $\dfrac{50}{50} + \dfrac{100}{50} =$

26. $\dfrac{2}{6} + \dfrac{2}{6} + \dfrac{2}{6} =$

27. $\dfrac{8}{9} + \dfrac{8}{9} =$

28. $\dfrac{35}{60} + \dfrac{45}{60} =$

29. $\dfrac{21}{25} + \dfrac{40}{25} =$

30. $\dfrac{16}{24} + \dfrac{10}{24} + \dfrac{2}{24} =$

31. $\begin{array}{r} \frac{3}{8} \\ + \frac{4}{8} \\ \hline \end{array}$

32. $\begin{array}{r} \frac{5}{7} \\ \frac{3}{7} \\ + \frac{4}{7} \\ \hline \end{array}$

33. $\begin{array}{r} \frac{5}{9} \\ + \frac{1}{9} \\ \hline \end{array}$

34. $\begin{array}{r} \frac{7}{10} \\ + \frac{7}{10} \\ \hline \end{array}$

35. $\begin{array}{r} \frac{8}{15} \\ \frac{10}{15} \\ + \frac{2}{15} \\ \hline \end{array}$

Application

To complete her market research, Wanling asked 12 people about where they work. She made a circle graph. Since she asked 12 people, she divided the circle graph into 12 equal parts.

Example Four people said that they worked in a restaurant. How many sections did Wanling use to show what fraction of the people work in a restaurant? Write the fraction. Reduce if possible.

Since 4 of the 12 people work in a restaurant, she used 4 sections.

$$\frac{4}{12} = \frac{1}{3}$$

Solve. Reduce if possible.

1. How many sections did she use for a retail store? Write the fraction.

   Answer_____

2. How many sections did she use for restaurants and retail stores together? Write the fraction.

   Answer_____

3. How many sections did she use for a hospital? Write the fraction.

   Answer_____

4. What fraction shows how many people work in a school?

   Answer_____

5. What fraction of the people Wanling spoke to work in a retail store, a restaurant, and an office?

   Answer_____

6. If you add the fractions for all of the places the people Wanling spoke to work, what is the total?

   Answer_____

Adding Mixed Numbers

You know that a mixed number has a whole number and a fraction. When adding mixed numbers, you need to add the whole numbers together and the fractions together.

Use These Steps

Add $3\frac{2}{9} + 2\frac{1}{9}$

1. Line up the fractions and the whole numbers in columns.

$$\begin{array}{r} 3\frac{2}{9} \\ +\,2\frac{1}{9} \\ \hline \end{array}$$

2. Add the fractions.

$$\begin{array}{r} 3\frac{2}{9} \\ +\,2\frac{1}{9} \\ \hline \frac{3}{9} \end{array}$$

3. Add the whole numbers. Reduce the fraction to lowest terms.

$$\begin{array}{r} 3\frac{2}{9} \\ +\,2\frac{1}{9} \\ \hline 5\frac{3}{9} = 5\frac{1}{3} \end{array}$$

Add. Reduce if possible.

1. $4\frac{1}{6} + 5\frac{2}{6} =$

$$\begin{array}{r} 4\frac{1}{6} \\ +\,5\frac{2}{6} \\ \hline 9\frac{3}{6} = 9\frac{1}{2} \end{array}$$

2. $1\frac{1}{4} + 7\frac{1}{4} =$

3. $2\frac{3}{8} + 5\frac{4}{8} =$

4. $6\frac{3}{10} + 3\frac{5}{10} =$

5.
$$\begin{array}{r} 16\frac{15}{20} \\ +\,5\frac{4}{20} \\ \hline \end{array}$$

6.
$$\begin{array}{r} 23\frac{13}{25} \\ +\,18\frac{7}{25} \\ \hline \end{array}$$

7.
$$\begin{array}{r} 30\frac{2}{10} \\ +\,33\frac{5}{10} \\ \hline \end{array}$$

8.
$$\begin{array}{r} 42\frac{20}{50} \\ +\,37\frac{10}{50} \\ \hline \end{array}$$

9. $6\frac{3}{12} + 4\frac{1}{12} + 7\frac{2}{12} =$

$$\begin{array}{r} 6\frac{3}{12} \\ 4\frac{1}{12} \\ +\,7\frac{2}{12} \\ \hline 17\frac{6}{12} = 17\frac{1}{2} \end{array}$$

10. $10\frac{2}{7} + 13\frac{1}{7} + 22\frac{2}{7} =$

11. $3\frac{1}{10} + 5\frac{3}{10} + 8\frac{1}{10} =$

Adding Mixed Numbers

Sometimes when you add mixed numbers, the fraction part of the answer is an improper fraction. When this happens, change the improper fraction to a whole or mixed number. Then add the result to the whole number of the answer.

Use These Steps

Add $3\frac{3}{5} + 2\frac{4}{5}$

1. Line up the mixed numbers. Add the fractions. Add the whole numbers.

$$3\frac{3}{5}$$
$$+2\frac{4}{5}$$
$$\overline{5\frac{7}{5}}$$

2. The fraction part of the answer is an improper fraction. Change it to a mixed number.

$$\frac{7}{5} = 1\frac{2}{5}$$

3. Add the result to the whole number part of the answer.

$$5 + 1\frac{2}{5} = 6\frac{2}{5}$$

Add. Change any improper fraction to a mixed number. Reduce if possible.

1. $2\frac{1}{6} + 4\frac{5}{6} =$

$$2\frac{1}{6}$$
$$+4\frac{5}{6}$$
$$\overline{6\frac{6}{6}} = 6 + 1 = 7$$

2. $5\frac{3}{4} + 5\frac{3}{4} =$

3. $9\frac{9}{10} + 15\frac{5}{10} =$

4. $7\frac{2}{9} + 19\frac{8}{9} =$

5.
$$16\frac{3}{5}$$
$$14\frac{4}{5}$$
$$+\ 9\frac{3}{5}$$

6.
$$29\frac{9}{10}$$
$$42\frac{6}{10}$$
$$+37\frac{8}{10}$$

7.
$$56\frac{8}{25}$$
$$32\frac{19}{25}$$
$$+69\frac{23}{25}$$

8.
$$25\frac{50}{100}$$
$$13\frac{25}{100}$$
$$+\ 7\frac{25}{100}$$

9. Phil made sales calls for $1\frac{1}{2}$ hours on Monday, $2\frac{1}{2}$ hours on Tuesday, and $1\frac{1}{2}$ hours on Wednesday. How many hours did he make sales calls all together?

10. Jana drove $3\frac{7}{10}$ miles from work to the supermarket, $1\frac{3}{10}$ miles to the hardware store, and $6\frac{1}{10}$ miles back home. How far did she drive in all?

Answer_____

Answer_____

Adding Mixed Numbers, Whole Numbers, and Fractions

When adding mixed numbers, whole numbers, and fractions, be sure to add all of the whole numbers together and all of the fractions together. Reduce answers if possible.

Use These Steps

Add $3\frac{3}{4} + \frac{3}{4} + 6$

1. Add the fractions. Add the whole numbers.

$$3\frac{3}{4}$$
$$\frac{3}{4}$$
$$\underline{+6}$$
$$9\frac{6}{4}$$

2. Change the improper fraction to a mixed number.

$$\frac{6}{4} = 1\frac{2}{4}$$

3. Add the result to the whole number part of the sum. Reduce.

$$9 + 1\frac{2}{4} = 10\frac{2}{4} = 10\frac{1}{2}$$

Add. Reduce if possible.

1.
$$2\frac{3}{8}$$
$$\frac{7}{8}$$
$$\underline{+4}$$
$$6\frac{10}{8} = 6 + 1\frac{2}{8} = 7\frac{2}{8} = 7\frac{1}{4}$$

2.
$$3\frac{2}{5}$$
$$7$$
$$\underline{+\ \frac{4}{5}}$$

3.
$$\frac{6}{10}$$
$$9\frac{7}{10}$$
$$\underline{+6}$$

4. $\frac{15}{16} + 14\frac{13}{16} + \frac{4}{16} =$

5. $17\frac{8}{9} + \frac{4}{9} + 16\frac{2}{9} =$

6. $2\frac{7}{12} + 8\frac{8}{12} + 7 =$

7. Lenore designs clothing for working women. One outfit she designed uses $3\frac{1}{8}$ yards of material for the jacket, 4 yards for the dress, and $\frac{5}{8}$ yard for the scarf. How many yards of material are used in all?

8. Lenore designed a coat that uses $2\frac{3}{8}$ yards, 2 yards, and $\frac{3}{8}$ yard of three different fabrics. How many yards in all are needed for the coat?

Answer _____

Answer _____

Mixed Review

Reduce each fraction to lowest terms. Write LT if the fraction is in lowest terms.

1. $\frac{7}{8} =$

2. $\frac{9}{2} =$

3. $2\frac{12}{4} =$

4. $6\frac{3}{5} =$

5. $1\frac{1}{3} =$

6. $\frac{15}{20} =$

7. $7\frac{5}{4} =$

8. $3\frac{2}{3} =$

9. $\frac{21}{7} =$

10. $\frac{2}{2} =$

Add. Reduce if possible.

11. $\frac{2}{9} + \frac{3}{9} =$

12. $\frac{5}{8} + \frac{1}{8} =$

13. $\frac{4}{5} + \frac{3}{5} =$

14. $\frac{9}{14} + \frac{7}{14} + \frac{3}{14} =$

15. $8\frac{3}{8} + 3\frac{7}{8} =$

16. $5\frac{7}{10} + 4\frac{3}{10} =$

17. $2\frac{7}{12} + 8\frac{8}{12} =$

18. $19\frac{5}{6} + 12 + 1\frac{4}{6} =$

19.
$$10\frac{5}{16}$$
$$3\frac{2}{16}$$
$$+ \quad \frac{7}{16}$$

20.
$$4\frac{1}{2}$$
$$3\frac{1}{2}$$
$$+9\frac{1}{2}$$

21.
$$\frac{3}{4}$$
$$\frac{3}{4}$$
$$+\frac{1}{4}$$

22.
$$5$$
$$7\frac{7}{8}$$
$$+ 12\frac{6}{8}$$

23.
$$23\frac{10}{25}$$
$$15\frac{24}{25}$$
$$+ 32\frac{20}{25}$$

24. The bookcase in Alma's office is $62\frac{3}{4}$ inches high. The window is $\frac{3}{4}$ inch higher. How high is the top of the window from the floor?

25. The curtain rod in Alma's office is $1\frac{1}{4}$ inches higher than the window. How high is the curtain rod?

Answer _____

Answer _____

Problem Solving: Using a Ruler

The ruler below is divided into inches and fractions of an inch: halves, fourths, eighths, and sixteenths.

To find the sum of two measures on the ruler, first add the measures. Then find the answer on the ruler.

Example Find the sum of $1\frac{1}{2}$ inches and $2\frac{1}{2}$ inches on the ruler.

▷ **Step 1.** Add the measures.

$$1\frac{1}{2}$$
$$+2\frac{1}{2}$$
$$3\frac{2}{2} = 3 + 1 = 4 \text{ inches}$$

▷ **Step 2.** Find 4 inches on the ruler. Draw an arrow pointing to the answer and label it A.

Find each sum on the ruler above.

1. Find the sum of $\frac{1}{4}$ inch and $1\frac{1}{2}$ inches. Draw an arrow pointing to the answer and label it B.

2. Find the sum of $1\frac{5}{8}$ inches and 2 inches. Draw an arrow pointing to the answer and label it C.

Answer_____

Answer_____

3. Find 3 inches on the ruler. Add $2\frac{3}{4}$ inches more. Draw an arrow pointing to the answer and label it D.

4. Find $4\frac{1}{2}$ inches on the ruler. Add $1\frac{1}{16}$ inches more. Draw an arrow pointing to the answer and label it E.

Answer_____

Answer_____

Find each sum on the ruler below.

5. Find the sum of $\frac{3}{8}$ inch and $3\frac{3}{8}$ inches on the ruler. Draw an arrow and label it A.

   Answer_____

6. Find the sum of 4 inches and $\frac{1}{8}$ inch on the ruler. Draw an arrow and label it B.

   Answer_____

7. Find the sum of $1\frac{5}{16}$ inches and $2\frac{3}{16}$ inches on the ruler. Draw an arrow and label it C.

   Answer_____

8. Find the sum of $3\frac{1}{8}$ inches and $1\frac{7}{16}$ inches on the ruler. Draw an arrow and label it D.

   Answer_____

9. Find the sum of $\frac{7}{8}$ inch and $1\frac{7}{8}$ inches on the ruler. Draw an arrow and label it E.

   Answer_____

10. Find the sum of $2\frac{1}{2}$ inches and $2\frac{3}{4}$ inches on the ruler. Draw an arrow and label it F.

    Answer_____

11. Find $1\frac{5}{8}$ inches on the ruler. Add $2\frac{3}{4}$ inches more. Draw an arrow and label it G.

    Answer_____

12. Find $4\frac{9}{16}$ inches on the ruler. Add $1\frac{7}{16}$ inches more. Draw an arrow and label it H.

    Answer_____

Finding Common Denominators

When you have two fractions with different denominators, you may need to change the fractions to equal fractions in higher terms with a common denominator.

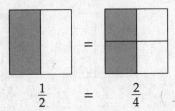

$$\frac{1}{2} \quad = \quad \frac{2}{4}$$

Use These Steps

Write $\frac{1}{3}$ and $\frac{5}{6}$ with common denominators.

1. Compare the denominators. 3 divides evenly into 6. The larger number, 6, works as the common denominator.

$$\frac{1}{3} = \frac{}{6}$$

$$\frac{5}{6} = \frac{}{6}$$

2. Change $\frac{1}{3}$ to a fraction in higher terms with 6 as the denominator.

$$\frac{1}{3} = \frac{2}{6}$$

$$\frac{5}{6} = \frac{5}{6}$$

Write each set of fractions with common denominators.

1. $\frac{1}{2}$ and $\frac{3}{10}$

$$\frac{1}{2} = \frac{5}{10}$$

$$\frac{3}{10} = \frac{3}{10}$$

2. $\frac{4}{5}$ and $\frac{7}{15}$

3. $\frac{2}{3}$ and $\frac{4}{9}$

4. $\frac{7}{12}$ and $\frac{5}{6}$

5. $\frac{3}{4}$ and $\frac{5}{8}$

6. $\frac{1}{2}$ and $\frac{5}{6}$

7. $\frac{7}{21}$ and $\frac{3}{7}$

8. $\frac{1}{5}$ and $\frac{3}{25}$

9. $\frac{3}{14}$ and $\frac{2}{7}$

10. $\frac{5}{8}$ and $\frac{7}{24}$

11. $\frac{9}{20}$ and $\frac{3}{10}$

12. $\frac{2}{9}$ and $\frac{5}{27}$

13. $\frac{1}{2}, \frac{3}{4}$, and $\frac{7}{8}$

$$\frac{1}{2} = \frac{4}{8}$$

$$\frac{3}{4} = \frac{6}{8}$$

$$\frac{7}{8} = \frac{7}{8}$$

14. $\frac{2}{3}, \frac{5}{6}$, and $\frac{1}{18}$

15. $\frac{1}{3}, \frac{3}{5}$, and $\frac{7}{15}$

Adding Fractions with Different Denominators

When fractions in an addition problem have different denominators, you must first change the fractions to equal fractions with common denominators. Then add the numerators.

$$\frac{1}{3} \ + \ \frac{3}{6} \ = \ \frac{2}{6} \ + \ \frac{3}{6} \ = \ \frac{5}{6}$$

Use These Steps

Add $\frac{1}{4} + \frac{3}{8}$

1. Compare the denominators. 4 will divide evenly into 8. 8 is the common denominator. Change 1/4 to higher terms with 8 as the common denominator.

$$\frac{1}{4} = \frac{1 \times 2}{4 \times 2} = \frac{2}{8}$$

2. The denominators are the same. Add the numerators.

$$\begin{aligned} \frac{1}{4} &= \frac{2}{8} \\ + \frac{3}{8} &= \frac{3}{8} \\ \hline &\frac{5}{8} \end{aligned}$$

Find common denominators. Change the fractions to higher terms. Then add.

1.
$$\frac{1}{5} + \frac{5}{10} =$$

$$\begin{aligned} \frac{1}{5} &= \frac{2}{10} \\ + \frac{5}{10} &= \frac{5}{10} \\ \hline &\frac{7}{10} \end{aligned}$$

2.
$$\frac{2}{6} + \frac{1}{2} =$$

3.
$$\frac{3}{14} + \frac{1}{7} =$$

4.
$$\frac{1}{4} + \frac{1}{2} =$$

5.
$$\begin{aligned} &\frac{5}{8} \\ &+ \frac{1}{4} \\ \hline \end{aligned}$$

6.
$$\begin{aligned} &\frac{1}{3} \\ &+ \frac{5}{9} \\ \hline \end{aligned}$$

7.
$$\begin{aligned} &\frac{3}{10} \\ &+ \frac{2}{5} \\ \hline \end{aligned}$$

8.
$$\begin{aligned} &\frac{1}{15} \\ &+ \frac{1}{5} \\ \hline \end{aligned}$$

9.
$$\begin{aligned} &\frac{1}{10} \\ &+ \frac{5}{20} \\ \hline \end{aligned}$$

Adding Fractions with Different Denominators

When you add fractions that have different denominators, you will need to find a common denominator. This means raising one or more of the fractions to higher terms.

Use These Steps

Add $\frac{3}{4} + \frac{1}{8} + \frac{1}{2}$

1. Change $\frac{3}{4}$ to higher terms with 8 as the denominator.

$$\frac{3}{4} = \frac{3 \times 2}{4 \times 2} = \frac{6}{8}$$

2. Change $\frac{1}{2}$ to higher terms with 8 as the denominator.

$$\frac{1}{2} = \frac{1 \times 4}{2 \times 4} = \frac{4}{8}$$

3. Add the fractions. Change the answer to a mixed number.

$$\frac{3}{4} = \frac{6}{8}$$
$$\frac{1}{8} = \frac{1}{8}$$
$$+\frac{1}{2} = \frac{4}{8}$$
$$\frac{11}{8} = 1\frac{3}{8}$$

Find common denominators. Then add. Reduce if possible.

1.
$$\frac{3}{10} + \frac{2}{5} + \frac{1}{2} =$$

$$\frac{3}{10} = \frac{3}{10}$$
$$\frac{2}{5} = \frac{4}{10}$$
$$+\frac{1}{2} = \frac{5}{10}$$
$$\frac{12}{10} = 1\frac{2}{10} = 1\frac{1}{5}$$

2.
$$\frac{1}{4} + \frac{1}{8} + \frac{3}{16} =$$

3.
$$\frac{5}{18} + \frac{3}{9} + \frac{2}{3} =$$

4.
$$\frac{1}{9} + \frac{1}{3} + \frac{5}{18} =$$

5.
$$\frac{1}{4} + \frac{2}{8} + \frac{5}{16} =$$

6.
$$\frac{2}{10} + \frac{1}{5} + \frac{1}{2} =$$

7.
$$\frac{6}{20}$$
$$\frac{2}{5}$$
$$+\frac{1}{4}$$

8.
$$\frac{5}{45}$$
$$\frac{1}{9}$$
$$+\frac{1}{5}$$

9.
$$\frac{5}{20}$$
$$\frac{4}{15}$$
$$+\frac{10}{60}$$

10.
$$\frac{1}{4}$$
$$\frac{10}{52}$$
$$+\frac{1}{13}$$

11.
$$\frac{9}{25}$$
$$\frac{17}{50}$$
$$+\frac{29}{100}$$

Adding Fractions with Different Denominators

When you add fractions with different denominators, first find a common denominator. Then add. Reduce if possible.

Use These Steps

Add $\frac{1}{7} + \frac{4}{14}$

1. Change $\frac{1}{7}$ to higher terms with 14 as the common denominator.

$$\frac{1}{7} = \frac{1 \times 2}{7 \times 2} = \frac{2}{14}$$

2. Add the fractions. Reduce.

$$\frac{1}{7} = \frac{2}{14}$$
$$+ \frac{4}{14} = \frac{4}{14}$$
$$\frac{6}{14} = \frac{3}{7}$$

Add. Reduce if possible.

1.

$$\frac{3}{14} + \frac{2}{7} =$$

$$\frac{3}{14} = \frac{3}{14}$$
$$+ \frac{2}{7} = \frac{4}{14}$$
$$\frac{7}{14} = \frac{1}{2}$$

2. $\frac{2}{15} + \frac{1}{5} =$

3. $\frac{1}{4} + \frac{3}{20} =$

4. $\frac{14}{25} + \frac{2}{5} =$

5.
$$\frac{2}{9}$$
$$+ \frac{5}{18}$$

6.
$$\frac{1}{3}$$
$$+ \frac{6}{12}$$

7.
$$\frac{3}{10}$$
$$+ \frac{1}{2}$$

8.
$$\frac{21}{50}$$
$$+ \frac{6}{25}$$

9.
$$\frac{1}{10}$$
$$+ \frac{15}{100}$$

10. $\frac{1}{4} + \frac{1}{2} + \frac{1}{8} =$

11. $\frac{2}{10} + \frac{1}{2} + \frac{1}{5} =$

12. $\frac{1}{3} + \frac{2}{6} + \frac{2}{12} =$

13. Joan, a nursing assistant, spent $\frac{1}{2}$ day helping patients on the first floor and $\frac{1}{4}$ day helping patients on the second floor of the hospital. What part of the day did she spend helping patients?

14. Chris spent $\frac{1}{6}$ of his paycheck on food and $\frac{1}{3}$ on rent. What fraction of his pay did he spend on food and rent?

Answer _____

Answer _____

Adding Fractions with Different Denominators

When the sum of two or more fractions is an improper fraction, be sure
to change the sum to a mixed or whole number.

Use These Steps

Add $\frac{2}{3} + \frac{5}{9}$

1. Change $\frac{2}{3}$ to higher terms with 9 as
   the common denominator.

   $$\frac{2}{3} = \frac{2 \times 3}{3 \times 3} = \frac{6}{9}$$

2. Add the fractions. Change the sum to
   a mixed number.

   $$\frac{2}{3} = \frac{6}{9}$$
   $$+\frac{5}{9} = \frac{5}{9}$$
   $$\frac{11}{9} = 1 + \frac{2}{9} = 1\frac{2}{9}$$

Add. Change improper fractions to mixed or whole numbers. Reduce if possible.

1.
$$\frac{5}{6} + \frac{1}{3} =$$

$$\frac{5}{6} = \frac{5}{6}$$
$$+\frac{1}{3} = \frac{2}{6}$$
$$\frac{7}{6} = 1 + \frac{1}{6} = 1\frac{1}{6}$$

2.
$$\frac{7}{8} + \frac{3}{4} =$$

3.
$$\frac{5}{6} + \frac{1}{2} =$$

4.
$$\frac{3}{8} + \frac{15}{16} =$$

5.
$$\frac{1}{4} + \frac{1}{3} + \frac{7}{12} =$$

6.
$$\frac{7}{10} + \frac{1}{2} + \frac{4}{5} =$$

7.
$$\frac{9}{24} + \frac{5}{8} + \frac{2}{3} =$$

8.
$$\frac{5}{8}$$
$$+\frac{3}{4}$$

9.
$$\frac{5}{7}$$
$$+\frac{9}{14}$$

10.
$$\frac{11}{12}$$
$$+\frac{2}{3}$$

11.
$$\frac{4}{5}$$
$$+\frac{11}{15}$$

12.
$$\frac{8}{10}$$
$$+\frac{10}{50}$$

13. In the candy store, Mr. Wilton packed
    three boxes of candy weighing $\frac{12}{16}$
    pound, $\frac{3}{4}$ pound, and $\frac{6}{8}$ pound.
    What was their total weight?

14. In the fabric store, Ms. Cline cut three
    pieces of ribbon that measured $\frac{4}{5}$ yard,
    $\frac{3}{10}$ yard, and $\frac{1}{2}$ yard. What was the
    combined length of the ribbon?

Answer_____

Answer_____

Mixed Review

Raise each fraction to higher terms.

1. $\dfrac{1}{4} = \dfrac{}{8}$

2. $\dfrac{3}{4} = \dfrac{}{12}$

3. $\dfrac{2}{3} = \dfrac{}{9}$

4. $\dfrac{5}{6} = \dfrac{}{18}$

5. $\dfrac{3}{5} = \dfrac{}{20}$

Reduce each fraction to lowest terms. Write LT if in lowest terms.

6. $\dfrac{6}{9} =$

7. $\dfrac{6}{10} =$

8. $\dfrac{3}{18} =$

9. $\dfrac{13}{25} =$

10. $\dfrac{8}{16} =$

Change each fraction to a whole or mixed number.

11. $\dfrac{6}{6} =$

12. $\dfrac{15}{12} =$

13. $\dfrac{9}{3} =$

14. $\dfrac{22}{7} =$

15. $\dfrac{45}{20} =$

Add. Reduce if possible.

16. $\dfrac{3}{8} + \dfrac{1}{8} =$

17. $\dfrac{7}{12} + \dfrac{5}{12} =$

18. $\dfrac{1}{9} + \dfrac{5}{9} + \dfrac{7}{9} =$

19. $\dfrac{2}{5} + \dfrac{1}{10} =$

20. $\dfrac{3}{16} + \dfrac{1}{4} =$

21. $\dfrac{5}{24} + \dfrac{1}{6} + \dfrac{1}{4} =$

22. $\dfrac{5}{7} + \dfrac{13}{14} =$

23. $\dfrac{2}{3} + \dfrac{11}{12} =$

24. $\dfrac{13}{18} + \dfrac{1}{2} + \dfrac{5}{6} =$

25. $\begin{array}{r} \frac{1}{2} \\ + \frac{1}{10} \\ \hline \end{array}$

26. $\begin{array}{r} 2\frac{9}{14} \\ + 3\frac{3}{14} \\ \hline \end{array}$

27. $\begin{array}{r} 6\frac{11}{12} \\ + 7\frac{11}{12} \\ \hline \end{array}$

28. $\begin{array}{r} \frac{2}{5} \\ + \frac{11}{25} \\ \hline \end{array}$

29. $\begin{array}{r} 3\frac{1}{20} \\ + 7\frac{9}{20} \\ \hline \end{array}$

Application

Dr. Cynthia Morgan works at a weight loss clinic. Each week she writes down the number of pounds her patients have lost.

Weight Loss Clinic					
	Week 1	Week 2	Week 3	Week 4	Total
Mona	$\frac{13}{16}$	$\frac{3}{4}$	$\frac{5}{8}$	$\frac{3}{8}$	$2\frac{9}{16}$
Theresa	$\frac{1}{2}$	$\frac{3}{4}$	$\frac{9}{16}$	$\frac{5}{16}$	
Lisa	$\frac{3}{4}$	$\frac{15}{16}$	$\frac{1}{2}$	$\frac{3}{8}$	
Janet	$\frac{3}{8}$	$\frac{1}{4}$	$\frac{7}{8}$	$\frac{3}{16}$	
Jay					

Example How much weight did Mona lose over the four weeks?

$$\frac{13}{16} = \frac{13}{16}$$
$$\frac{3}{4} = \frac{12}{16}$$
$$\frac{5}{8} = \frac{10}{16}$$
$$+\frac{3}{8} = \frac{6}{16}$$
$$\frac{41}{16} = 2\frac{9}{16}$$

Mona lost $2\frac{9}{16}$ pounds.

Solve. Reduce if possible.

1. How much weight did Theresa lose in all?

2. How much weight did Lisa lose in all?

Answer_____

Answer_____

3. How much weight did Janet lose in all?

4. Who lost the most weight?

Answer_____

Answer_____

Comparing Denominators

The common denominator in a fractions problem may not always be the largest denominator. You can also find the common denominator by multiplying the denominators.

When you have three fractions with different denominators, you can sometimes multiply two of the denominators by each other to find the common denominator. Make sure the third denominator will divide evenly into the new denominator.

Use These Steps

Write $\frac{2}{3}$ and $\frac{1}{4}$ with a common denominator.

1. Compare the denominators. Since 3 will not divide evenly into 4, multiply 3 x 4 to get the common denominator.

   $\frac{2}{3} = \frac{}{12}$

   $\frac{1}{4} = \frac{}{12}$

2. Raise the fractions to higher terms with 12 as the denominator.

   $\frac{2}{3} = \frac{8}{12}$

   $\frac{1}{4} = \frac{3}{12}$

Find the common denominator for each set of fractions. Raise each fraction to higher terms.

1. $\frac{1}{5}$ and $\frac{2}{3}$

   $\frac{1}{5} = \frac{3}{15}$

   $\frac{2}{3} = \frac{10}{15}$

2. $\frac{2}{5}$ and $\frac{1}{4}$

3. $\frac{1}{6}$ and $\frac{3}{5}$

4. $\frac{3}{7}$ and $\frac{1}{2}$

5. $\frac{1}{3}$, $\frac{1}{4}$, and $\frac{1}{6}$

   $\frac{1}{3} = \frac{4}{12}$

   $\frac{1}{4} = \frac{3}{12}$

   $\frac{1}{6} = \frac{2}{12}$

6. $\frac{1}{2}$, $\frac{2}{5}$, and $\frac{3}{7}$

7. $\frac{4}{9}$, $\frac{1}{3}$, and $\frac{2}{7}$

8. $\frac{5}{9}$ and $\frac{1}{4}$

9. $\frac{2}{3}$, $\frac{2}{7}$, and $\frac{5}{6}$

10. $\frac{3}{4}$ and $\frac{2}{9}$

11. $\frac{3}{8}$, $\frac{3}{5}$, and $\frac{2}{3}$

Adding Fractions with Different Denominators

When multiplying the denominators to find a common denominator, change all fractions to higher terms. Reduce the answer if possible.

Use These Steps

Add $\frac{1}{6} + \frac{3}{5}$

1. Multiply the denominators to find the common denominator.

$$\frac{1}{6} = \frac{}{30}$$
$$+\frac{3}{5} = \frac{}{30}$$

2. Raise both fractions to higher terms with 30 as the common denominator.

$$\frac{1}{6} = \frac{5}{30}$$
$$+\frac{3}{5} = \frac{18}{30}$$

3. Add.

$$\frac{1}{6} = \frac{5}{30}$$
$$+\frac{3}{5} = \frac{18}{30}$$
$$\frac{23}{30}$$

Add. Reduce if possible.

1.
$$\frac{1}{2} + \frac{1}{3} =$$
$$\frac{1}{2} = \frac{3}{6}$$
$$+\frac{1}{3} = \frac{2}{6}$$
$$\frac{5}{6}$$

2.
$$\frac{2}{6} + \frac{1}{4} =$$

3.
$$\frac{3}{8} + \frac{1}{3} =$$

4.
$$\frac{1}{4} + \frac{2}{7} =$$

5.
$$\frac{1}{4} + \frac{2}{5} =$$
$$\frac{1}{4} = \frac{5}{20}$$
$$+\frac{2}{5} = \frac{8}{20}$$
$$\frac{13}{20}$$

6.
$$\frac{2}{3} + \frac{1}{6} =$$

7.
$$\frac{2}{9} + \frac{1}{3} =$$

8.
$$\frac{1}{5}$$
$$+\frac{1}{3}$$

9.
$$\frac{3}{4}$$
$$+\frac{1}{6}$$

10.
$$\frac{1}{7}$$
$$+\frac{1}{2}$$

11.
$$\frac{5}{8}$$
$$+\frac{1}{5}$$

12.
$$\frac{3}{10}$$
$$+\frac{1}{3}$$

Adding Fractions with Different Denominators

Compare the denominators before adding. Find a common denominator and add only the numerators. If the answer is an improper fraction, change to a whole or mixed number. Reduce if possible.

Use These Steps

Add $\frac{3}{4} + \frac{1}{3}$

1. Multiply the denominators to find the common denominator.

$$\frac{3}{4} = \frac{}{12}$$
$$+\frac{1}{3} = \frac{}{12}$$

2. Raise each fraction to higher terms.

$$\frac{3}{4} = \frac{9}{12}$$
$$+\frac{1}{3} = \frac{4}{12}$$

3. Add. The sum is an improper fraction. Change to a mixed number.

$$\frac{3}{4} = \frac{9}{12}$$
$$+\frac{1}{3} = \frac{4}{12}$$
$$\frac{13}{12} = 1\frac{1}{12}$$

Add. Change improper fractions to whole or mixed numbers. Reduce if possible.

1.
$$\frac{7}{8} + \frac{2}{3} =$$

$$\frac{7}{8} = \frac{21}{24}$$
$$+\frac{2}{3} = \frac{16}{24}$$
$$\frac{37}{24} = 1\frac{13}{24}$$

2.
$$\frac{4}{5} + \frac{3}{4} =$$

3.
$$\frac{1}{3} + \frac{9}{10} =$$

4.
$$\frac{5}{6} + \frac{2}{7} =$$

5.
$$\frac{1}{2} + \frac{3}{4} + \frac{1}{5} =$$

$$\frac{1}{2} = \frac{10}{20}$$
$$\frac{3}{4} = \frac{15}{20}$$
$$+\frac{1}{5} = \frac{4}{20}$$
$$\frac{29}{20} = 1\frac{9}{20}$$

6.
$$\frac{7}{8} + \frac{3}{4} + \frac{2}{3} =$$

7.
$$\frac{2}{7} + \frac{3}{5} + \frac{1}{4} =$$

8. Wilfred's Caterers used $\frac{5}{6}$ pound of corned beef, $\frac{3}{4}$ pound of turkey, and $\frac{1}{2}$ pound of ham for a small lunch party. How much did the sandwich meat weigh in all?

9. For dessert, Wilfred's used $\frac{2}{3}$ pound of apples, $\frac{3}{4}$ pound of pears, and $\frac{1}{2}$ pound of oranges. How much did the fruit weigh in all?

Answer_____   Answer_____

Finding the Lowest Common Denominator

Another way to find a common denominator is by making a list of multiples of each denominator. A multiple of a number is the number multiplied by 1, 2, 3, and so on. For example, some multiples of 2 are 2, 4, 6, 8 and 10.

After listing multiples for each denominator, find the smallest number that appears on both lists. This number is the lowest common denominator (LCD) for the fractions.

Use These Steps

Add $\frac{1}{6} + \frac{3}{4}$

1. List multiples of each denominator. The smallest number on both lists is 12. 12 is the LCD.

$\frac{1}{6}$ 6 ⑫ 18 24

$\frac{3}{4}$ 4 8 ⑫ 16

2. Raise each fraction to higher terms with 12 as the LCD.

$\frac{1}{6} = \frac{2}{12}$

$+\frac{3}{4} = \frac{9}{12}$

3. Add.

$\frac{2}{12}$

$+\frac{9}{12}$

$\frac{11}{12}$

List the multiples of each denominator to find the LCD. Change the fractions. Then add. Reduce if possible.

1. $\frac{1}{6} + \frac{1}{9} =$

$\frac{1}{6}$ 6 12 ⑱ 24

$\frac{1}{9}$ 9 ⑱ 27

$\frac{1}{6} = \frac{3}{18}$

$+\frac{1}{9} = \frac{2}{18}$

$\frac{5}{18}$

2. $\frac{5}{6} + \frac{1}{4} =$

3. $\frac{5}{8} + \frac{3}{10} =$

4. $\frac{1}{12} + \frac{3}{16} =$

5.
$\frac{1}{6}$
$+\frac{7}{10}$

6.
$\frac{5}{12}$
$+\frac{17}{18}$

7.
$\frac{4}{9}$
$+\frac{7}{12}$

8.
$\frac{3}{8}$
$+\frac{5}{6}$

Mixed Review

Write each set of fractions with common denominators.

1. $\frac{1}{2}$ and $\frac{1}{4}$

2. $\frac{1}{3}$ and $\frac{2}{5}$

3. $\frac{6}{7}$ and $\frac{2}{21}$

4. $\frac{1}{6}$ and $\frac{5}{8}$

5. $\frac{5}{9}$ and $\frac{3}{10}$

Find a common denominator. Add. Change improper fractions to whole or mixed numbers. Reduce if possible.

6. $\frac{1}{6} + \frac{1}{3} =$

7. $\frac{3}{8} + \frac{1}{4} =$

8. $\frac{2}{9} + \frac{2}{3} =$

9. $\frac{7}{16} + \frac{3}{4} =$

10. $\frac{2}{3} + \frac{3}{4} =$

11. $\frac{5}{6} + \frac{3}{5} =$

12. $\frac{3}{5} + \frac{1}{4} =$

13. $\frac{1}{2} + \frac{7}{9} =$

14. $\begin{array}{r} \frac{7}{10} \\ + \frac{4}{5} \\ \hline \end{array}$

15. $\begin{array}{r} \frac{5}{8} \\ + \frac{1}{2} \\ \hline \end{array}$

16. $\begin{array}{r} \frac{2}{7} \\ + \frac{1}{4} \\ \hline \end{array}$

17. $\begin{array}{r} \frac{1}{5} \\ + \frac{1}{3} \\ \hline \end{array}$

18. $\begin{array}{r} \frac{3}{4} \\ + \frac{2}{3} \\ \hline \end{array}$

19. $\frac{4}{5} + \frac{3}{10} + \frac{1}{2} =$

20. $\frac{3}{4} + \frac{3}{8} + \frac{3}{16} =$

21. $\frac{5}{6} + \frac{1}{3} + \frac{2}{9} =$

22. $\begin{array}{r} \frac{11}{12} \\ \frac{1}{4} \\ + \frac{2}{3} \\ \hline \end{array}$

23. $\begin{array}{r} \frac{4}{15} \\ \frac{2}{5} \\ + \frac{1}{2} \\ \hline \end{array}$

24. $\begin{array}{r} \frac{3}{7} \\ \frac{2}{21} \\ + \frac{6}{14} \\ \hline \end{array}$

25. $\begin{array}{r} \frac{1}{2} \\ \frac{3}{4} \\ + \frac{5}{6} \\ \hline \end{array}$

26. $\begin{array}{r} \frac{8}{9} \\ \frac{3}{18} \\ + \frac{1}{3} \\ \hline \end{array}$

Adding Mixed Numbers

When you add mixed numbers, you may need to find a common denominator.

Use These Steps

Add $5\frac{1}{3} + 2\frac{1}{8}$

1. Find a common denominator for the fractions.

$$5\frac{1}{3} = 5\frac{}{24}$$
$$+2\frac{1}{8} = 2\frac{}{24}$$

2. Raise each fraction to higher terms with the new denominator.

$$5\frac{1}{3} = 5\frac{8}{24}$$
$$+2\frac{1}{8} = 2\frac{3}{24}$$

3. Add the fractions. Add the whole numbers.

$$5\frac{1}{3} = 5\frac{8}{24}$$
$$+2\frac{1}{8} = 2\frac{3}{24}$$
$$7\frac{11}{24}$$

Add. Reduce if possible.

1.
$$2\frac{1}{4} + 3\frac{1}{8} =$$
$$2\frac{1}{4} = 2\frac{2}{8}$$
$$+3\frac{1}{8} = 3\frac{1}{8}$$
$$5\frac{3}{8}$$

2. $3\frac{2}{3} + 4\frac{1}{9} =$

3. $6\frac{4}{7} + 5\frac{9}{14} =$

4. $7\frac{1}{2} + 12\frac{5}{6} =$

5. $3\frac{2}{3} + 4\frac{1}{4} =$

6. $1\frac{5}{8} + 4\frac{1}{6} =$

7. $8\frac{3}{5} + 9\frac{2}{7} =$

8. $10\frac{3}{10} + 4\frac{1}{3} =$

9.
$$7\frac{1}{6} + 2\frac{2}{3} + 4\frac{7}{9} =$$
$$7\frac{1}{6} = 7\frac{3}{18}$$
$$2\frac{2}{3} = 2\frac{12}{18}$$
$$+4\frac{7}{9} = 4\frac{14}{18}$$
$$13\frac{29}{18} = 14\frac{11}{18}$$

10. $1\frac{1}{2} + 6\frac{3}{4} + 2\frac{5}{6} =$

11. $9\frac{1}{5} + 6\frac{7}{10} + 3\frac{1}{2} =$

Adding Mixed Numbers, Whole Numbers, and Fractions

When adding mixed numbers, whole numbers, and fractions, compare the denominators of the fractions. Then find a common denominator and raise fractions to higher terms.

Use These Steps

Add $2\frac{1}{2} + \frac{5}{6} + 3$

1. Compare the denominators. 2 divides evenly into 6. Raise $\frac{1}{2}$ to higher terms with 6 as the denominator.

$$2\frac{1}{2} = 2\frac{3}{6}$$
$$\frac{5}{6} = \frac{5}{6}$$
$$\underline{+3 = 3}$$

2. Add the fractions. Add the whole numbers.

$$2\frac{1}{2} = 2\frac{3}{6}$$
$$\frac{5}{6} = \frac{5}{6}$$
$$\underline{+3 = 3}$$
$$5\frac{8}{6}$$

3. Change the improper fraction in the sum to a mixed number. Add the new mixed number to the whole number. Reduce.

$$5\frac{8}{6} = 5 + 1\frac{2}{6} = 6\frac{2}{6} = 6\frac{1}{3}$$

Add. Reduce if possible.

1.

$$3\frac{7}{8} + \frac{1}{3} + 6 =$$

$$3\frac{7}{8} = 3\frac{21}{24}$$
$$\frac{1}{3} = \frac{8}{24}$$
$$\underline{+6 = 6}$$
$$9\frac{29}{24} = 9 + 1\frac{5}{24} = 10\frac{5}{24}$$

2.

$$4\frac{1}{2} + 7 =$$

3.

$$8\frac{3}{4} + \frac{5}{6} =$$

4.

$$7 + 2\frac{1}{8} + \frac{3}{7} =$$

5.

$$\frac{9}{10} + 3\frac{1}{5} + 20 =$$

6.

$$\frac{5}{12} + 2\frac{1}{6} + 4 =$$

7.

$$\begin{array}{r} 3 \\ \frac{5}{6} \\ +2\frac{1}{2} \\ \hline \end{array}$$

8.

$$\begin{array}{r} 15\frac{1}{2} \\ 7 \\ +2\frac{3}{12} \\ \hline \end{array}$$

9.

$$\begin{array}{r} 8\frac{9}{10} \\ 6 \\ +2\frac{8}{15} \\ \hline \end{array}$$

10.

$$\begin{array}{r} \frac{1}{4} \\ \frac{1}{6} \\ +9\frac{1}{12} \\ \hline \end{array}$$

11.

$$\begin{array}{r} 18 \\ 24\frac{2}{5} \\ +12\frac{7}{30} \\ \hline \end{array}$$

Problem Solving: Using Time Records

Several parents serve as teachers' aides in the Southside Elementary School. Reiko writes down the hours worked each day. At the end of the week, she adds the hours to get the total hours each person worked.

Aide	November 5					Hours Worked Total
	M	Tu	W	Th	F	
Tim	$2\frac{2}{3}$	$2\frac{1}{3}$	3	$4\frac{3}{4}$	$3\frac{1}{4}$	16
Jorge	$3\frac{3}{4}$	$5\frac{1}{2}$	$6\frac{1}{3}$	$3\frac{3}{4}$	$5\frac{2}{3}$	
Sue	$6\frac{1}{3}$	7	$6\frac{1}{2}$	$4\frac{1}{2}$	$5\frac{2}{3}$	
Rachel	$6\frac{2}{3}$	$5\frac{2}{3}$	$5\frac{1}{2}$	$5\frac{1}{2}$	$5\frac{2}{3}$	

Example Find the total hours Tim worked the week of November 5. Write the amount in the chart.

Step 1. Multiply 3×4 to find the common denominator. Change all fractions to higher terms with 12 as the denominator. Add.

$$2\frac{2}{3} = 2\frac{8}{12}$$
$$2\frac{1}{3} = 2\frac{4}{12}$$
$$3 \quad = 3$$
$$4\frac{3}{4} = 4\frac{9}{12}$$
$$+\,3\frac{1}{4} = 3\frac{3}{12}$$
$$\overline{14\frac{24}{12}}$$

Step 2. Change $\frac{24}{12}$ to 2. Add 2 to 14.

$$14 + 2 = 16$$

The week of November 5, Tim worked a total of 16 hours. 16 is written in the total column at the end of Tim's row.

Solve. Reduce if possible.

1. Find the total hours that Jorge worked. Write the amount in the chart.

Answer_____

2. Find the total hours for Sue. Write the total in the chart.

Answer_____

3. Find the total hours Rachel worked. Write this total in the chart.

Answer_____

4. Find the grand total of the hours all four teachers' aides worked.

Answer_____

Example

During the week of September 24, the teachers' aides worked a grand total of 48 hours. Ray worked 12 hours that week. What fraction of the grand total did Ray work during the week of September 24?

Aide	September			
	3	10	17	24
Ray	0	$8\frac{1}{2}$	17	12
June	5	$5\frac{1}{2}$	15	6
Carlos	3	2	$4\frac{1}{2}$	$12\frac{3}{4}$
Kenji	7	8	$13\frac{1}{2}$	$17\frac{1}{4}$
Total	15	24	50	48

Step 1. Set up a fraction with the number of hours Ray worked, 12, as the numerator. The grand total, 48, is the denominator.

$$\frac{12}{48}$$

Step 2. Reduce the fraction to lowest terms.

$$\frac{12}{48} = \frac{1}{4}$$

Ray worked $\frac{1}{4}$ of the grand total during the week of September 24.

Solve. Reduce if possible.

5. What fraction of the grand total for the week of September 17 did June work?

Answer_____

6. What fraction of the grand total for the week of September 10 did Kenji work?

Answer_____

7. What fraction of the grand total for the week of September 3 did Carlos work?

Answer_____

8. What fraction of the grand total for the week of September 10 did Carlos work?

Answer_____

Unit 2 Review

Add. Change improper fractions to mixed or whole numbers. Reduce if possible.

1. $\frac{1}{3} + \frac{1}{3} =$

2. $\frac{1}{4} + \frac{2}{4} =$

3. $\frac{3}{8} + \frac{2}{8} =$

4. $\frac{12}{15} + \frac{2}{15} =$

5. $\frac{1}{16}$
$+ \frac{12}{16}$

6. $\frac{7}{10}$
$+ \frac{2}{10}$

7. $\frac{4}{25}$
$+ \frac{13}{25}$

8. $\frac{3}{50}$
$+ \frac{26}{50}$

9. $\frac{14}{100}$
$+ \frac{27}{100}$

10. $\frac{2}{6} + \frac{1}{6} =$

11. $\frac{5}{9} + \frac{5}{9} =$

12. $\frac{7}{11} + \frac{5}{11} =$

13. $\frac{4}{5} + \frac{3}{5} + \frac{4}{5} =$

14. $\frac{2}{7}$
$+ \frac{5}{7}$

15. $\frac{5}{8}$
$+ \frac{7}{8}$

16. $\frac{3}{6}$
$+ \frac{4}{6}$

17. $\frac{3}{10}$
$+ \frac{3}{10}$

18. $\frac{5}{12}$
$+ \frac{7}{12}$

19. $3\frac{1}{2} + 2\frac{1}{2} =$

20. $16\frac{3}{8} + 10\frac{7}{8} =$

21. $21\frac{2}{9} + 29\frac{4}{9} =$

22. $1\frac{9}{10} + 2 + \frac{7}{10} =$

23. $5\frac{1}{4}$
$+ 6\frac{1}{4}$

24. $10\frac{7}{8}$
$+ 12\frac{5}{8}$

25. $9\frac{7}{10}$
$+ 15\frac{1}{10}$

26. $18\frac{4}{18}$
$+ 3\frac{16}{18}$

27. $7\frac{3}{20}$
$+ 4\frac{9}{20}$

28. $\frac{2}{5} + \frac{3}{10} =$

29. $\frac{3}{16} + \frac{1}{2} =$

30. $\frac{5}{18} + \frac{3}{9} =$

31. $\frac{3}{4} + \frac{1}{8} =$

32. $\frac{2}{7}$
$+ \frac{1}{14}$

33. $\frac{1}{2}$
$+ \frac{5}{12}$

34. $\frac{1}{5}$
$+ \frac{1}{10}$

35. $\frac{4}{15}$
$+ \frac{2}{3}$

36. $\frac{19}{25}$
$+ \frac{1}{5}$

Add. Change improper fractions to mixed or whole numbers. Reduce if possible.

37. $\frac{1}{3} + \frac{1}{6} =$

38. $\frac{1}{2} + \frac{5}{10} =$

39. $\frac{3}{12} + \frac{5}{6} =$

40. $\frac{2}{3} + \frac{5}{6} + \frac{1}{2} =$

41.
$$\frac{4}{16}$$
$$+ \frac{3}{8}$$

42.
$$\frac{2}{3}$$
$$+ \frac{5}{12}$$

43.
$$\frac{2}{7}$$
$$+ \frac{15}{21}$$

44.
$$\frac{7}{30}$$
$$+ \frac{14}{15}$$

45.
$$\frac{1}{2}$$
$$+ \frac{9}{10}$$

46. $\frac{2}{6} + \frac{1}{4} =$

47. $\frac{5}{8} + \frac{2}{3} =$

48. $\frac{3}{4} + \frac{1}{7} =$

49. $\frac{3}{10} + \frac{2}{3} + \frac{1}{2} =$

50.
$$\frac{1}{2}$$
$$+ \frac{2}{3}$$

51.
$$\frac{3}{4}$$
$$+ \frac{5}{6}$$

52.
$$\frac{2}{5}$$
$$+ \frac{1}{3}$$

53.
$$\frac{5}{9}$$
$$+ \frac{1}{2}$$

54.
$$\frac{5}{6}$$
$$+ \frac{3}{8}$$

55. $3\frac{1}{2} + 6\frac{2}{3} =$

56. $3\frac{3}{5} + 9\frac{1}{4} + 2 =$

57. $\frac{1}{8} + 14\frac{2}{6} + 3 =$

58.
$$5\frac{1}{4}$$
$$+ 6\frac{1}{3}$$

59.
$$1\frac{2}{5}$$
$$+ 9\frac{3}{4}$$

60.
$$8\frac{9}{10}$$
$$+ 6\frac{5}{6}$$

61.
$$15\frac{1}{9}$$
$$+ 2\frac{1}{2}$$

62.
$$27\frac{5}{6}$$
$$+ 19\frac{1}{8}$$

Below is a list of the problems in this review and the pages on which the skills are taught. If you missed any problems, turn to the pages listed and practice the skills. Then correct the problems you missed in the Unit Review.

Problems	Pages		Problems	Pages
1-9	41-42		37-45	57-59
10-18	44-46		46-54	62-65
19-27	49-51		55-62	67-68
28-36	55-56			

Unit 3 SUBTRACTING FRACTIONS

Subtraction problems with fractions usually ask you to find the difference between two numbers or how much is left after using part of something. You may have needed to subtract fractions when doing inventory or figuring distance on a car trip.

In this unit you will learn how to subtract fractions and mixed numbers, how to subtract fractions from whole numbers, and how to solve word problems using fractions.

Getting Ready

You should be familiar with the skills on this page and the next before you begin this unit. To check your answers, turn to page 182.

 When subtracting, you may need to borrow.

Subtract.

1.	2.	3.	4.	5.
15	92	40	700	401
− 7	− 39	− 18	− 26	− 193
8				

6.	7.	8.	9.	10.
831	284	3,106	8,000	26,002
− 256	− 194	− 928	− 6,241	− 9,607

To raise a fraction to higher terms with a given denominator, multiply the numerator and denominator by the same number.

Write each fraction using the given denominator.

11.
$$\frac{3}{4} = \frac{6}{8}$$

12.
$$\frac{1}{2} = \frac{}{10}$$

13.
$$\frac{2}{3} = \frac{}{12}$$

14.
$$\frac{3}{5} = \frac{}{15}$$

15.
$$\frac{3}{7} = \frac{}{21}$$

16.
$$\frac{4}{9} = \frac{}{27}$$

17.
$$\frac{1}{10} = \frac{}{30}$$

18.
$$\frac{5}{8} = \frac{}{40}$$

19.
$$\frac{7}{12} = \frac{}{48}$$

20.
$$\frac{5}{15} = \frac{}{60}$$

For review, see Unit 1, pages 19–20.

 Before adding or subtracting fractions, you may need to find a common denominator.

Write each set of fractions with a common denominator.

21.
$\frac{1}{4}$ and $\frac{1}{2}$
$\frac{1}{4}$ and $\frac{2}{4}$

22.
$\frac{2}{3}$ and $\frac{3}{4}$

23.
$\frac{5}{7}$ and $\frac{3}{5}$

24.
$3\frac{3}{12}$ and $1\frac{1}{4}$

25.
$2\frac{1}{10}$ and $6\frac{3}{5}$

26.
$\frac{3}{8}$ and $\frac{5}{6}$

27.
$2\frac{4}{9}$ and $5\frac{1}{18}$

28.
$\frac{3}{10}$ and $\frac{3}{25}$

29.
$\frac{2}{3}$ and $\frac{2}{9}$

30.
$\frac{1}{6}$ and $\frac{1}{4}$

For review, see Unit 1, page 25.

 To reduce fractions to lowest terms, divide the numerator and the denominator by the same number.

Reduce each fraction to lowest terms. If the fraction is in lowest terms, write LT.

31.
$$\frac{3}{6} = \frac{1}{2}$$

32.
$$\frac{10}{11} =$$

33.
$$\frac{8}{12} =$$

34.
$$2\frac{15}{25} =$$

35.
$$5\frac{7}{15} =$$

36.
$$\frac{2}{9} =$$

37.
$$\frac{4}{8} =$$

38.
$$\frac{4}{16} =$$

39.
$$2\frac{7}{21} =$$

40.
$$\frac{10}{35} =$$

For review, see Unit 1, pages 15–16.

Subtracting Fractions with the Same Denominator

To subtract fractions with the same denominator, subtract only the numerators. Keep the denominator.

$$\frac{5}{6} \quad - \quad \frac{4}{6} \quad = \quad \frac{1}{6}$$

Use These Steps

Subtract $\frac{5}{8} - \frac{2}{8}$

1. The denominators are the same. Write the denominator under the fraction bar.

$$\frac{5}{8} - \frac{2}{8} = \frac{}{8}$$

2. Subtract only the numerators. $5 - 2 = 3$. Write the difference over the denominator.

$$\frac{5}{8} - \frac{2}{8} = \frac{3}{8}$$

Shade in the figures to show the fractions. Subtract the fractions. Then shade in the final figure to show the difference.

1.

$$\frac{7}{8} - \frac{4}{8} = \frac{3}{8}$$

2.

$$\frac{3}{5} - \frac{1}{5} =$$

3.

$$\frac{7}{9} - \frac{3}{9} =$$

4.

$$\frac{4}{6} - \frac{3}{6} =$$

Subtract.

5. $\frac{5}{9} - \frac{3}{9} = \frac{2}{9}$

6. $\frac{4}{6} - \frac{3}{6} =$

7. $\frac{4}{7} - \frac{1}{7} =$

8. $\frac{4}{5} - \frac{2}{5} =$

Subtracting Fractions with the Same Denominator

Fraction problems may be set up horizontally or vertically. Be sure the denominators are the same and subtract only the numerators.

Use These Steps

Subtract
$$\frac{7}{10}$$
$$-\frac{4}{10}$$

1. The denominators are the same. Write the denominator under the fraction bar.

$$\frac{7}{10}$$
$$-\frac{4}{10}$$
$$\overline{\frac{}{10}}$$

2. Subtract only the numerators. $7 - 4 = 3$. Write the difference over the denominator.

$$\frac{7}{10}$$
$$-\frac{4}{10}$$
$$\frac{3}{10}$$

Subtract.

1.
$$\frac{7}{14}$$
$$-\frac{4}{14}$$
$$\frac{3}{14}$$

2.
$$\frac{9}{16}$$
$$-\frac{2}{16}$$

3.
$$\frac{15}{25}$$
$$-\frac{9}{25}$$

4.
$$\frac{11}{12}$$
$$-\frac{4}{12}$$

5.
$$\frac{5}{7}$$
$$-\frac{3}{7}$$

6. $\frac{6}{9} - \frac{2}{9} =$

7. $\frac{8}{10} - \frac{1}{10} =$

8. $\frac{13}{15} - \frac{5}{15} =$

9. $\frac{17}{20} - \frac{10}{20} =$

10.
$$\frac{29}{30}$$
$$-\frac{18}{30}$$

11.
$$\frac{11}{50}$$
$$-\frac{8}{50}$$

12.
$$\frac{31}{42}$$
$$-\frac{12}{42}$$

13.
$$\frac{9}{11}$$
$$-\frac{6}{11}$$

14.
$$\frac{99}{100}$$
$$-\frac{68}{100}$$

15. $\frac{60}{75} - \frac{37}{75} =$

16. $\frac{50}{63} - \frac{25}{63} =$

17. $\frac{18}{35} - \frac{9}{35} =$

18. $\frac{12}{18} - \frac{7}{18} =$

19. Louise's Diner had $\frac{3}{4}$ pound of butter. The chef used $\frac{2}{4}$ pound for breakfast. How much butter is left?

20. Roland had $\frac{7}{8}$ yard of plastic tubing. He used $\frac{4}{8}$ yard. How much plastic tubing was left?

Answer _____

Answer _____

Subtracting and Reducing Fractions

When subtracting fractions, you may get an answer that can be reduced.
Always reduce answers to lowest terms.

Use These Steps

Subtract $\dfrac{3}{16} - \dfrac{1}{16}$

1. The denominators are the same. Write the denominator under the fraction bar.

$$\frac{3}{16} - \frac{1}{16} = \frac{}{16}$$

2. Subtract the numerators. Write the difference over the denominator.

$$\frac{3}{16} - \frac{1}{16} = \frac{2}{16}$$

3. Reduce the answer to lowest terms.

$$\frac{2}{16} = \frac{2 \div 2}{16 \div 2} = \frac{1}{8}$$

Subtract. Reduce to lowest terms.

1.
$$\frac{4}{9} - \frac{1}{9} =$$
$$\frac{3}{9} = \frac{3 \div 3}{9 \div 3} = \frac{1}{3}$$

2.
$$\frac{10}{12} - \frac{1}{12} =$$

3.
$$\frac{5}{8} - \frac{3}{8} =$$

4.
$$\frac{7}{10} - \frac{2}{10} =$$

5.
$$\frac{3}{4} - \frac{1}{4} =$$

6.
$$\frac{5}{6} - \frac{3}{6} =$$

7.
$$\frac{13}{14} - \frac{7}{14} =$$

8.
$$\frac{12}{15} - \frac{2}{15} =$$

9.
$$\frac{4}{6}$$
$$-\frac{1}{6}$$

10.
$$\frac{7}{8}$$
$$-\frac{1}{8}$$

11.
$$\frac{5}{10}$$
$$-\frac{3}{10}$$

12.
$$\frac{17}{20}$$
$$-\frac{2}{20}$$

13.
$$\frac{20}{21}$$
$$-\frac{6}{21}$$

14.
$$\frac{20}{27}$$
$$-\frac{2}{27}$$

15.
$$\frac{24}{30}$$
$$-\frac{19}{30}$$

16.
$$\frac{34}{35}$$
$$-\frac{20}{35}$$

17.
$$\frac{46}{50}$$
$$-\frac{21}{50}$$

18.
$$\frac{90}{100}$$
$$-\frac{15}{100}$$

19. Jim's Nursery had $\frac{3}{4}$ ton of topsoil. Jim used $\frac{1}{4}$ ton to make potting soil. How much topsoil did he have left?

20. Anne bought $\frac{9}{16}$ bushel of peaches. She used $\frac{7}{16}$ bushel to make jam to sell at the Farmer's Market. How much did she have left?

Answer _____

Answer _____

Subtracting Mixed Numbers

You know that a mixed number has a whole number and a fraction. When subtracting mixed numbers, subtract the fractions and then the whole numbers. Reduce the answer if possible.

Use These Steps

Subtract $3\frac{5}{9} - 1\frac{2}{9}$

1. Line up the fractions and the whole numbers in columns.

$$3\frac{5}{9}$$
$$-1\frac{2}{9}$$

2. Subtract the fractions.

$$3\frac{5}{9}$$
$$-1\frac{2}{9}$$
$$\frac{3}{9}$$

3. Subtract the whole numbers. Reduce the fraction to lowest terms.

$$3\frac{5}{9}$$
$$-1\frac{2}{9}$$
$$2\frac{3}{9} = 2\frac{1}{3}$$

Subtract. Reduce if possible.

1.
$5\frac{5}{6} - 1\frac{2}{6} =$

$5\frac{5}{6}$
$-1\frac{2}{6}$
$\overline{4\frac{3}{6}} = 4\frac{1}{2}$

2.
$10\frac{7}{8} - 5\frac{5}{8} =$

3.
$7\frac{3}{4} - 1\frac{1}{4} =$

4.
$15\frac{11}{12} - 8\frac{8}{12} =$

5.
$18\frac{17}{20}$
$-15\frac{2}{20}$

6.
$13\frac{23}{28}$
$-2\frac{19}{28}$

7.
$26\frac{27}{30}$
$-19\frac{12}{30}$

8.
$15\frac{30}{45}$
$-11\frac{21}{45}$

9.
$31\frac{20}{50}$
$-27\frac{15}{50}$

10.
$7\frac{9}{10} - 4\frac{3}{10} =$

11.
$13\frac{7}{16} - 2\frac{4}{16} =$

12.
$15\frac{11}{15} - 9\frac{8}{15} =$

13.
$20\frac{15}{18} - 6\frac{3}{18} =$

14. Willie bought $2\frac{7}{8}$ yards of material to make seat covers for his truck. He used $1\frac{3}{8}$ yards for one seat cover. How many yards does he have left?

15. Willie also bought $12\frac{3}{4}$ yards of trim. He used $6\frac{1}{4}$ yards for one seat cover. How much trim does he have left?

Answer_____

Answer_____

Application

Adrienne works at the city animal shelter. Her job is to feed the dogs and cats twice a day. She measures the animals' food from large bags.

Example Adrienne used $12\frac{3}{8}$ pounds of dog food from a bag that had $21\frac{7}{8}$ pounds in it. How much was left in the bag?

To find the amount left, subtract. Reduce to lowest terms.

$$21\frac{7}{8}$$
$$-12\frac{3}{8}$$
$$9\frac{4}{8} = 9\frac{1}{2}$$

There were $9\frac{1}{2}$ pounds of dog food left in the bag.

Solve. Reduce if possible.

1. Adrienne needed $12\frac{7}{8}$ pounds of puppy food to feed the puppies. The open bag of food only had $10\frac{3}{8}$ pounds in it. How much more puppy food did she need?

   Answer_____

2. It takes $10\frac{5}{16}$ pounds of cat food to feed all the cats in the shelter. Adrienne gets this amount from a bag that has $14\frac{9}{16}$ pounds in it. How much is left in the bag after she feeds all the cats?

   Answer_____

3. Adrienne gives each of the animals water from a container that holds $15\frac{2}{3}$ cups. She uses $10\frac{1}{3}$ cups. How many cups of water are left in the container?

   Answer_____

4. Adrienne checks the amount of food left at the end of each day. Today she counted $50\frac{3}{4}$ pounds of dog food and $28\frac{1}{4}$ pounds of cat food. How much more dog food than cat food is left?

   Answer_____

Subtracting Fractions from Mixed Numbers

When you subtract a fraction from a mixed number, first subtract the fractions. Since there is no whole number to subtract, bring down the whole number part of the mixed number into the answer.

Use These Steps

Subtract $5\frac{4}{10} - \frac{2}{10}$

1. Line up the fractions.

$$5\frac{4}{10}$$
$$-\ \frac{2}{10}$$

2. Subtract the fractions. Bring down the whole number.

$$5\frac{4}{10}$$
$$-\ \frac{2}{10}$$
$$5\frac{2}{10}$$

3. Reduce the fraction to lowest terms.

$$5\frac{2}{10} = 5\frac{1}{5}$$

Subtract. Reduce if possible.

1.
$$3\frac{5}{16} - \frac{3}{16} =$$
$$3\frac{5}{16}$$
$$-\ \frac{3}{16}$$
$$3\frac{2}{16} = 3\frac{1}{8}$$

2. $9\frac{7}{12} - \frac{1}{12} =$

3. $11\frac{2}{3} - \frac{1}{3} =$

4. $4\frac{9}{15} - \frac{4}{15} =$

5.
$$36\frac{18}{25}$$
$$-\ \frac{3}{25}$$

6.
$$42\frac{12}{21}$$
$$-\ \frac{5}{21}$$

7.
$$50\frac{26}{32}$$
$$-\ \frac{16}{32}$$

8.
$$61\frac{48}{49}$$
$$-\ \frac{34}{49}$$

9.
$$79\frac{33}{100}$$
$$-\ \frac{24}{100}$$

10. $12\frac{9}{10} - \frac{3}{10} =$

11. $20\frac{5}{18} - \frac{2}{18} =$

12. $14\frac{11}{20} - \frac{1}{20} =$

13. $22\frac{9}{17} - \frac{2}{17} =$

14.
$$59\frac{14}{15}$$
$$-\ \frac{12}{15}$$

15.
$$32\frac{9}{16}$$
$$-\ \frac{5}{16}$$

16.
$$44\frac{20}{27}$$
$$-\ \frac{2}{27}$$

17.
$$95\frac{27}{50}$$
$$-\ \frac{2}{50}$$

18.
$$102\frac{60}{75}$$
$$-\ \frac{15}{75}$$

Subtracting Whole Numbers from Mixed Numbers

When you subtract a whole number from a mixed number, first bring down the fraction. Then subtract the whole numbers.

Use These Steps

Subtract $9\frac{7}{8} - 3$

1. Line up the whole numbers.

$$9\frac{7}{8}$$
$$-3$$

2. Bring down the fraction.

$$9\frac{7}{8}$$
$$-3$$
$$\overline{\frac{7}{8}}$$

3. Subtract the whole numbers.

$$9\frac{7}{8}$$
$$-3$$
$$\overline{6\frac{7}{8}}$$

Subtract.

1.
$$12\frac{5}{11} - 9 =$$
$$12\frac{5}{11}$$
$$-9$$
$$\overline{3\frac{5}{11}}$$

2.
$$15\frac{2}{3} - 7 =$$

3.
$$19\frac{1}{7} - 13 =$$

4.
$$5\frac{2}{9} - 3 =$$

5.
$$57\frac{9}{16}$$
$$-32$$

6.
$$84\frac{22}{35}$$
$$-19$$

7.
$$99\frac{9}{10}$$
$$-80$$

8.
$$117\frac{27}{50}$$
$$-94$$

9.
$$125\frac{73}{100}$$
$$-46$$

10.
$$23\frac{7}{13} - 14 =$$

11.
$$30\frac{10}{21} - 15 =$$

12.
$$25\frac{9}{20} - 18 =$$

13.
$$41\frac{12}{25} - 37 =$$

14. Joseph had $3\frac{1}{2}$ pounds of grass seed. He used 2 pounds on a bare patch of lawn in front of City Hall. How much did he have left?

15. Joseph had $1\frac{3}{4}$ gallons of paint. He used 1 gallon to paint the entrance to City Hall. How much paint did he have left?

Answer _____

Answer _____

Mixed Review

Reduce each fraction to lowest terms.

1.
$$\frac{12}{16} =$$

2.
$$\frac{2}{10} =$$

3.
$$\frac{6}{9} =$$

4.
$$\frac{2}{4} =$$

5.
$$\frac{16}{18} =$$

Add or subtract. Reduce if possible.

6.
$$\frac{3}{5} + \frac{1}{5} =$$

7.
$$3\frac{6}{9} - \frac{3}{9} =$$

8.
$$\frac{5}{6} - \frac{2}{6} =$$

9.
$$1\frac{5}{8} + 5\frac{1}{8} =$$

10.
$$\frac{1}{7} + \frac{3}{7} =$$

11.
$$2\frac{3}{10} + 4\frac{3}{10} =$$

12.
$$5\frac{7}{12} - 1\frac{1}{12} =$$

13.
$$\frac{8}{15} - \frac{3}{15} =$$

14.
$$14\frac{3}{20}$$
$$+ 18\frac{2}{20}$$

15.
$$1\frac{8}{9}$$
$$- \frac{2}{9}$$

16.
$$\frac{12}{25}$$
$$- \frac{7}{25}$$

17.
$$1\frac{3}{13}$$
$$+ 9\frac{7}{13}$$

18.
$$\frac{9}{14}$$
$$- \frac{5}{14}$$

19.
$$\frac{11}{35}$$
$$+ \frac{16}{35}$$

20.
$$2\frac{16}{27}$$
$$- 2\frac{13}{27}$$

21.
$$5\frac{4}{30}$$
$$+ 6\frac{16}{30}$$

22.
$$10\frac{8}{21}$$
$$- 1\frac{5}{21}$$

23.
$$\frac{15}{42}$$
$$- \frac{9}{42}$$

24.
$$2\frac{9}{10} + 3 =$$

25.
$$\frac{7}{16} - \frac{3}{16} =$$

26.
$$10\frac{7}{18} + 3\frac{2}{18} =$$

27.
$$\frac{6}{7} - \frac{3}{7} =$$

28.
$$21\frac{3}{5}$$
$$- 5$$

29.
$$4\frac{19}{49}$$
$$+ \frac{22}{49}$$

30.
$$\frac{63}{75}$$
$$- \frac{13}{75}$$

31.
$$12\frac{27}{64}$$
$$- 4\frac{19}{64}$$

32.
$$43\frac{98}{100}$$
$$+ 7\frac{1}{100}$$

33.
$$19\frac{2}{3} - 11 =$$

34.
$$\frac{6}{20} + \frac{3}{20} =$$

35.
$$\frac{7}{10} - \frac{5}{10} =$$

36.
$$6\frac{5}{12} - 3\frac{1}{12} =$$

Problem Solving: Using a Ruler

The ruler below is divided into inches and fractions of an inch: halves, fourths, eighths, and sixteenths.

To find the distance between two points on the ruler, first find the distance from zero for both points. Then subtract.

Example How far is point F from point A?

Step 1. Find point F. The nearest whole inch mark to the left is 2. The mark at the arrow is $\frac{3}{4}$ inch from 2. Point F is $2\frac{3}{4}$ inches from zero.

Step 2. Find point A. The nearest whole inch mark to the left is zero. The mark at the arrow is $\frac{1}{4}$ inch from zero. Point A is $\frac{1}{4}$ inch from zero.

Step 3. Subtract. Reduce to lowest terms.

$$\begin{array}{r} 2\frac{3}{4} \\ - \ \frac{1}{4} \\ \hline 2\frac{2}{4} = 2\frac{1}{2} \end{array}$$

Point F is $2\frac{1}{2}$ inches from point A.

Use the ruler to answer the questions. Reduce if possible.

1. How far from point B is point I?

2. How far from point A is point J?

Answer_____

Answer_____

3. How far from point B is point G?

4. How far from point C is point D?

Answer_____

Answer_____

Use the ruler to answer the questions. Reduce if possible.

5. How far from point D is point E?

Answer_____

6. How far from point F is point J?

Answer_____

7. How far from point C is point F?

Answer_____

8. How far from point G is point I?

Answer_____

9. Mike drew a line from point H to point J on the ruler. How long was the line he drew?

Answer_____

10. Tony drew a line from point A to point H on the ruler. How long was the line he drew?

Answer_____

Solve. Reduce if possible.

11. Sam makes and sells picture frames. He has a piece of picture frame molding that is $4\frac{1}{2}$ inches long. If he cuts off $3\frac{1}{2}$ inches, how much molding will he have left?

Answer_____

12. Sam is making a picture frame that is $6\frac{1}{4}$ inches long. He has a piece of molding that is $9\frac{3}{4}$ inches long. If he cuts off $6\frac{1}{4}$ inches, how much will he have left?

Answer_____

13. Sam's assistant measured a large photograph to frame. It is $34\frac{1}{4}$ inches wide and $36\frac{3}{4}$ inches long. What is the difference between its height and its width?

Answer_____

14. A large poster that needs a frame is $52\frac{5}{8}$ inches tall and $49\frac{1}{8}$ inches wide. How much greater is the height than the width?

Answer_____

Changing Whole Numbers to Mixed Numbers

To change a whole number to a mixed number, you will need to borrow 1 from the whole number. Change the 1 to an improper fraction.

$$2 = 1\frac{4}{4}$$

Use These Steps

Change 4 to a mixed number with 6 as the denominator.

1. Borrow 1 from 4.

$$4 - 1 = 3$$

2. Change 1 to an improper fraction with 6 as the denominator.

$$1 = \frac{6}{6}$$

3. Write $\frac{6}{6}$ next to the 3.

$$3\frac{6}{6}$$

Change each whole number to a mixed number with the given denominator.

1. $1 = \dfrac{\boxed{3}}{3}$

2. $1 = \dfrac{\square}{5}$

3. $1 = \dfrac{\square}{10}$

4. $1 = \dfrac{\square}{7}$

5. $2 = 1\dfrac{\boxed{2}}{2}$

6. $3 = 2\dfrac{\square}{5}$

7. $7 = 6\dfrac{\square}{10}$

8. $9 = 8\dfrac{\square}{12}$

9. $6 = 5\dfrac{\square}{7}$

10. $4 = 3\dfrac{\square}{6}$

11. $5 = 4\dfrac{\square}{4}$

12. $8 = 7\dfrac{\square}{9}$

13. $12 = 11\dfrac{\square}{3}$

14. $15 = 14\dfrac{\square}{16}$

15. $10 = 9\dfrac{\square}{14}$

16. $17 = 16\dfrac{\square}{15}$

17. $27 = \boxed{26}\dfrac{\boxed{5}}{5}$

18. $99 = \square\dfrac{\square}{12}$

19. $14 = \square\dfrac{\square}{17}$

20. $19 = \square\dfrac{\square}{20}$

21. $121 = \square\dfrac{\square}{8}$

22. $136 = \square\dfrac{\square}{11}$

23. $140 = \square\dfrac{\square}{18}$

24. $59 = \square\dfrac{\square}{21}$

25. $100 = \square\dfrac{\square}{25}$

26. $90 = \square\dfrac{\square}{30}$

27. $101 = \square\dfrac{\square}{49}$

28. $128 = \square\dfrac{\square}{100}$

Subtracting Fractions from One

To subtract a fraction from 1, you must change the 1 to an improper fraction. Use the denominator of the fraction being subtracted.

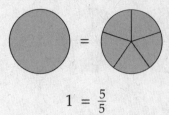

$$1 = \frac{5}{5}$$

Use These Steps

Subtract $1 - \frac{2}{5}$

1. Set up the problem.

$$\begin{array}{r} 1 \\ - \frac{2}{5} \\ \hline \end{array}$$

2. Change 1 to an improper fraction with 5 as the denominator. 5 is the denominator of the fraction being subtracted.

$$1 = \frac{5}{5}$$

3. Subtract the fractions.

$$\begin{array}{r} 1 = \frac{5}{5} \\ - \frac{2}{5} = \frac{2}{5} \\ \hline \frac{3}{5} \end{array}$$

Change 1 to an improper fraction with the given denominator.

1. $1 = \dfrac{\boxed{9}}{9}$

2. $1 = \dfrac{\boxed{}}{6}$

3. $1 = \dfrac{\boxed{}}{10}$

4. $1 = \dfrac{\boxed{}}{15}$

5. $1 = \dfrac{\boxed{}}{50}$

Subtract.

6. $1 - \dfrac{3}{7} =$

$$\begin{array}{r} 1 = \frac{7}{7} \\ - \frac{3}{7} = \frac{3}{7} \\ \hline \frac{4}{7} \end{array}$$

7. $1 - \dfrac{7}{12} =$

8. $1 - \dfrac{11}{15} =$

9. $1 - \dfrac{12}{25} =$

10.
$$\begin{array}{r} 1 \\ - \frac{5}{6} \\ \hline \end{array}$$

11.
$$\begin{array}{r} 1 \\ - \frac{10}{19} \\ \hline \end{array}$$

12.
$$\begin{array}{r} 1 \\ - \frac{6}{11} \\ \hline \end{array}$$

13.
$$\begin{array}{r} 1 \\ - \frac{14}{17} \\ \hline \end{array}$$

14.
$$\begin{array}{r} 1 \\ - \frac{29}{30} \\ \hline \end{array}$$

15. $1 - \dfrac{2}{3} =$

16. $1 - \dfrac{9}{10} =$

17. $1 - \dfrac{3}{8} =$

18. $1 - \dfrac{7}{20} =$

Subtracting Fractions from Whole Numbers

To subtract a fraction from a whole number, you must borrow 1 from the whole number. Change 1 to an improper fraction. Use the denominator of the fraction being subtracted.

Use These Steps

Subtract $5 - \frac{1}{2}$

1. Set up the problem.

$$5$$
$$- \frac{1}{2}$$

2. Borrow 1 from 5. $5 - 1 = 4$. Change the borrowed 1 to an improper fraction with 2 as the denominator.

$$5 = 4\frac{2}{2}$$
$$- \frac{1}{2} = \frac{1}{2}$$

3. Subtract the fractions. Bring down the whole number, 4.

$$5 = 4\frac{2}{2}$$
$$- \frac{1}{2} = \frac{1}{2}$$
$$\overline{\qquad 4\frac{1}{2}}$$

Subtract.

1.
$$2 - \frac{2}{3} =$$
$$2 = 1\frac{3}{3}$$
$$- \frac{2}{3} = \frac{2}{3}$$
$$\overline{\qquad 1\frac{1}{3}}$$

2. $5 - \frac{3}{4} =$

3. $4 - \frac{3}{10} =$

4. $8 - \frac{4}{9} =$

5.
$$30$$
$$- \frac{11}{18}$$

6.
$$26$$
$$- \frac{19}{20}$$

7.
$$37$$
$$- \frac{13}{21}$$

8.
$$40$$
$$- \frac{3}{25}$$

9.
$$53$$
$$- \frac{12}{35}$$

10. $10 - \frac{3}{5} =$

11. $13 - \frac{5}{6} =$

12. $15 - \frac{7}{12} =$

13. $21 - \frac{2}{15} =$

14.
$$94$$
$$- \frac{10}{49}$$

15.
$$30$$
$$- \frac{18}{29}$$

16.
$$76$$
$$- \frac{3}{50}$$

17.
$$81$$
$$- \frac{37}{75}$$

18.
$$25$$
$$- \frac{81}{100}$$

Subtracting Fractions from Mixed Numbers

When you subtract a fraction from a mixed number, the fraction part of the mixed number may be smaller than the fraction being subtracted. When the whole number part is 1, change the 1 to an improper fraction.

Use These Steps

Subtract $1\frac{4}{9} - \frac{7}{9}$

1. Set up the problem.

$$1\frac{4}{9}$$
$$-\ \frac{7}{9}$$

2. Change 1 to an improper fraction with 9 as the denominator. Add $\frac{9}{9}$ to $\frac{4}{9}$.

$$1\frac{4}{9} = \frac{9}{9} + \frac{4}{9} = \frac{13}{9}$$
$$-\ \frac{7}{9} = \qquad\quad \frac{7}{9}$$

3. Subtract from the new fraction, $\frac{13}{9}$. Reduce.

$$1\frac{4}{9} = \frac{13}{9}$$
$$-\ \frac{7}{9} = \frac{7}{9}$$
$$\qquad \frac{6}{9} = \frac{2}{3}$$

Subtract. Reduce if possible.

1.

$$1\frac{5}{12} - \frac{9}{12} =$$
$$1\frac{5}{12} = \frac{12}{12} + \frac{5}{12} = \frac{17}{12}$$
$$-\ \frac{9}{12} = \qquad\qquad \frac{9}{12}$$
$$\qquad\qquad\qquad \frac{8}{12} = \frac{2}{3}$$

2. $1\frac{2}{7} - \frac{5}{7} =$

3. $1\frac{1}{4} - \frac{3}{4} =$

4. $1\frac{6}{11} - \frac{9}{11} =$

5.

$$1\frac{8}{15}$$
$$-\ \frac{9}{15}$$

6.

$$1\frac{10}{21}$$
$$-\ \frac{20}{21}$$

7.

$$1\frac{15}{32}$$
$$-\ \frac{19}{32}$$

8.

$$1\frac{13}{50}$$
$$-\ \frac{29}{50}$$

9.

$$1\frac{15}{63}$$
$$-\ \frac{30}{63}$$

10. $1\frac{11}{18} - \frac{17}{18} =$

11. $1\frac{29}{42} - \frac{31}{42} =$

12. $1\frac{15}{76} - \frac{40}{76} =$

13. $1\frac{26}{100} - \frac{37}{100} =$

14.

$$1\frac{2}{7}$$
$$-\ \frac{3}{7}$$

15.

$$1\frac{7}{10}$$
$$-\ \frac{9}{10}$$

16.

$$1\frac{5}{16}$$
$$-\ \frac{9}{16}$$

17.

$$1\frac{11}{25}$$
$$-\ \frac{21}{25}$$

18.

$$1\frac{23}{54}$$
$$-\ \frac{40}{54}$$

Subtracting Fractions from Mixed Numbers

When you subtract a fraction from a mixed number, you may have to borrow from the whole number. Change the borrowed 1 to an improper fraction. Use the denominator of the fraction being subtracted.

Use These Steps

Subtract $4\frac{1}{10}$

$\quad -\ \frac{3}{10}$

1. Since $\frac{3}{10}$ is greater than $\frac{1}{10}$, borrow 1 from the 4. Change the borrowed 1 to an improper fraction with 10 as the denominator. $1 = \frac{10}{10}$.

$4\frac{1}{10} = 3\frac{1}{10} + \frac{10}{10}$

2. Add the mixed number and the fraction.

$3\frac{1}{10} + \frac{10}{10} = 3\frac{11}{10}$

3. Subtract the fractions. Bring down the whole number. Reduce.

$3\frac{11}{10}$

$-\ \frac{3}{10}$

$3\frac{8}{10} = 3\frac{4}{5}$

Subtract. Reduce if possible.

1.

$11\frac{5}{11} = 10\frac{16}{11}$

$-\ \frac{6}{11} = \quad \frac{6}{11}$

$\qquad\qquad 10\frac{10}{11}$

2. $31\frac{2}{8}$
$-\ \frac{5}{8}$

3. $12\frac{1}{6}$
$-\ \frac{5}{6}$

4. $20\frac{4}{12}$
$-\ \frac{7}{12}$

5. $45\frac{3}{15}$
$-\ \frac{11}{15}$

6.

$7\frac{2}{9} - \frac{4}{9} =$

$7\frac{2}{9} = 6\frac{11}{9}$

$-\ \frac{4}{9} = \quad \frac{4}{9}$

$\qquad\quad 6\frac{7}{9}$

7. $4\frac{3}{10} - \frac{7}{10} =$

8. $6\frac{1}{4} - \frac{3}{4} =$

9. $2\frac{3}{7} - \frac{6}{7} =$

10. $17\frac{2}{21} - \frac{3}{21} =$

11. $40\frac{9}{18} - \frac{13}{18} =$

12. $13\frac{7}{30} - \frac{11}{30} =$

13. $72\frac{17}{50} - \frac{20}{50} =$

14. $18\frac{2}{63}$
$-\ \frac{4}{63}$

15. $25\frac{18}{72}$
$-\ \frac{27}{72}$

16. $31\frac{25}{75}$
$-\ \frac{70}{75}$

17. $6\frac{3}{90}$
$-\ \frac{43}{90}$

18. $12\frac{12}{100}$
$-\ \frac{92}{100}$

Subtracting Mixed Numbers from Mixed Numbers

When subtracting a mixed number from a mixed number, the fraction on top may be smaller than the fraction on the bottom. When this happens, you will need to borrow from the whole number on top.

Use These Steps

Subtract $6\frac{2}{7} - 3\frac{4}{7}$

1. Set up the problem. Since $\frac{4}{7}$ is greater than $\frac{2}{7}$, borrow 1 from the 6. Change the borrowed 1 to an improper fraction with 7 as the denominator. $1 = \frac{7}{7}$.

$$6\frac{2}{7} = 5\frac{2}{7} + \frac{7}{7}$$
$$-3\frac{4}{7}$$

2. Add $5\frac{2}{7}$ to $\frac{7}{7}$.

$$5\frac{2}{7} + \frac{7}{7} = 5\frac{9}{7}$$

3. Subtract the fractions. Then subtract the whole numbers.

$$5\frac{9}{7}$$
$$-3\frac{4}{7}$$
$$\overline{\;2\frac{5}{7}\;}$$

Subtract. Reduce if possible.

1.
$$8\frac{1}{3} - 4\frac{2}{3} =$$

$$8\frac{1}{3} = 7\frac{4}{3}$$
$$-4\frac{2}{3} = 4\frac{2}{3}$$
$$\overline{\;3\frac{2}{3}\;}$$

2.
$$5\frac{1}{4} - 3\frac{3}{4} =$$

3.
$$6\frac{5}{7} - 1\frac{6}{7} =$$

4.
$$3\frac{1}{5} - 1\frac{2}{5} =$$

5.
$$10\frac{3}{8}$$
$$-\;5\frac{7}{8}$$

6.
$$13\frac{1}{6}$$
$$-12\frac{3}{6}$$

7.
$$19\frac{2}{10}$$
$$-\;9\frac{3}{10}$$

8.
$$25\frac{10}{15}$$
$$-15\frac{13}{15}$$

9.
$$30\frac{6}{19}$$
$$-24\frac{10}{19}$$

10. Lloyd began his trip with $18\frac{1}{4}$ gallons of gas in the tank of his car. He used $16\frac{3}{4}$ gallons. How many gallons does he have left in his gas tank?

11. Marsha's high-jump record last year was $52\frac{7}{10}$ inches. This year she jumped $59\frac{3}{10}$ inches. How much higher was her record this year?

Answer_____

Answer_____

Application

Martha works for ACE Upholstering Company. She needs to recover Mrs. Chapman's wing-backed chair.

Back
Wing
Arm
Cushion
Skirt

Example Martha has a piece of fabric that measures 8 yards long to recover the chair. She needs $2\frac{1}{2}$ yards for both arms. How much will she have left for the rest of the chair?

$$8 \quad = 7\frac{2}{2}$$
$$-\ 2\frac{1}{2} = 2\frac{1}{2}$$
$$\overline{\phantom{-2\frac{1}{2}=\ } 5\frac{1}{2}}$$

She has $5\frac{1}{2}$ yards of fabric left.

Solve.

1. Martha needs one piece $1\frac{1}{2}$ yards long to make the cover for the back of the chair. How much will she have left from $5\frac{1}{2}$ yards after cutting off $1\frac{1}{2}$ yards?

   Answer_____

2. Martha needs $\frac{1}{6}$ yard of fabric to make each side of the skirt around the bottom of the chair. If she has $\frac{5}{6}$ yard of fabric, how much will she have left after cutting off the first $\frac{1}{6}$ yard?

   Answer_____

3. The fabric Martha is using is 54 inches or $4\frac{1}{2}$ feet wide. The width of the cushion is 2 feet. How much fabric will she have left if she cuts off two pieces for the cushion?

   Answer_____

4. If Martha has 3 yards of fabric, how much will be left if she cuts off $1\frac{3}{8}$ yard for the wings?

   Answer_____

Mixed Review

Add or subtract. Reduce if possible.

1.
$$\frac{1}{6} + \frac{5}{6} =$$

2.
$$7\frac{2}{5} - \frac{2}{5} =$$

3.
$$2\frac{5}{8} - 1\frac{1}{8} =$$

4.
$$\frac{2}{3} + \frac{2}{3} =$$

5.
$$6\frac{3}{4}$$
$$-\ 2\frac{1}{4}$$

6.
$$9\frac{1}{2}$$
$$+\ 3\frac{1}{2}$$

7.
$$12\frac{5}{7}$$
$$-\ \ \frac{2}{7}$$

8.
$$\frac{5}{12}$$
$$+\ \frac{7}{12}$$

9.
$$\frac{15}{16}$$
$$-\ \frac{3}{16}$$

Change each whole number to a mixed number with the given denominator.

10.
$$9 = 8\frac{\square}{2}$$

11.
$$6 = 5\frac{\square}{3}$$

12.
$$18 = \square\frac{\square}{9}$$

13.
$$20 = \square\frac{\square}{10}$$

14.
$$29 = \square\frac{\square}{35}$$

Add or subtract. Reduce if possible.

15.
$$1 - \frac{3}{4} =$$

16.
$$2 - \frac{2}{5} =$$

17.
$$14 + \frac{17}{20} =$$

18.
$$20 - \frac{3}{16} =$$

19.
$$12\frac{3}{10}$$
$$-\ 7\frac{7}{10}$$

20.
$$17\frac{1}{6}$$
$$+\ \ 3\frac{5}{6}$$

21.
$$7\frac{9}{11}$$
$$-\ 2\frac{10}{11}$$

22.
$$1\frac{13}{15}$$
$$+\ \ \frac{14}{15}$$

23.
$$8\frac{2}{9}$$
$$-\ 3\frac{7}{9}$$

24.
$$24\frac{5}{12} + 6\frac{1}{12} =$$

25.
$$13\frac{5}{16} - 12\frac{9}{16} =$$

26.
$$6\frac{3}{4} + 1\frac{1}{4} =$$

27.
$$19\frac{2}{21} - \frac{4}{21} =$$

28.
$$1\frac{1}{3}$$
$$-\ \ \frac{2}{3}$$

29.
$$2\frac{31}{50}$$
$$-\ 1\frac{41}{50}$$

30.
$$20\frac{7}{32}$$
$$+\ 11\frac{5}{32}$$

31.
$$1\frac{15}{64}$$
$$-\ \ \frac{7}{64}$$

32.
$$27\frac{23}{100}$$
$$-\ \ \frac{17}{100}$$

Subtracting Fractions with Different Denominators

When subtracting fractions, the denominators may be different. When this happens, you need to raise fractions to higher terms with the same common denominator. Then subtract the numerators.

When one denominator will divide evenly into the other, use the larger denominator as the common denominator.

$$\frac{3}{4} - \frac{1}{2} = \frac{3}{4} - \frac{2}{4} = \frac{1}{4}$$

Use These Steps

Subtract $\frac{5}{8} - \frac{1}{4}$

1. The denominators are different. Since 4 divides evenly into 8, write 8 as the common denominator.

$$\frac{1}{4} = \frac{}{4 \times 2} = \frac{}{8}$$

2. Raise $\frac{1}{4}$ to higher terms with 8 as the denominator.

$$\frac{1}{4} = \frac{1 \times 2}{4 \times 2} = \frac{2}{8}$$

3. Subtract the numerators. Write the difference over the denominator.

$$\frac{5}{8} = \frac{5}{8}$$
$$-\frac{1}{4} = \frac{2}{8}$$
$$\frac{3}{8}$$

Subtract. Reduce if possible.

1. $\frac{9}{10} - \frac{1}{5} =$

$$\frac{9}{10} = \frac{9}{10}$$
$$-\frac{1}{5} = \frac{2}{10}$$
$$\frac{7}{10}$$

2. $\frac{8}{12} - \frac{1}{4}$

3. $\frac{2}{3} - \frac{2}{9} =$

4. $\frac{5}{7} - \frac{1}{14} =$

5. $\frac{7}{15}$
$-\frac{1}{5}$

6. $\frac{5}{9}$
$-\frac{5}{18}$

7. $\frac{9}{10}$
$-\frac{7}{20}$

8. $\frac{3}{4}$
$-\frac{9}{16}$

9. $\frac{11}{20}$
$-\frac{2}{5}$

10. $\frac{17}{18} - \frac{5}{6} =$

11. $\frac{7}{10} - \frac{1}{2} =$

12. $\frac{9}{20} - \frac{1}{4} =$

13. $\frac{11}{14} - \frac{1}{2} =$

Subtracting Fractions with Different Denominators

Find a common denominator. Subtract only the numerators.
Reduce the fraction if possible.

Use These Steps

Subtract $\frac{9}{10} - \frac{2}{5}$

1. Raise $\frac{2}{5}$ to higher terms with 10 as the denominator.

$$\frac{2}{5} = \frac{2 \times 2}{5 \times 2} = \frac{4}{10}$$

2. Subtract the numerators. Write the difference over the denominator.

$$\frac{9}{10} = \frac{9}{10}$$
$$-\frac{2}{5} = \frac{4}{10}$$
$$\frac{5}{10}$$

3. Reduce the answer to lowest terms.

$$\frac{5}{10} = \frac{1}{2}$$

Subtract. Reduce if possible.

1.
$$\frac{7}{12} - \frac{1}{3} =$$

$$\frac{7}{12} = \frac{7}{12}$$
$$-\frac{1}{3} = \frac{4}{12}$$
$$\frac{3}{12} = \frac{1}{4}$$

2.
$$\frac{1}{2} - \frac{1}{8} =$$

3.
$$\frac{2}{3} - \frac{1}{9} =$$

4.
$$\frac{11}{14} - \frac{2}{7} =$$

5.
$$\frac{3}{4}$$
$$-\frac{3}{16}$$

6.
$$\frac{19}{20}$$
$$-\frac{1}{5}$$

7.
$$\frac{11}{18}$$
$$-\frac{1}{3}$$

8.
$$\frac{5}{7}$$
$$-\frac{8}{21}$$

9.
$$\frac{19}{24}$$
$$-\frac{1}{6}$$

10.
$$\frac{3}{5} - \frac{2}{25} =$$

11.
$$\frac{24}{27} - \frac{2}{9} =$$

12.
$$\frac{29}{30} - \frac{5}{6} =$$

13.
$$\frac{5}{8} - \frac{7}{40} =$$

14. Janie spent $\frac{1}{2}$ hour writing a newspaper article and $\frac{1}{4}$ hour editing it. How much longer did she spend writing than editing?

15. During their lunch break, Viola walked $\frac{4}{5}$ mile and Rhonda walked $\frac{7}{10}$ mile. How much farther did Viola walk than Rhonda?

Answer_____

Answer_____

Subtracting Fractions with Different Denominators

When you subtract fractions, you can find a common denominator by multiplying the denominators. Make sure that each of the old denominators divides into the common denominator. Then raise each fraction to higher terms with the new denominator.

Use These Steps

Subtract $\dfrac{1}{3} - \dfrac{1}{4}$

1. Multiply 3 times 4 to find a common denominator.
$3 \times 4 = 12$.

$$\dfrac{1}{3} = \dfrac{}{12}$$
$$-\dfrac{1}{4} = \dfrac{}{12}$$

2. Raise each fraction to higher terms with 12 as the denominator.

$$\dfrac{1}{3} = \dfrac{4}{12}$$
$$-\dfrac{1}{4} = \dfrac{3}{12}$$

3. Subtract the numerators. Write the difference over the denominator.

$$\dfrac{1}{3} = \dfrac{4}{12}$$
$$-\dfrac{1}{4} = \dfrac{3}{12}$$
$$\dfrac{1}{12}$$

Subtract.

1. $\dfrac{3}{5} - \dfrac{1}{2} =$

$$\dfrac{3}{5} = \dfrac{6}{10}$$
$$-\dfrac{1}{2} = \dfrac{5}{10}$$
$$\dfrac{1}{10}$$

2. $\dfrac{3}{4} - \dfrac{1}{3} =$

3. $\dfrac{2}{3} - \dfrac{1}{2} =$

4. $\dfrac{4}{5} - \dfrac{2}{3} =$

5. $\dfrac{5}{6}$
$-\dfrac{1}{5}$

6. $\dfrac{3}{8}$
$-\dfrac{1}{3}$

7. $\dfrac{4}{7}$
$-\dfrac{1}{2}$

8. $\dfrac{2}{3}$
$-\dfrac{3}{10}$

9. $\dfrac{3}{4}$
$-\dfrac{2}{5}$

10. $\dfrac{3}{7} - \dfrac{1}{6} =$

11. $\dfrac{2}{3} - \dfrac{2}{7} =$

12. $\dfrac{5}{7} - \dfrac{1}{2} =$

13. $\dfrac{8}{9} - \dfrac{3}{4} =$

14. $\dfrac{4}{7}$
$-\dfrac{2}{5}$

15. $\dfrac{7}{9}$
$-\dfrac{1}{2}$

16. $\dfrac{3}{4}$
$-\dfrac{1}{5}$

17. $\dfrac{3}{5}$
$-\dfrac{1}{4}$

18. $\dfrac{5}{8}$
$-\dfrac{1}{3}$

Subtracting Fractions Using the LCD

To find the lowest common denominator (LCD), list several multiples of each denominator. Find the smallest number that appears on both lists. This number is the LCD. Make sure that each of the old denominators divides evenly into the new denominator. Then subtract.

Use These Steps

Subtract $\dfrac{3}{8} - \dfrac{1}{6}$

1. List multiples of each denominator. The smallest number on both lists is 24.

$\dfrac{3}{8}$ 8 16 ⓐ24 32 40

$\dfrac{1}{6}$ 6 12 18 ⓐ24 30

2. Raise each fraction to higher terms with 24 as the LCD.

$$\dfrac{3}{8} = \dfrac{9}{24}$$
$$-\dfrac{1}{6} = \dfrac{4}{24}$$

3. Subtract the numerators. Write the difference over the denominator.

$$\dfrac{3}{8} = \dfrac{9}{24}$$
$$-\dfrac{1}{6} = \dfrac{4}{24}$$
$$\dfrac{5}{24}$$

Subtract. Use the LCD.

1.
$$\dfrac{3}{4} - \dfrac{1}{6} =$$

$\dfrac{3}{4}$ 4 8 ⓐ12 16

$\dfrac{1}{6}$ 6 ⓐ12 18

$$\dfrac{3}{4} = \dfrac{9}{12}$$
$$-\dfrac{1}{6} = \dfrac{2}{12}$$
$$\dfrac{7}{12}$$

2.
$$\dfrac{5}{6} - \dfrac{4}{9} =$$

3.
$$\dfrac{7}{10} - \dfrac{1}{4} =$$

4.
$$\dfrac{7}{8} - \dfrac{7}{12} =$$

5.
$$\dfrac{13}{18}$$
$$-\dfrac{5}{12}$$

6.
$$\dfrac{9}{10}$$
$$-\dfrac{2}{3}$$

7.
$$\dfrac{7}{9}$$
$$-\dfrac{7}{12}$$

8.
$$\dfrac{14}{15}$$
$$-\dfrac{5}{9}$$

9.
$$\dfrac{11}{12}$$
$$-\dfrac{3}{16}$$

Mixed Review

Subtract. Reduce if possible.

1. $\dfrac{4}{5} - \dfrac{3}{8} =$

2. $\dfrac{5}{6} - \dfrac{1}{8} =$

3. $\dfrac{5}{8} - \dfrac{1}{2} =$

4. $\dfrac{3}{4} - \dfrac{3}{7} =$

5. $\dfrac{9}{10} - \dfrac{5}{8} =$

6. $\dfrac{4}{7} - \dfrac{2}{5} =$

7. $\dfrac{3}{10} - \dfrac{1}{5} =$

8. $\dfrac{2}{3} - \dfrac{5}{14} =$

9. $\begin{array}{r} \dfrac{6}{7} \\ -\dfrac{1}{2} \\ \hline \end{array}$

10. $\begin{array}{r} \dfrac{10}{13} \\ -\dfrac{1}{3} \\ \hline \end{array}$

11. $\begin{array}{r} \dfrac{7}{8} \\ -\dfrac{7}{12} \\ \hline \end{array}$

12. $\begin{array}{r} \dfrac{7}{12} \\ -\dfrac{1}{6} \\ \hline \end{array}$

13. $\begin{array}{r} \dfrac{2}{3} \\ -\dfrac{1}{9} \\ \hline \end{array}$

14. $\begin{array}{r} \dfrac{2}{3} \\ -\dfrac{2}{9} \\ \hline \end{array}$

15. $\begin{array}{r} \dfrac{7}{10} \\ -\dfrac{1}{4} \\ \hline \end{array}$

16. $\begin{array}{r} \dfrac{3}{4} \\ -\dfrac{1}{6} \\ \hline \end{array}$

17. $\begin{array}{r} \dfrac{5}{9} \\ -\dfrac{1}{2} \\ \hline \end{array}$

18. $\begin{array}{r} \dfrac{5}{6} \\ -\dfrac{3}{5} \\ \hline \end{array}$

19. $\dfrac{14}{15} - \dfrac{5}{9} =$

20. $\dfrac{13}{18} - \dfrac{5}{12} =$

21. $\dfrac{1}{4} - \dfrac{1}{5} =$

22. $\dfrac{19}{20} - \dfrac{3}{4} =$

23. $\dfrac{5}{6} - \dfrac{3}{4} =$

24. $\dfrac{2}{3} - \dfrac{1}{10} =$

25. $\dfrac{11}{12} - \dfrac{4}{9} =$

26. $\dfrac{13}{15} - \dfrac{1}{5} =$

Problem Solving: Using a Map

The map shows the distance in miles between four towns. For example, the distance between Prairie and Keene is $6\frac{3}{10}$ miles.

| **Example** | Bob sells insurance. Bob is traveling from Prairie to Fort Smith. After driving for $6\frac{4}{10}$ miles he stopped for a cup of coffee. How many more miles does he have to drive to Fort Smith? |

▷ **Step 1.** Find the distance from Prairie to Fort Smith on the map.

$$10\frac{9}{10} \text{ miles}$$

▷ **Step 2.** To find how many more miles Bob has to drive, subtract. Reduce.

$$
\begin{aligned}
  &10\frac{9}{10} \\
- \ &6\frac{4}{10} \\
\hline
  &4\frac{5}{10} = 4\frac{1}{2}
\end{aligned}
$$

Bob has to drive $4\frac{1}{2}$ more miles to Fort Smith.

Solve. Reduce if possible.

1. The distance from Fort Smith to Newton is $3\frac{3}{10}$ miles. How much farther is Junction from Fort Smith than Newton is?

2. The distance from Fort Smith to Keene is 12 miles. The distance from Fort Smith to Newton is $3\frac{3}{10}$ miles. How far is it from Newton to Keene?

Answer_____

Answer_____

Solve. Reduce if possible.

3. The distance from Fort Smith to Keene is how many more miles than the distance from Fort Smith to Prairie?

Answer_____

4. One day the road from Fort Smith to Newton was closed. Bob took a detour through Junction. How far did he travel to get to Newton?

Answer_____

5. Bob knows a short cut from Newton to Prairie. The short cut is $7\frac{1}{10}$ miles long. The long way is 15 miles long. How many miles will he save if he uses the short cut instead of traveling through Keene?

Answer_____

6. The distance across Lake Sue from Junction to Wood is $5\frac{1}{2}$ miles. How much shorter is it to cross the lake by boat than to go the 10 miles around the lake to Wood?

Answer_____

7. How much farther is it from Wood to Newton than it is from Wood to Keene?

Answer_____

8. Bob's sister's house is $2\frac{1}{10}$ miles past Keene on the way to Wood. Does she live closer to Wood or to Keene?

Answer_____

9. Bob's car broke down one day $2\frac{3}{10}$ miles past Keene on the way to Wood. How many miles did a tow truck from Wood have to come to pick up Bob's car?

Answer_____

10. Bob drove $42\frac{1}{10}$ miles last week. This week he drove $3\frac{7}{10}$ miles less than last week. How many miles did he drive this week?

Answer_____

Subtracting Mixed Numbers

When subtracting mixed numbers, you may need to find a common denominator for the fractions before you can subtract.

Use These Steps

Subtract $3\frac{1}{2} - 1\frac{1}{3}$

1. Find a common denominator by multiplying the two denominators.
$2 \times 3 = 6$.

$$3\frac{1}{2} = 3\frac{}{6}$$
$$-1\frac{1}{3} = 1\frac{}{6}$$

2. Raise each fraction to higher terms with 6 as the denominator.

$$3\frac{1}{2} = 3\frac{3}{6}$$
$$-1\frac{1}{3} = 1\frac{2}{6}$$

3. Subtract the fractions. Subtract the whole numbers.

$$3\frac{1}{2} = 3\frac{3}{6}$$
$$-1\frac{1}{3} = 1\frac{2}{6}$$
$$2\frac{1}{6}$$

Subtract. Reduce if possible.

1.
$$4\frac{3}{8} - 2\frac{1}{4} =$$
$$4\frac{3}{8} = 4\frac{3}{8}$$
$$-2\frac{1}{4} = 2\frac{2}{8}$$
$$2\frac{1}{8}$$

2.
$$7\frac{2}{3} - 3\frac{1}{6} =$$

3.
$$5\frac{3}{4} - 2\frac{1}{2} =$$

4.
$$9\frac{3}{5} - 7\frac{1}{10} =$$

5.
$$12\frac{3}{4}$$
$$- \ 2\frac{1}{3}$$

6.
$$15\frac{5}{6}$$
$$- 10\frac{3}{5}$$

7.
$$20\frac{7}{10}$$
$$- \ 8\frac{1}{3}$$

8.
$$13\frac{5}{9}$$
$$- \ 1\frac{1}{2}$$

9.
$$12\frac{3}{8}$$
$$- \ 5\frac{1}{4}$$

10. Kho sells quilts at crafts fairs. Kho has $3\frac{3}{4}$ yards of blue material to make a quilt. She will use $1\frac{2}{3}$ yards for blocks and the rest for the border. How much material will she use for the border?

11. Kho has $4\frac{7}{8}$ yards of green material for a quilt. She will use $1\frac{2}{3}$ yards for blocks and the rest for the lining. How much will she use for the lining?

Answer _____

Answer _____

Subtracting Mixed Numbers with Borrowing

When subtracting mixed numbers, you may need to find a common denominator. Then, if the fraction you are subtracting is greater than the one you are subtracting from, you will need to borrow.

Use These Steps

Subtract $18\frac{2}{7} - 10\frac{1}{2}$

1. Find a common denominator. Raise each fraction to higher terms.

$$18\frac{2}{7} = 18\frac{4}{14}$$
$$-10\frac{1}{2} = 10\frac{7}{14}$$

2. Since $\frac{7}{14}$ is greater than $\frac{4}{14}$, borrow 1 from 18.

$$18\frac{2}{7} = 18\frac{4}{14} = 17\frac{18}{14}$$
$$-10\frac{1}{2} = 10\frac{7}{14} = 10\frac{7}{14}$$

3. Subtract the fractions. Subtract the whole numbers.

$$17\frac{18}{14}$$
$$-10\frac{7}{14}$$
$$\overline{7\frac{11}{14}}$$

Subtract. Reduce if possible.

1.
$$7\frac{2}{3} - 6\frac{8}{9} =$$
$$7\frac{2}{3} = 7\frac{6}{9} = 6\frac{15}{9}$$
$$-6\frac{8}{9} = 6\frac{8}{9} = 6\frac{8}{9}$$
$$\overline{\frac{7}{9}}$$

2.
$$9\frac{1}{2} - 6\frac{7}{8} =$$

3.
$$10\frac{1}{6} - 2\frac{3}{8} =$$

4.
$$27\frac{2}{9}$$
$$-18\frac{3}{4}$$

5.
$$30\frac{1}{10}$$
$$-15\frac{3}{5}$$

6.
$$14\frac{3}{8}$$
$$-6\frac{11}{12}$$

7.
$$33\frac{2}{11} - 19\frac{1}{2} =$$

8.
$$25\frac{1}{5} - 9\frac{1}{3} =$$

9.
$$18\frac{3}{10} - 17\frac{3}{4} =$$

10.
$$50\frac{9}{25}$$
$$-14\frac{4}{5}$$

11.
$$86\frac{5}{9}$$
$$-49\frac{5}{6}$$

12.
$$132\frac{9}{20}$$
$$-75\frac{3}{4}$$

Subtracting Mixed Numbers with Borrowing

When subtracting mixed numbers with different denominators, change the fractions to higher terms with common denominators. Then borrow.

Use These Steps

Subtract $2\frac{1}{5} - 1\frac{4}{15}$

1. Find a common denominator. Raise each fraction to higher terms.

$$2\frac{1}{5} = 2\frac{3}{15}$$
$$-1\frac{4}{15} = 1\frac{4}{15}$$

2. Since $\frac{4}{15}$ is greater than $\frac{3}{15}$, borrow 1 from the 2.

$$-\ 2\frac{1}{5} = 2\frac{3}{15} = 1\frac{18}{15}$$
$$-1\frac{4}{15} = 1\frac{4}{15} = 1\frac{4}{15}$$

3. Subtract the fractions. Subtract the whole numbers.

$$1\frac{18}{15}$$
$$-1\frac{4}{15}$$
$$\overline{\frac{14}{15}}$$

Subtract. Reduce if possible.

1.

$$6\frac{1}{10} - 2\frac{1}{6} =$$

$$6\frac{1}{10} = 6\frac{3}{30} = 5\frac{33}{30}$$
$$-\ 2\frac{1}{6} = 2\frac{5}{30} = 2\frac{5}{30}$$
$$\overline{3\frac{28}{30} = 3\frac{14}{15}}$$

2.

$$4\frac{2}{7} - 1\frac{1}{3} =$$

3.

$$9\frac{2}{5} - 3\frac{1}{2} =$$

4.

$$12\frac{1}{12} - 5\frac{5}{6} =$$

5.

$$10\frac{3}{8} - 9\frac{5}{6} =$$

6.

$$15\frac{1}{10} - 11\frac{2}{5} =$$

7.

$$20\frac{3}{20} - 7\frac{1}{4} =$$

8.

$$9\frac{1}{7} - 3\frac{4}{21} =$$

9.

$$14\frac{1}{6} - 8\frac{7}{30} =$$

Subtracting Mixed Numbers and Fractions

When the fraction you are subtracting is greater than the fraction you are subtracting from, you will need to borrow.

Use These Steps

Subtract $1\frac{1}{3} - \frac{1}{2}$

1. Find a common denominator.

$$1\frac{1}{3} = 1\frac{2}{6}$$
$$-\ \frac{1}{2} = \ \frac{3}{6}$$

2. Since $\frac{3}{6}$ is greater than $\frac{2}{6}$, borrow 1.

$$1\frac{1}{3} = 1\frac{2}{6} = \frac{8}{6}$$
$$-\ \frac{1}{2} = \ \frac{3}{6} = \frac{3}{6}$$

3. Subtract the fractions.

$$\frac{8}{6}$$
$$-\ \frac{3}{6}$$
$$\frac{5}{6}$$

Subtract. Reduce if possible.

1.
$$1\frac{1}{10} - \frac{5}{6} =$$
$$1\frac{1}{10} = 1\frac{3}{30} = \frac{33}{30}$$
$$-\ \ \frac{5}{6} = \ \frac{25}{30} = \frac{25}{30}$$
$$\frac{8}{30} = \frac{4}{15}$$

2.
$$3\frac{2}{5} - \frac{7}{8} =$$

3.
$$1\frac{3}{7} - \frac{3}{4} =$$

4.
$$4\frac{1}{2} - \frac{2}{3} =$$

5.
$$9\frac{3}{8} - \frac{1}{2} =$$

6.
$$1\frac{1}{9} - \frac{1}{6} =$$

7.
$$5\frac{2}{5} - \frac{9}{10} =$$

8.
$$10\frac{5}{12} - \frac{5}{6} =$$

9.
$$2\frac{3}{11} - \frac{1}{3} =$$

Unit 3 *Review*

Subtract. Reduce if possible.

1.
$$\begin{array}{r} \frac{11}{13} \\ -\ \frac{2}{13} \\ \hline \end{array}$$

2.
$$\begin{array}{r} \frac{7}{10} \\ -\ \frac{1}{10} \\ \hline \end{array}$$

3.
$$\begin{array}{r} \frac{5}{8} \\ -\ \frac{3}{8} \\ \hline \end{array}$$

4.
$$\begin{array}{r} \frac{4}{5} \\ -\ \frac{3}{5} \\ \hline \end{array}$$

5.
$$\begin{array}{r} \frac{5}{9} \\ -\ \frac{2}{9} \\ \hline \end{array}$$

6. $\dfrac{10}{15} - \dfrac{5}{15} =$

7. $\dfrac{5}{6} - \dfrac{1}{6} =$

8. $\dfrac{19}{21} - \dfrac{12}{21} =$

9. $\dfrac{17}{30} - \dfrac{2}{30} =$

10.
$$\begin{array}{r} 12\frac{3}{10} \\ -\ 4\frac{1}{10} \\ \hline \end{array}$$

11.
$$\begin{array}{r} 7\frac{3}{4} \\ -\ 5\frac{1}{4} \\ \hline \end{array}$$

12.
$$\begin{array}{r} 25\frac{9}{16} \\ -\ 11\frac{3}{16} \\ \hline \end{array}$$

13.
$$\begin{array}{r} 19\frac{14}{18} \\ -\ 16\frac{2}{18} \\ \hline \end{array}$$

14.
$$\begin{array}{r} 8\frac{7}{20} \\ -\ 2\frac{3}{20} \\ \hline \end{array}$$

15. $10\frac{7}{8} - \dfrac{5}{8} =$

16. $4\frac{15}{25} - 3 =$

17. $18\frac{30}{35} - \dfrac{18}{35} =$

18. $2\frac{22}{40} - \dfrac{7}{40} =$

19.
$$\begin{array}{r} 5\frac{4}{30} \\ -\ \frac{1}{30} \\ \hline \end{array}$$

20.
$$\begin{array}{r} 8\frac{20}{27} \\ -\ \frac{2}{27} \\ \hline \end{array}$$

21.
$$\begin{array}{r} 60\frac{47}{50} \\ -\ 30 \\ \hline \end{array}$$

22.
$$\begin{array}{r} 5\frac{17}{42} \\ -\ \frac{10}{42} \\ \hline \end{array}$$

23.
$$\begin{array}{r} 14\frac{10}{11} \\ -\ 6 \\ \hline \end{array}$$

24. $1 - \dfrac{5}{6} =$

25. $1 - \dfrac{7}{10} =$

26. $1 - \dfrac{3}{4} =$

27. $1 - \dfrac{1}{3} =$

Subtract. Reduce if possible.

28.
$$4 - \frac{1}{2} =$$

29.
$$6 - \frac{1}{3} =$$

30.
$$3 - \frac{3}{4} =$$

31.
$$6 - \frac{2}{9} =$$

32.
$$\begin{array}{r} 8 \\ -\ \frac{3}{10} \\ \hline \end{array}$$

33.
$$\begin{array}{r} 10 \\ -\ \frac{2}{5} \\ \hline \end{array}$$

34.
$$\begin{array}{r} 18 \\ -\ \frac{1}{6} \\ \hline \end{array}$$

35.
$$\begin{array}{r} 11 \\ -\ \frac{4}{7} \\ \hline \end{array}$$

36.
$$\begin{array}{r} 13 \\ -\ \frac{5}{12} \\ \hline \end{array}$$

37.
$$5\frac{1}{3} - 1\frac{2}{3} =$$

38.
$$1\frac{4}{9} - \frac{7}{9} =$$

39.
$$7\frac{1}{4} - \frac{3}{4} =$$

40.
$$12\frac{4}{11} - 3\frac{5}{11} =$$

41.
$$\begin{array}{r} 1\frac{5}{9} \\ -\ \frac{7}{9} \\ \hline \end{array}$$

42.
$$\begin{array}{r} 8\frac{3}{10} \\ -\ 2\frac{7}{10} \\ \hline \end{array}$$

43.
$$\begin{array}{r} 2\frac{1}{5} \\ -\ \frac{3}{5} \\ \hline \end{array}$$

44.
$$\begin{array}{r} 1\frac{1}{6} \\ -\ \frac{3}{6} \\ \hline \end{array}$$

45.
$$\begin{array}{r} 10\frac{3}{20} \\ -\ 5\frac{7}{20} \\ \hline \end{array}$$

46.
$$\frac{2}{3} - \frac{1}{6} =$$

47.
$$\frac{3}{7} - \frac{5}{14} =$$

48.
$$\frac{11}{12} - \frac{3}{4} =$$

49.
$$\frac{4}{5} - \frac{8}{20} =$$

50.
$$\begin{array}{r} \frac{1}{2} \\ -\ \frac{1}{3} \\ \hline \end{array}$$

51.
$$\begin{array}{r} \frac{3}{4} \\ -\ \frac{3}{5} \\ \hline \end{array}$$

52.
$$\begin{array}{r} \frac{9}{10} \\ -\ \frac{2}{3} \\ \hline \end{array}$$

53.
$$\begin{array}{r} \frac{3}{7} \\ -\ \frac{1}{6} \\ \hline \end{array}$$

54.
$$\begin{array}{r} \frac{7}{8} \\ -\ \frac{2}{3} \\ \hline \end{array}$$

55.
$$\frac{3}{4} - \frac{1}{6} =$$

56.
$$\frac{3}{10} - \frac{1}{4} =$$

57.
$$\frac{5}{8} - \frac{1}{12} =$$

58.
$$\frac{7}{10} - \frac{3}{8} =$$

Subtract. Reduce if possible.

59.
$$5\frac{1}{3}$$
$$-\ 2\frac{1}{4}$$

60.
$$10\frac{3}{5}$$
$$-\ 7\frac{1}{10}$$

61.
$$13\frac{5}{6}$$
$$-\ 2\frac{1}{4}$$

62.
$$8\frac{2}{3}$$
$$-7\frac{5}{12}$$

63.
$$6\frac{8}{15}$$
$$-1\frac{1}{2}$$

64. $21\frac{3}{10} - 2\frac{1}{4} =$

65. $18\frac{7}{9} - 13\frac{1}{3} =$

66. $10\frac{3}{4} - 5\frac{1}{6} =$

67. $9\frac{7}{15} - 2\frac{2}{5} =$

68.
$$15\frac{3}{7}$$
$$-\ 6\frac{1}{2}$$

69.
$$4\frac{1}{2}$$
$$-2\frac{5}{8}$$

70.
$$16\frac{1}{10}$$
$$-\ 3\frac{3}{4}$$

71. $10\frac{1}{9} - 6\frac{3}{4} =$

72. $31\frac{5}{11} - 18\frac{2}{3} =$

73. $17\frac{1}{6} - 3\frac{3}{5} =$

74.
$$1\frac{2}{9}$$
$$-\ \frac{1}{4}$$

75.
$$5\frac{2}{5}$$
$$-\ \frac{5}{8}$$

76.
$$2\frac{1}{12}$$
$$-\ \frac{3}{10}$$

Below is a list of the problems in this review and the pages on which the skills are taught. If you missed any problems, turn to the pages listed and practice the skills. Then correct the problems you missed in the Unit Review.

Problems	Pages	Problems	Pages
1-14	75-78	46-58	93-96
15-23	80-81	59-67	100
24-27	86	68-73	101-102
28-36	87	74-76	103
37-45	88-90		

Unit MULTIPLYING FRACTIONS

Have you ever had to double a recipe, change a fraction of a yard to inches, or figure the cost of clothes at a $\frac{1}{3}$-off sale? All of these problems can be solved by multiplying fractions.

In this unit you will learn how to multiply fractions, whole numbers, and mixed numbers. You will be able to solve word problems using fractions.

Getting Ready

You should be familiar with the skills on this page and the next before you begin this unit. To check your answers, turn to page 193.

 Knowing the multiplication facts will help make multiplying fractions easier.

Multiply.

1. $3 \times 4 = $ **12**	**2.** $6 \times 2 = $	**3.** $1 \times 5 = $	**4.** $2 \times 9 = $
5. $7 \times 3 = $	**6.** $4 \times 5 = $	**7.** $3 \times 2 = $	**8.** $5 \times 8 = $
9. $9 \times 3 = $	**10.** $3 \times 3 = $	**11.** $6 \times 7 = $	**12.** $4 \times 8 = $
13. $7 \times 9 = $	**14.** $5 \times 3 = $	**15.** $2 \times 5 = $	**16.** $4 \times 4 = $

For review, see pages 85–87 in **Math Skills for the Workforce, Whole Numbers.**

Often after multiplying fractions, you need to reduce answers to lowest terms.

Reduce each fraction to lowest terms. If the fraction is in lowest terms, write LT.

17.
$\frac{2}{12} = \frac{1}{6}$

18.
$\frac{6}{20} =$

19.
$\frac{4}{63} =$

20.
$\frac{18}{32} =$

21.
$\frac{3}{9} =$

22.
$\frac{12}{28} =$

23.
$\frac{15}{32} =$

24.
$\frac{16}{20} =$

25.
$\frac{12}{45} =$

26.
$\frac{14}{42} =$

27.
$\frac{20}{25} =$

28.
$\frac{9}{10} =$

29.
$\frac{2}{14} =$

30.
$\frac{8}{16} =$

31.
$\frac{10}{50} =$

For review, see Unit 1, pages 15–16.

 When you get an improper fraction as an answer, you need to change the improper fraction to a whole or mixed number.

Change each improper fraction to a whole or mixed number. Reduce if possible.

32.
$\frac{11}{2} =$
$$\frac{5}{2)\overline{11}} = 5\frac{1}{2}$$
$$\frac{-10}{1}$$

33.
$\frac{16}{5} =$

34.
$\frac{72}{4} =$

35.
$\frac{29}{3} =$

36.
$\frac{51}{6} =$

37.
$\frac{40}{12} =$

38.
$\frac{27}{8} =$

39.
$\frac{42}{7} =$

40.
$\frac{49}{9} =$

41.
$\frac{53}{10} =$

42.
$\frac{18}{3} =$

43.
$\frac{22}{11} =$

44.
$\frac{25}{4} =$

45.
$\frac{30}{14} =$

46.
$\frac{21}{20} =$

47.
$\frac{50}{16} =$

48.
$\frac{96}{24} =$

49.
$\frac{92}{8} =$

50.
$\frac{45}{15} =$

51.
$\frac{54}{13} =$

For review, see Unit 1, pages 33–34.

Multiplying Fractions by Fractions

Multiplying fractions is a way to find a part of something. If you have half a gallon of ice cream and you want to give half of it to a friend, you can find out what part of the ice cream you will give away by multiplying. Your friend will get $\frac{1}{2}$ of $\frac{1}{2}$. When working with fractions, *of* means to multiply.

$$\frac{1}{2} \quad \times \quad \frac{1}{2} \quad = \quad \frac{1}{4}$$

Use These Steps

Find $\frac{1}{2}$ of $\frac{3}{4}$

1. Set up the problem.

$$\frac{1}{2} \times \frac{3}{4} =$$

2. Multiply the numerators.

$$\frac{1}{2} \times \frac{3}{4} = \frac{3}{}$$

3. Multiply the denominators.

$$\frac{1}{2} \times \frac{3}{4} = \frac{3}{8}$$

Multiply the fractions and shade in the figures given to show the answers.

1.
$$\frac{1}{2} \text{ of } \frac{1}{3} = \frac{1}{2} \times \frac{1}{3} = \frac{1}{6}$$

2.
$$\frac{1}{2} \text{ of } \frac{1}{4} =$$

3.
$$\frac{3}{4} \text{ of } \frac{1}{2} =$$

4.
$$\frac{2}{3} \text{ of } \frac{1}{3} =$$

5.
$$\frac{3}{5} \text{ of } \frac{1}{2} =$$

6.
$$\frac{1}{3} \text{ of } \frac{3}{4} =$$

7.
$$\frac{3}{4} \times \frac{1}{4} =$$

8.
$$\frac{7}{8} \times \frac{1}{3} =$$

9.
$$\frac{1}{5} \times \frac{1}{2} =$$

Multiplying Fractions by Fractions

To multiply fractions, set up the problem horizontally. Multiply the numerators and then multiply the denominators. Reduce if possible.

Use These Steps

Multiply $\frac{1}{3} \times \frac{3}{5}$

1. **Multiply the numerators.**

$$\frac{1}{3} \times \frac{3}{5} = \frac{3}{}$$

2. **Multiply the denominators.**

$$\frac{1}{3} \times \frac{3}{5} = \frac{3}{15}$$

3. **Reduce the answer to lowest terms.**

$$\frac{3}{15} = \frac{1}{5}$$

Multiply. Reduce if possible.

1. $\frac{1}{4} \times \frac{2}{5} = \frac{2}{20} = \frac{1}{10}$

2. $\frac{1}{2} \times \frac{5}{6} =$

3. $\frac{1}{3} \times \frac{3}{7} =$

4. $\frac{1}{8} \times \frac{1}{2} =$

5. $\frac{3}{4} \times \frac{2}{3} =$

6. $\frac{2}{3} \times \frac{2}{7} =$

7. $\frac{3}{5} \times \frac{3}{4} =$

8. $\frac{2}{9} \times \frac{2}{9} =$

9. $\frac{3}{7} \times \frac{4}{7} =$

10. $\frac{5}{6} \times \frac{1}{4} =$

11. $\frac{2}{5} \times \frac{2}{5} =$

12. $\frac{5}{8} \times \frac{1}{10} =$

13. $\frac{2}{9} \times \frac{5}{6} =$

14. $\frac{1}{3} \times \frac{1}{3} =$

15. $\frac{4}{7} \times \frac{1}{2} =$

16. $\frac{3}{4} \times \frac{7}{8} =$

17. $\frac{1}{6} \times \frac{5}{6} =$

18. $\frac{2}{5} \times \frac{5}{8} =$

19. $\frac{6}{7} \times \frac{5}{7} =$

20. $\frac{2}{3} \times \frac{3}{10} =$

21. $\frac{3}{4} \times \frac{3}{4} =$

22. $\frac{1}{7} \times \frac{1}{6} =$

23. $\frac{5}{6} \times \frac{4}{5} =$

24. $\frac{5}{8} \times \frac{3}{8} =$

25. Alex bought $\frac{3}{4}$ pound of potato salad. He and his friends ate $\frac{1}{2}$ of it while watching a football game. How much potato salad did they eat?

26. Daniel drinks $\frac{1}{2}$ quart of milk a day. His younger sister only drinks $\frac{1}{3}$ as much as her brother. How much milk does Daniel's sister drink a day?

Answer_____

Answer_____

Application

This table shows the average number of cassettes, CDs, and albums sold each day at River City Records. For example, 15 CDs are $\frac{3}{20}$ of total sales.

River City Records

Item	Number Sold	Fraction of Total Sales
Cassettes	40	$\frac{2}{5}$
CDs	15	$\frac{3}{20}$
Albums	45	$\frac{9}{20}$
Total Items Sold	100	

Example $\frac{1}{2}$ of all the cassettes sold are country and western music. What fraction of the total sales is this?

Cassettes are $\frac{2}{5}$ of the total sales. Country and western music is $\frac{1}{2}$ of the cassettes.

$$\frac{1}{2} \times \frac{2}{5} = \frac{2}{10} = \frac{1}{5}$$

$\frac{1}{5}$ of total sales are country and western cassettes.

Solve. Reduce if possible.

1. $\frac{1}{4}$ of the cassettes sold are rap. What fraction of the total sales is this?

   Answer_____

2. $\frac{1}{8}$ of the cassettes sold are classical music. What fraction of the total sales is this?

   Answer_____

3. $\frac{1}{5}$ of the CDs sold are classical music. What fraction of the total sales is this?

   Answer_____

4. $\frac{3}{5}$ of the CDs sold are rock music. What fraction of the total sales is this?

   Answer_____

5. $\frac{1}{3}$ of the albums sold are country and western. What fraction of the total sales is this?

   Answer_____

6. $\frac{4}{9}$ of the albums sold are rock music. What fraction of the total sales is this?

   Answer_____

Multiplying Three Fractions

When multiplying three fractions, multiply the first two numerators. Then multiply that answer by the last numerator. Multiply the denominators the same way.

Use These Steps

Multiply $\dfrac{1}{2} \times \dfrac{2}{3} \times \dfrac{3}{4}$

1. Multiply the first two numerators. Then multiply that answer by the last numerator.

2. Multiply the first two denominators. Then multiply that answer by the last denominator.

3. Reduce the answer to lowest terms.

$$\overset{2}{\overbrace{\dfrac{1}{2} \times \dfrac{2}{3}}} \times \dfrac{3}{4} = \dfrac{6}{\ }$$

$$\underset{6}{\underbrace{\dfrac{1}{2} \times \dfrac{2}{3}}} \times \dfrac{3}{4} = \dfrac{6}{24}$$

$$\dfrac{6}{24} = \dfrac{1}{4}$$

Multiply. Reduce if possible.

1. $\dfrac{1}{3} \times \dfrac{2}{3} \times \dfrac{1}{4} = \dfrac{2}{36} = \dfrac{1}{18}$

2. $\dfrac{1}{2} \times \dfrac{2}{5} \times \dfrac{1}{3} =$

3. $\dfrac{3}{4} \times \dfrac{3}{4} \times \dfrac{2}{3} =$

4. $\dfrac{1}{6} \times \dfrac{2}{5} \times \dfrac{1}{2} =$

5. $\dfrac{2}{3} \times \dfrac{3}{7} \times \dfrac{2}{3} =$

6. $\dfrac{3}{8} \times \dfrac{1}{2} \times \dfrac{5}{6} =$

7. $\dfrac{1}{4} \times \dfrac{2}{5} \times \dfrac{3}{5} =$

8. $\dfrac{2}{9} \times \dfrac{2}{3} \times \dfrac{1}{4} =$

9. $\dfrac{4}{5} \times \dfrac{5}{6} \times \dfrac{2}{3} =$

10. $\dfrac{4}{9} \times \dfrac{1}{2} \times \dfrac{3}{5} =$

11. $\dfrac{3}{4} \times \dfrac{2}{7} \times \dfrac{2}{3} =$

12. $\dfrac{1}{4} \times \dfrac{3}{5} \times \dfrac{5}{6} =$

13. $\dfrac{3}{7} \times \dfrac{4}{7} \times \dfrac{1}{2} =$

14. $\dfrac{2}{5} \times \dfrac{7}{10} \times \dfrac{1}{2} =$

15. $\dfrac{3}{10} \times \dfrac{2}{5} \times \dfrac{1}{4} =$

16. $\dfrac{5}{8} \times \dfrac{3}{4} \times \dfrac{2}{3} =$

17. $\dfrac{1}{5} \times \dfrac{3}{7} \times \dfrac{7}{9} =$

18. $\dfrac{3}{20} \times \dfrac{2}{3} \times \dfrac{1}{3} =$

19. $\dfrac{5}{12} \times \dfrac{1}{2} \times \dfrac{2}{5} =$

20. $\dfrac{3}{4} \times \dfrac{1}{6} \times \dfrac{12}{13} =$

21. $\dfrac{1}{8} \times \dfrac{4}{5} \times \dfrac{15}{16} =$

Multiplying Fractions Using Cancellation

You can sometimes make a multiplication problem easier if you cancel before you multiply. To cancel, divide a numerator and a denominator by the same number.

Use These Steps

Multiply $\frac{4}{5} \times \frac{1}{2}$

1. Cancel by dividing the numerator of the first fraction, 4, and the denominator of the second fraction, 2, by 2. Cross out the 4 and the 2 and write the new numbers.

$$\frac{\overset{2}{\cancel{4}}}{5} \times \frac{1}{\underset{1}{\cancel{2}}} =$$

2. Multiply the numerators of the new fractions.

$$\frac{\overset{2}{\cancel{4}}}{5} \times \frac{1}{\underset{1}{\cancel{2}}} = \frac{2}{}$$

3. Multiply the denominators of the new fractions.

$$\frac{\overset{2}{\cancel{4}}}{5} \times \frac{1}{\underset{1}{\cancel{2}}} = \frac{2}{5}$$

Cancel and multiply. Reduce if possible.

1. $\frac{1}{\underset{3}{\cancel{9}}} \times \frac{\overset{1}{\cancel{3}}}{5} = \frac{1}{15}$

2. $\frac{3}{8} \times \frac{4}{7} =$

3. $\frac{5}{7} \times \frac{3}{5} =$

4. $\frac{2}{3} \times \frac{6}{7} =$

5. $\frac{3}{4} \times \frac{6}{7} =$

6. $\frac{3}{14} \times \frac{4}{7} =$

7. $\frac{3}{8} \times \frac{4}{9} =$

8. $\frac{4}{15} \times \frac{10}{13} =$

9. $\frac{3}{20} \times \frac{5}{8} =$

10. $\frac{1}{6} \times \frac{12}{17} =$

11. $\frac{4}{15} \times \frac{10}{21} =$

12. $\frac{21}{25} \times \frac{9}{14} =$

13. $\frac{1}{10} \times \frac{25}{27} =$

14. $\frac{3}{16} \times \frac{4}{7} =$

15. $\frac{14}{15} \times \frac{11}{35} =$

16. $\frac{6}{11} \times \frac{2}{9} =$

17. $\frac{7}{50} \times \frac{10}{11} =$

18. $\frac{9}{26} \times \frac{13}{14} =$

19. $\frac{8}{9} \times \frac{1}{32} =$

20. $\frac{14}{15} \times \frac{4}{49} =$

21. $\frac{13}{15} \times \frac{4}{39} =$

22. $\frac{3}{25} \times \frac{5}{7} =$

23. $\frac{9}{10} \times \frac{1}{3} =$

24. $\frac{7}{8} \times \frac{16}{19} =$

Multiplying Fractions Using Cancellation

Sometimes you can cancel more than one time when you are multiplying fractions.

Use These Steps

Multiply $\frac{5}{6} \times \frac{3}{10}$

1. Cancel once by dividing the numerator of the first fraction, 5, and the denominator of the second fraction, 10, by 5. Cross out the 5 and the 10. Write the new numbers.

$$\frac{\overset{1}{\cancel{5}}}{6} \times \frac{3}{\underset{2}{\cancel{10}}} =$$

2. Cancel again by dividing the numerator of the second fraction, 3, and the denominator of the first fraction, 6, by 3. Cross out the 3 and the 6. Write the new numbers.

$$\frac{\overset{1}{\cancel{5}}}{\underset{2}{\cancel{6}}} \times \frac{\overset{1}{\cancel{3}}}{\underset{2}{\cancel{10}}} =$$

3. Multiply the new numerators and the new denominators.

$$\frac{\overset{1}{\cancel{5}}}{\underset{2}{\cancel{6}}} \times \frac{\overset{1}{\cancel{3}}}{\underset{2}{\cancel{10}}} = \frac{1}{4}$$

Cancel and multiply. Reduce if possible.

1. $\dfrac{\overset{3}{\cancel{9}}}{\underset{6}{\cancel{12}}} \times \dfrac{\overset{1}{\cancel{2}}}{\underset{1}{\cancel{3}}} = \dfrac{3}{6} = \dfrac{1}{2}$

2. $\dfrac{4}{5} \times \dfrac{10}{16} =$

3. $\dfrac{3}{4} \times \dfrac{12}{15} =$

4. $\dfrac{3}{6} \times \dfrac{18}{21} =$

5. $\dfrac{15}{16} \times \dfrac{14}{15} =$

6. $\dfrac{7}{9} \times \dfrac{6}{21} =$

7. $\dfrac{9}{10} \times \dfrac{12}{27} =$

8. $\dfrac{7}{8} \times \dfrac{24}{28} =$

9. $\dfrac{4}{9} \times \dfrac{3}{14} =$

10. $\dfrac{22}{24} \times \dfrac{8}{11} =$

11. $\dfrac{17}{18} \times \dfrac{12}{34} =$

12. $\dfrac{16}{27} \times \dfrac{9}{20} =$

13. $\dfrac{5}{12} \times \dfrac{4}{5} =$

14. $\dfrac{10}{21} \times \dfrac{7}{20} =$

15. $\dfrac{33}{42} \times \dfrac{6}{22} =$

16. $\dfrac{7}{24} \times \dfrac{12}{35} =$

17. The mechanic used a bolt $\frac{15}{16}$ inch long to put in a new water pump. He needed another bolt $\frac{2}{3}$ as long to put on a license plate. How long was the bolt he used for the license plate?

18. Kenny can mow his back yard in $\frac{3}{4}$ hour. He can mow the front yard in $\frac{2}{3}$ that time. How long does it take Kenny to mow his front yard?

Answer_____

Answer_____

Multiplying Three Fractions Using Cancellation

When multiplying three fractions, you may be able to cancel several times. Be sure you have canceled all possible numbers before you start to multiply.

Use These Steps

Multiply $\dfrac{5}{6} \times \dfrac{3}{4} \times \dfrac{2}{5}$

1. Start with the numerator of the first fraction, 5. Cancel the numerator of the first fraction with the denominator of the third fraction, 5.

$$\dfrac{\overset{1}{\cancel{5}}}{6} \times \dfrac{3}{4} \times \dfrac{2}{\underset{1}{\cancel{5}}} =$$

2. Cancel the denominator of the first fraction, 6, with the numerator of the second fraction, 3.

$$\dfrac{\overset{1}{\cancel{5}}}{\underset{2}{\cancel{6}}} \times \dfrac{\overset{1}{\cancel{3}}}{4} \times \dfrac{2}{\underset{1}{\cancel{5}}} =$$

3. Cancel the numerator of the third fraction, 2, with the denominator of the second fraction, 4. Multiply the new fractions.

$$\dfrac{\overset{1}{\cancel{5}}}{\underset{2}{\cancel{6}}} \times \dfrac{\overset{1}{\cancel{3}}}{\underset{2}{\cancel{4}}} \times \dfrac{\overset{1}{\cancel{2}}}{\underset{1}{\cancel{5}}} = \dfrac{1}{4}$$

Cancel and multiply. Reduce if possible.

1. $\dfrac{\overset{2}{\cancel{4}}}{\underset{5}{\cancel{25}}} \times \dfrac{\overset{1}{\cancel{7}}}{\underset{5}{\cancel{10}}} \times \dfrac{\overset{4}{\cancel{20}}}{\underset{3}{\cancel{21}}} = \dfrac{8}{75}$

2. $\dfrac{21}{24} \times \dfrac{8}{35} \times \dfrac{5}{9} =$

3. $\dfrac{8}{10} \times \dfrac{26}{32} \times \dfrac{12}{13} =$

4. $\dfrac{11}{45} \times \dfrac{18}{33} \times \dfrac{1}{2} =$

5. $\dfrac{6}{12} \times \dfrac{10}{30} \times \dfrac{5}{14} =$

6. $\dfrac{15}{36} \times \dfrac{12}{15} \times \dfrac{5}{6} =$

7. $\dfrac{9}{10} \times \dfrac{8}{9} \times \dfrac{3}{4} =$

8. $\dfrac{7}{16} \times \dfrac{6}{21} \times \dfrac{3}{14} =$

9. $\dfrac{5}{8} \times \dfrac{4}{27} \times \dfrac{3}{50} =$

10. $\dfrac{2}{3} \times \dfrac{15}{16} \times \dfrac{4}{5} =$

11. $\dfrac{13}{20} \times \dfrac{5}{39} \times \dfrac{8}{9} =$

12. $\dfrac{24}{35} \times \dfrac{7}{8} \times \dfrac{20}{21} =$

13. $\dfrac{1}{2} \times \dfrac{6}{7} \times \dfrac{7}{12} =$

14. $\dfrac{4}{5} \times \dfrac{25}{32} \times \dfrac{2}{15} =$

15. $\dfrac{17}{50} \times \dfrac{10}{51} \times \dfrac{2}{3} =$

16. $\dfrac{11}{12} \times \dfrac{36}{55} \times \dfrac{5}{9} =$

17. $\dfrac{3}{100} \times \dfrac{75}{81} \times \dfrac{9}{10} =$

18. $\dfrac{7}{15} \times \dfrac{45}{49} \times \dfrac{2}{5} =$

Mixed Review

Add, subtract, or multiply. Cancel and reduce if possible.

1. $\frac{3}{4} \times \frac{1}{2} =$

2. $\frac{2}{3} - \frac{1}{3} =$

3. $\frac{5}{9} + \frac{4}{9} =$

4. $\frac{1}{8} \times \frac{1}{6} =$

5. $\frac{3}{5} \times \frac{5}{6} =$

6. $\frac{5}{8} - \frac{3}{8} =$

7. $\frac{5}{7} + \frac{3}{7} =$

8. $\frac{1}{4} \times \frac{3}{8} =$

9. $\frac{3}{10} + \frac{2}{10} =$

10. $\frac{1}{2} \times \frac{1}{2} =$

11. $\frac{2}{3} \times \frac{4}{7} =$

12. $\frac{7}{12} - \frac{3}{12} =$

13. $\frac{5}{6} \times \frac{12}{13} =$

14. $\frac{3}{7} \times \frac{4}{6} =$

15. $\frac{4}{10} - \frac{2}{10} =$

16. $\frac{4}{21} \times \frac{7}{9} =$

17. $\frac{7}{16} \times \frac{4}{14} =$

18. $\frac{4}{20} + \frac{6}{20} =$

19. $\frac{19}{25} - \frac{4}{25} =$

20. $\frac{7}{30} + \frac{1}{30} =$

21. $\frac{2}{9} \times \frac{3}{8} =$

22. $\frac{11}{15} \times \frac{5}{22} =$

23. $\frac{7}{12} \times \frac{2}{21} =$

24. $\frac{3}{20} \times \frac{5}{9} =$

25. $\frac{1}{2} \times \frac{4}{5} \times \frac{2}{3} =$

26. $\frac{3}{8} \times \frac{4}{7} \times \frac{1}{2} =$

27. $\frac{1}{3} \times \frac{1}{4} \times \frac{1}{5} =$

28. $\frac{3}{10} \times \frac{4}{9} \times \frac{1}{8} =$

29. $\frac{16}{20} \times \frac{10}{15} \times \frac{5}{8} =$

30. $\frac{1}{7} \times \frac{21}{25} \times \frac{10}{12} =$

31. $\frac{2}{30} \times \frac{6}{10} \times \frac{5}{18} =$

32. $\frac{12}{13} \times \frac{26}{30} \times \frac{5}{8} =$

33. $\frac{20}{24} \times \frac{6}{7} \times \frac{4}{5} =$

34. Aurelio owns Southside Flowers. He had $\frac{13}{16}$ pound of potting soil. He used $\frac{7}{16}$ pound to repot an African violet. How much potting soil did he have left?

35. Aurelio mixed $\frac{2}{3}$ gallon of fertilizer. If he sprayed $\frac{1}{2}$ of the fertilizer on transplants, what part of a gallon does he have left?

Answer_____

Answer_____

Multiplying Whole Numbers and Fractions

Multiplying a whole number by a fraction is one way to find part of a whole. For example, to find one half of a dozen, multiply $\frac{1}{2}$ by 12. Remember, when working with fractions, *of* means to multiply.

$$\frac{1}{2} \times 12 = \frac{1}{\underset{1}{2}} \times \frac{\overset{6}{\cancel{12}}}{1} = \frac{6}{1} = 6$$

$$\boxed{1 \text{ dozen} = 12}$$

Use These Steps

Find $\frac{1}{3}$ of a dozen.

1. Set up the problem. Write 12 as an improper fraction with a denominator of 1.

    $$\frac{1}{3} \times \frac{12}{1} =$$

2. Cancel. Multiply the new fractions.

    $$\frac{1}{\underset{1}{3}} \times \frac{\overset{4}{\cancel{12}}}{1} = \frac{4}{1}$$

3. The answer is an improper fraction. Change to a whole number by dividing the numerator by the denominator.

    $$\frac{4}{1} = 4$$

Set up each problem. Cancel and multiply. Use the information in the boxes to help you.

$$\boxed{1 \text{ yard} = 36 \text{ inches} \qquad 1 \text{ day} = 24 \text{ hours} \qquad 1 \text{ week} = 7 \text{ days} \qquad 1 \text{ year} = 52 \text{ weeks}}$$

1. $\frac{1}{2}$ of a yard = ___18___ inches

    $$\frac{1}{2} \times 36 = \frac{1}{\underset{1}{2}} \times \frac{\overset{18}{\cancel{36}}}{1} = \frac{18}{1} = 18$$

2. $\frac{1}{3}$ of a yard = _____ inches

3. $\frac{3}{4}$ of a yard = _____ inches

4. $\frac{2}{3}$ of a yard = _____ inches

5. $\frac{1}{2}$ of a day = _____ hours

6. $\frac{1}{3}$ of a day = _____ hours

7. $\frac{3}{4}$ of a day = _____ hours

8. $\frac{6}{7}$ of a week = _____ days

9. $\frac{1}{4}$ of a year = _____ weeks

10. $\frac{3}{4}$ of a year = _____ weeks

Multiplying Whole Numbers and Fractions

To multiply a whole number and a fraction, first write the whole number over 1. Then multiply the numerators and the denominators. Remember to change answers that are improper fractions to whole or mixed numbers.

Use These Steps

Multiply $\frac{1}{3} \times 13$

1. Set up the problem. Write 13 as $\frac{13}{1}$.

$$\frac{1}{3} \times \frac{13}{1} =$$

2. Multiply the numerators. Multiply the denominators.

$$\frac{1}{3} \times \frac{13}{1} = \frac{13}{3}$$

3. The answer is an improper fraction. Change to a mixed number by dividing the numerator by the denominator.

$$\frac{13}{3} = 4\frac{1}{3}$$

Multiply. Cancel and reduce if possible.

1. $\frac{2}{3} \times 15 =$

$$\frac{2}{\overset{1}{\cancel{3}}} \times \frac{\overset{5}{\cancel{15}}}{1} = \frac{10}{1} = 10$$

2. $10 \times \frac{1}{2} =$

3. $8 \times \frac{3}{4} =$

4. $12 \times \frac{1}{4} =$

5. $\frac{2}{7} \times 14 =$

6. $\frac{3}{8} \times 16 =$

7. $\frac{1}{6} \times 18 =$

8. $\frac{4}{5} \times 20 =$

9. $11 \times \frac{1}{2} =$

10. $17 \times \frac{2}{9} =$

11. $\frac{5}{8} \times 15 =$

12. $\frac{2}{3} \times 10 =$

13. $\frac{3}{14} \times 6 =$

14. $18 \times \frac{9}{10} =$

15. $20 \times \frac{5}{6} =$

16. $19 \times \frac{1}{2} =$

17. $\frac{3}{10} \times 20 =$

18. $\frac{2}{7} \times 21 =$

19. $\frac{1}{4} \times 2 =$

20. $\frac{1}{6} \times 5 =$

Multiplying Mixed Numbers and Whole Numbers

When multiplying mixed and whole numbers, remember to change both numbers to improper fractions.

Use These Steps

Multiply $3\frac{1}{6} \times 4$

1. Write $3\frac{1}{6}$ as an improper fraction.

$$3\frac{1}{6} = \frac{19}{6}$$

2. Write 4 as an improper fraction.

$$4 = \frac{4}{1}$$

3. Cancel. Multiply. Change the answer to a mixed number.

$$\frac{19}{\cancel{6}_{3}} \times \frac{\cancel{4}^{2}}{1} = \frac{38}{3} = 12\frac{2}{3}$$

Multiply. Cancel and reduce if possible.

1.
$$2\frac{1}{3} \times 4 =$$
$$\frac{7}{3} \times \frac{4}{1} = \frac{28}{3} = 9\frac{1}{3}$$

2.
$$4\frac{2}{5} \times 5 =$$

3.
$$1\frac{1}{8} \times 10 =$$

4.
$$2\frac{5}{9} \times 9 =$$

5.
$$6\frac{2}{3} \times 3 =$$

6.
$$5\frac{1}{2} \times 10 =$$

7.
$$2\frac{3}{7} \times 21 =$$

8.
$$9\frac{3}{4} \times 2 =$$

9.
$$5 \times 3\frac{1}{2} =$$

10.
$$4 \times 7\frac{5}{6} =$$

11.
$$8 \times 3\frac{1}{10} =$$

12.
$$6 \times 6\frac{2}{3} =$$

13.
$$2 \times 1\frac{7}{10} =$$

14.
$$4 \times 3\frac{7}{12} =$$

15.
$$3 \times 5\frac{1}{4} =$$

16.
$$2 \times 9\frac{4}{5} =$$

17.
$$3\frac{6}{7} \times 14 =$$

18.
$$12 \times 1\frac{3}{4} =$$

19.
$$12 \times 2\frac{9}{10} =$$

20.
$$7\frac{1}{7} \times 7 =$$

21. Lupe processed 10 catalog orders in one hour. How many orders can she process in $2\frac{1}{2}$ hours?

22. Jacob ran $2\frac{7}{10}$ miles each day for 5 days. How many miles did he run all together?

Answer_____

Answer_____

Problem Solving: Figuring Overtime

When you are paid at an hourly rate for regular time and at time and a half for overtime, you can use multiplication to figure your total pay. *Time and a half* means that you get paid your regular rate plus one half your regular rate.

MARCY'S RESTAURANT

Employee	Regular	Overtime
Kenichi	$ 6	$ 9
Marina	$ 8	
Nestor	$ 12	
Rita	$ 10	
Edward	$ 16	

Example   Employees at Marcy's Restaurant are paid time and a half for overtime hours. Overtime hours are hours worked over 40 hours per week.

What is Kenichi's overtime pay rate?

▶ **Step 1.**   Find Kenichi's regular pay in the chart.

$6 per hour

▶ **Step 2.**   Multiply by $1\frac{1}{2}$ to find his overtime rate.

$$6 \times 1\frac{1}{2} = \frac{\overset{3}{\cancel{6}}}{1} \times \frac{3}{\underset{1}{\cancel{2}}} = \frac{9}{1} = 9$$

Kenichi's overtime pay rate is $9 per hour.

Solve. Fill in the chart.

1. Find Marina's overtime pay rate.

2. Find Nestor's overtime pay rate.

Answer_____

Answer_____

3. Find Rita's overtime pay rate.

4. Find Edward's overtime pay rate.

Answer_____

Answer_____

MILLER TIRE FACTORY

EMPLOYEE	OVERTIME RATE	OVERTIME HOURS	OVERTIME PAY
Oscar	$ 6	$3 \frac{1}{2}$	
Carl	$ 9	$5 \frac{2}{3}$	
Ruthie	$ 15	$2 \frac{1}{3}$	
James	$ 18	$8 \frac{1}{2}$	
Mike	$ 12	$5 \frac{3}{4}$	$ 69

Example Employees at Miller Tire Factory are paid by the hour. When they work over 40 hours a week, they get time and a half for those hours.

Mike worked $5 \frac{3}{4}$ hours overtime this week. How much will he earn in overtime pay?

▶ **Step 1.** Find Mike's overtime pay rate on the chart.

$12

▶ **Step 2.** Multiply to find Mike's overtime pay.

$$12 \times 5 \frac{3}{4} = \frac{\overset{3}{\cancel{12}}}{1} \times \frac{23}{\underset{1}{\cancel{4}}} = \frac{69}{1} = 69$$

Mike will get $69 in overtime pay.

Solve. Fill in the chart.

1. Oscar worked $3 \frac{1}{2}$ hours overtime last week. What was his overtime pay?

   Answer_____

2. Carl worked $5 \frac{2}{3}$ hours overtime. What was his overtime pay?

   Answer_____

3. Ruthie worked $2 \frac{1}{3}$ hours overtime. What was her overtime pay?

   Answer_____

4. James worked $8 \frac{1}{2}$ hours overtime. What was his overtime pay?

   Answer_____

Multiplying Mixed Numbers and Fractions

When multiplying mixed numbers and fractions, change the mixed number to an improper fraction. Cancel if possible. Change answers that are improper fractions to mixed numbers.

Use These Steps

Multiply $6\frac{3}{7} \times \frac{3}{5}$

1. Write $6\frac{3}{7}$ as an improper fraction.

$$6\frac{3}{7} = \frac{45}{7}$$

2. Cancel. Multiply the numerators. Multiply the denominators.

$$\frac{\overset{9}{\cancel{45}}}{7} \times \frac{3}{\underset{1}{\cancel{5}}} = \frac{27}{7}$$

3. Change the answer to a mixed number.

$$\frac{27}{7} = 3\frac{6}{7}$$

Multiply. Cancel and reduce if possible.

1. $3\frac{1}{5} \times \frac{3}{4} =$

$$\frac{\overset{4}{\cancel{16}}}{5} \times \frac{3}{\underset{1}{\cancel{4}}} = \frac{12}{5} = 2\frac{2}{5}$$

2. $4\frac{3}{8} \times \frac{5}{7} =$

3. $5\frac{2}{5} \times \frac{1}{4} =$

4. $7\frac{1}{9} \times \frac{3}{4} =$

5. $2\frac{1}{2} \times \frac{3}{10} =$

6. $1\frac{1}{3} \times \frac{3}{16} =$

7. $6\frac{1}{3} \times \frac{3}{5} =$

8. $3\frac{2}{7} \times \frac{1}{7} =$

9. $\frac{3}{8} \times 4\frac{1}{6} =$

10. $3\frac{7}{9} \times \frac{3}{4} =$

11. $\frac{9}{10} \times 5\frac{2}{3} =$

12. $4\frac{1}{4} \times \frac{12}{13} =$

13. $\frac{1}{2} \times 9\frac{2}{3} =$

14. $\frac{7}{8} \times 3\frac{1}{14} =$

15. $\frac{5}{12} \times 10\frac{1}{10} =$

16. $\frac{7}{15} \times 4\frac{3}{21} =$

17. $6\frac{1}{3} \times \frac{2}{9} =$

18. $\frac{8}{11} \times 2\frac{1}{2} =$

Multiplying Mixed Numbers and Mixed Numbers

When multiplying mixed numbers, change both mixed numbers to improper fractions. Cancel if possible. Multiply. Change answers that are improper fractions to whole or mixed numbers.

Use These Steps

Multiply $2\frac{1}{7} \times 1\frac{2}{5}$

1. Write $2\frac{1}{7}$ as an improper fraction.

$$2\frac{1}{7} = \frac{15}{7}$$

2. Write $1\frac{2}{5}$ as an improper fraction.

$$1\frac{2}{5} = \frac{7}{5}$$

3. Cancel. Multiply. Change the answer to a whole number.

$$\overset{3}{\cancel{\frac{15}{7}}} \times \overset{1}{\cancel{\frac{7}{5}}} = \frac{3}{1} = 3$$

Multiply. Cancel and reduce if possible.

1.
$$3\frac{1}{9} \times 5\frac{1}{4} =$$
$$\overset{7}{\underset{3}{\cancel{\frac{28}{9}}}} \times \overset{7}{\underset{1}{\cancel{\frac{21}{4}}}} = \frac{49}{3} = 16\frac{1}{3}$$

2.
$$9\frac{4}{5} \times 3\frac{4}{7} =$$

3.
$$4\frac{7}{8} \times 9\frac{1}{3} =$$

4.
$$2\frac{3}{4} \times 2\frac{5}{11} =$$

5.
$$4\frac{1}{5} \times 3\frac{1}{3} =$$

6.
$$1\frac{1}{5} \times 2\frac{5}{6} =$$

7.
$$5\frac{1}{3} \times 6\frac{1}{8} =$$

8.
$$1\frac{1}{2} \times 7\frac{1}{3} =$$

9.
$$3\frac{1}{10} \times 4\frac{2}{7} =$$

10.
$$1\frac{5}{9} \times 2\frac{9}{14} =$$

11.
$$5\frac{1}{7} \times 2\frac{1}{10} =$$

12.
$$1\frac{1}{12} \times 3\frac{3}{5} =$$

13.
$$7\frac{1}{8} \times 6\frac{2}{3} =$$

14.
$$5\frac{1}{11} \times 4\frac{1}{2} =$$

15.
$$9\frac{3}{8} \times 8\frac{8}{25} =$$

Application

Robert is a baker. He has a recipe that makes 1 dozen large brownies. He needs to make $3\frac{1}{2}$ dozen brownies for a baby shower. He will need to use $3\frac{1}{2}$ times as much of each ingredient listed in the recipe.

```
Fudge Brownies
               Serves: 1 dozen
½ cup butter              2 eggs
1¼ cups sugar             ⅛ teaspoon salt
¾ cup flour
½ teaspoon baking powder
1½ ounces unsweetened chocolate
¾ cup chopped nuts


Stir and bake at 350° for 25 minutes.
```

Example How many cups of butter will Robert need to make $3\frac{1}{2}$ dozen brownies?

$$\tfrac{1}{2} \text{ cup} \times 3\tfrac{1}{2} = \tfrac{1}{2} \times \tfrac{7}{2} = \tfrac{7}{4} = 1\tfrac{3}{4}$$

Robert needs $1\frac{3}{4}$ cups butter.

Solve. Reduce if possible.

1. How many ounces of unsweetened chocolate will Robert need to make $3\frac{1}{2}$ dozen brownies?

   Answer_____

2. How many cups of sugar will Robert need to make $3\frac{1}{2}$ dozen brownies?

   Answer_____

3. How many cups of flour will Robert need to make $3\frac{1}{2}$ dozen brownies?

   Answer_____

4. How many teaspoons of salt will he need to make $3\frac{1}{2}$ dozen brownies?

   Answer_____

5. For a bank opening, Robert needs to make 5 dozen brownies. How many cups of butter will he need?

   Answer_____

6. How many cups of chopped nuts will he need to make 5 dozen brownies?

   Answer_____

Unit 4 *Review*

Multiply. Reduce if possible.

1. $\dfrac{1}{3} \times \dfrac{2}{3} =$

2. $\dfrac{1}{2} \times \dfrac{1}{3} =$

3. $\dfrac{1}{4} \times \dfrac{1}{3} =$

4. $\dfrac{3}{5} \times \dfrac{1}{2} =$

5. $\dfrac{5}{9} \times \dfrac{1}{4} =$

6. $\dfrac{4}{5} \times \dfrac{4}{5} =$

7. $\dfrac{5}{6} \times \dfrac{7}{8} =$

8. $\dfrac{7}{10} \times \dfrac{1}{2} =$

9. $\dfrac{1}{2} \times \dfrac{1}{3} \times \dfrac{1}{4} =$

10. $\dfrac{3}{5} \times \dfrac{1}{4} \times \dfrac{3}{7} =$

11. $\dfrac{1}{5} \times \dfrac{3}{4} \times \dfrac{1}{4} =$

12. $\dfrac{2}{3} \times \dfrac{3}{5} \times \dfrac{5}{8} =$

13. $\dfrac{1}{10} \times \dfrac{5}{6} \times \dfrac{2}{7} =$

14. $\dfrac{4}{9} \times \dfrac{1}{3} \times \dfrac{3}{5} =$

Multiply. Cancel and reduce if possible.

15. $\dfrac{1}{3} \times \dfrac{3}{7} =$

16. $\dfrac{4}{5} \times \dfrac{10}{12} =$

17. $\dfrac{3}{8} \times \dfrac{4}{9} =$

18. $\dfrac{2}{15} \times \dfrac{5}{6} =$

19. $\dfrac{4}{10} \times \dfrac{3}{8} =$

20. $\dfrac{2}{7} \times \dfrac{3}{10} =$

21. $\dfrac{5}{14} \times \dfrac{7}{10} =$

22. $\dfrac{1}{6} \times \dfrac{6}{7} =$

23. $\dfrac{1}{4} \times \dfrac{2}{5} =$

24. $\dfrac{2}{7} \times \dfrac{7}{9} =$

25. $\dfrac{3}{16} \times \dfrac{8}{9} =$

26. $\dfrac{1}{8} \times \dfrac{8}{9} =$

27. $\dfrac{4}{9} \times \dfrac{3}{4} \times \dfrac{3}{5} =$

28. $\dfrac{8}{10} \times \dfrac{12}{14} \times \dfrac{7}{16} =$

29. $\dfrac{3}{25} \times \dfrac{5}{12} \times \dfrac{8}{9} =$

30. $\dfrac{11}{45} \times \dfrac{18}{33} \times \dfrac{1}{2} =$

31. $\dfrac{6}{12} \times \dfrac{10}{30} \times \dfrac{5}{14} =$

32. $\dfrac{15}{36} \times \dfrac{12}{15} \times \dfrac{5}{6} =$

33. $\dfrac{5}{8} \times \dfrac{1}{6} \times \dfrac{9}{10} =$

34. $\dfrac{4}{11} \times \dfrac{5}{12} \times \dfrac{11}{15} =$

35. $\dfrac{4}{15} \times \dfrac{7}{12} \times \dfrac{3}{4} =$

Multiply. Cancel and reduce if possible.

36.
$$\frac{1}{2} \times 10 =$$

37.
$$\frac{2}{3} \times 12 =$$

38.
$$\frac{5}{6} \times 18 =$$

39.
$$\frac{4}{5} \times 30 =$$

40.
$$5 \times \frac{2}{3} =$$

41.
$$7 \times \frac{1}{4} =$$

42.
$$9 \times \frac{2}{5} =$$

43.
$$11 \times \frac{1}{2} =$$

44.
$$20 \times \frac{2}{5} =$$

45.
$$\frac{4}{9} \times 6 =$$

46.
$$42 \times \frac{1}{6} =$$

47.
$$\frac{5}{14} \times 28 =$$

Multiply. Cancel and reduce if possible.

48.
$$1\frac{1}{2} \times 3 =$$

49.
$$6 \times 5\frac{2}{3} =$$

50.
$$4 \times 2\frac{3}{8} =$$

51.
$$3\frac{6}{7} \times 9 =$$

52.
$$2\frac{1}{3} \times \frac{3}{5} =$$

53.
$$\frac{5}{9} \times 2\frac{1}{3} =$$

54.
$$\frac{7}{15} \times 5\frac{1}{14} =$$

55.
$$4\frac{5}{11} \times \frac{2}{7} =$$

56.
$$1\frac{1}{6} \times 2\frac{5}{7} =$$

57.
$$2\frac{2}{3} \times 5\frac{1}{4} =$$

58.
$$5\frac{1}{7} \times 2\frac{1}{6} =$$

59.
$$1\frac{1}{5} \times 6\frac{2}{3} =$$

Below is a list of the problems in this review and the pages on which the skills are taught. If you missed any problems, turn to the pages listed and practice the skills. Then correct the problems you missed in the Unit Review.

Unit 5   Dividing Fractions

Have you ever needed to divide $\frac{1}{2}$ a cake equally among four people, divide a pound of peanuts into $\frac{1}{4}$-pound packages, or cut a 6-foot piece of wood into $1\frac{1}{2}$-foot pieces? All of these problems can be solved by dividing fractions.

You will find that knowing how to multiply fractions will help you learn how to divide fractions.

In this unit, you will learn how to work division problems with fractions, whole numbers, and mixed numbers, and how to solve word problems using fractions.

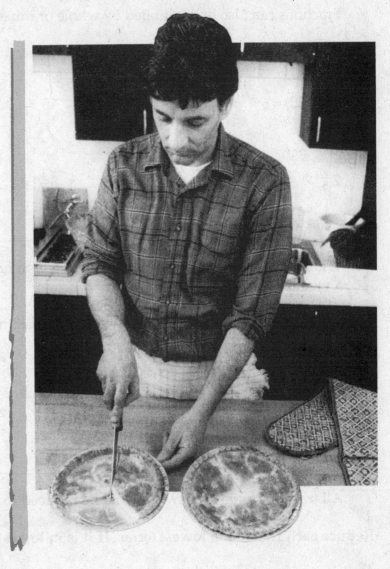

Getting Ready

You should be familiar with the skills on this page and the next before you begin this unit. To check your answers, turn to page 198.

 Knowing how to multiply fractions is the first step in learning how to divide fractions.

Multiply these fractions by canceling.

1.
$$\frac{1}{\underset{1}{\cancel{2}}} \times \frac{\overset{2}{\cancel{4}}}{9} = \frac{2}{9}$$

2.
$$\frac{2}{3} \times \frac{6}{7} =$$

3.
$$\frac{5}{8} \times \frac{16}{20} =$$

4.
$$\frac{3}{4} \times \frac{8}{9} =$$

5.
$$\frac{1}{3} \times \frac{3}{12} =$$

6.
$$\frac{3}{8} \times \frac{4}{21} =$$

7.
$$\frac{11}{16} \times \frac{4}{9} =$$

8.
$$\frac{7}{11} \times \frac{33}{49} =$$

9.
$$\frac{4}{15} \times \frac{3}{7} =$$

10.
$$\frac{5}{6} \times \frac{24}{35} =$$

For review, see Unit 4, pages 113–114.

Getting Ready

 Fractions can also be multiplied by whole or mixed numbers.

Multiply. Cancel and reduce if possible.

11. $\frac{1}{5} \times 30 = 6$ **12.** $17 \times \frac{1}{4} =$ **13.** $\frac{2}{3} \times 45 =$ **14.** $24 \times \frac{1}{6} =$ **15.** $\frac{3}{7} \times 21 =$

16. $2\frac{1}{5} \times \frac{10}{11} =$ **17.** $\frac{7}{10} \times 1\frac{1}{7} =$ **18.** $\frac{8}{9} \times 3\frac{1}{2} =$ **19.** $7\frac{3}{4} \times \frac{2}{3} =$ **20.** $4\frac{1}{10} \times \frac{5}{7} =$

For review, see Unit 4, pages 118 and 122.

 When your answer is an improper fraction, you need to change it to a whole or mixed number.

Change each improper fraction to a whole or mixed number. Reduce if possible.

21. $\frac{10}{2} = 5$ **22.** $\frac{13}{5} =$ **23.** $\frac{17}{3} =$ **24.** $\frac{15}{4} =$ **25.** $\frac{20}{5} =$

26. $\frac{31}{6} =$ **27.** $\frac{9}{4} =$ **28.** $\frac{15}{10} =$ **29.** $\frac{18}{9} =$ **30.** $\frac{48}{12} =$

For review, see Unit 1, pages 33–34.

 All fractions in your answer should be reduced to lowest terms.

Reduce each fraction to lowest terms. If it is in lowest terms, write LT.

31. $\frac{2}{4} = \frac{1}{2}$ **32.** $\frac{3}{8} =$ **33.** $\frac{3}{9} =$ **34.** $\frac{6}{12} =$ **35.** $\frac{7}{8} =$

36. $\frac{4}{10} =$ **37.** $\frac{6}{9} =$ **38.** $\frac{15}{20} =$ **39.** $\frac{21}{49} =$ **40.** $\frac{16}{24} =$

For review, see Unit 1, pages 15–16.

To divide mixed numbers, you will need to know how to change a mixed number to an improper fraction.

Change each mixed number to an improper fraction.

41. $1\frac{1}{2} = \frac{3}{2}$ **42.** $2\frac{2}{3} =$ **43.** $4\frac{1}{4} =$ **44.** $3\frac{2}{5} =$ **45.** $5\frac{3}{8} =$

For review, see Unit 1, pages 35–36.

Dividing Fractions by Fractions

To find out how many equal parts are in a fraction, you may need to divide a fraction by a fraction.

For example, if you have $\frac{3}{4}$ yard of material to divide equally into $\frac{1}{4}$-yard pieces, how many pieces will you get? To find how many $\frac{1}{4}$s are in $\frac{3}{4}$s, divide $\frac{3}{4}$ by $\frac{1}{4}$.

To divide by a fraction, invert (turn upside down) the fraction you are dividing by (the fraction to the right of the division sign). When you invert $\frac{1}{4}$, you get $\frac{4}{1}$. Change the division sign to a multiplication sign and multiply.

$$\frac{3}{4} \div \frac{1}{4} = \frac{3}{4} \times \frac{4}{1} = \frac{12}{4} = 3 \text{ pieces}$$

Use These Steps

Divide $\frac{1}{2} \div \frac{1}{8}$

1. Invert the fraction to the right of the division sign.

$$\frac{1}{8} \diagup \frac{8}{1}$$

2. Change the division sign to a multiplication sign. Multiply by the new fraction, $\frac{8}{1}$. Cancel.

$$\frac{1}{\underset{1}{2}} \times \frac{\overset{4}{\cancel{8}}}{1} = \frac{4}{1}$$

3. Change the answer to a whole number.

$$\frac{4}{1} = 4$$

Divide. Cancel and reduce if possible.

1.

$$\frac{5}{6} \div \frac{1}{6} = \frac{5}{\underset{1}{\cancel{6}}} \times \frac{\overset{1}{\cancel{6}}}{1} = \frac{5}{1} = 5$$

2.

$$\frac{3}{4} \div \frac{1}{8} =$$

3. $\frac{2}{5} \div \frac{1}{10} =$

4. $\frac{2}{3} \div \frac{1}{3} =$

5. $\frac{3}{8} \div \frac{1}{16} =$

6. $\frac{7}{10} \div \frac{1}{20} =$

7. $\frac{6}{9} \div \frac{1}{9} =$

8. $\frac{3}{7} \div \frac{1}{21} =$

9. $\frac{5}{9} \div \frac{1}{18} =$

10. $\frac{2}{3} \div \frac{1}{6} =$

Dividing Fractions by Fractions

When you divide fractions, always invert the fraction to the right of the division sign and then multiply.

Use These Steps

Divide $\frac{4}{5} \div \frac{2}{7}$

1. Invert the fraction to the right of the division sign.

$$\frac{2}{7} \diagdown \frac{7}{2}$$

2. Multiply by the new fraction. Cancel.

$$\frac{\overset{2}{\cancel{4}}}{5} \times \frac{7}{\underset{1}{\cancel{2}}} = \frac{14}{5}$$

3. Change the answer to a mixed number.

$$\frac{14}{5} = 2\frac{4}{5}$$

Divide. Cancel and reduce if possible.

1. $\frac{3}{4} \div \frac{3}{5} =$

$\frac{\overset{1}{\cancel{3}}}{4} \times \frac{5}{\underset{1}{\cancel{3}}} = \frac{5}{4} = 1\frac{1}{4}$

2. $\frac{5}{9} \div \frac{1}{4} =$

3. $\frac{4}{7} \div \frac{3}{8} =$

4. $\frac{7}{10} \div \frac{7}{12} =$

5. $\frac{1}{3} \div \frac{2}{3} =$

$\frac{1}{\underset{1}{\cancel{3}}} \times \frac{\overset{1}{\cancel{3}}}{2} = \frac{1}{2}$

6. $\frac{2}{5} \div \frac{5}{9} =$

7. $\frac{1}{4} \div \frac{1}{3} =$

8. $\frac{3}{7} \div \frac{3}{5} =$

9. $\frac{2}{3} \div \frac{3}{4} =$

10. $\frac{9}{10} \div \frac{2}{5} =$

11. $\frac{5}{8} \div \frac{3}{4} =$

12. $\frac{7}{9} \div \frac{1}{6} =$

13. $\frac{5}{8} \div \frac{2}{5} =$

14. $\frac{4}{5} \div \frac{10}{11} =$

15. $\frac{5}{6} \div \frac{1}{3} =$

16. $\frac{1}{8} \div \frac{1}{4} =$

17. Karen has $\frac{1}{2}$ yard of wire that she wants to cut into $\frac{1}{4}$-yard pieces. How many pieces will she get?

18. If Karen cuts her $\frac{1}{2}$ yard of wire into $\frac{1}{6}$-yard pieces, how many pieces will she get?

Answer_____

Answer_____

Dividing Whole Numbers by Fractions

To divide a whole number by a fraction, change the whole number to an improper fraction with a denominator of 1. Then invert the fraction to the right of the division sign and multiply the new fractions.

For example, if you have 3 acres of land and want to find out how many $\frac{1}{4}$-acre plots you have, divide 3 by $\frac{1}{4}$.

3											
$\frac{1}{4}$	$\frac{1}{4}$	$\frac{1}{4}$	$\frac{1}{4}$	$\frac{1}{4}$	$\frac{1}{4}$	$\frac{1}{4}$	$\frac{1}{4}$	$\frac{1}{4}$	$\frac{1}{4}$	$\frac{1}{4}$	$\frac{1}{4}$

$3 \div \frac{1}{4} = \frac{3}{1} \times \frac{4}{1} = \frac{12}{1} = 12$ plots

Use These Steps

Divide $4 \div \frac{1}{6}$

1. Change the whole number, 4, to an improper fraction with a denominator of 1.

   $4 = \frac{4}{1}$

2. Invert the fraction to the right of the division sign.

   $\frac{1}{6} \diagup \frac{6}{1}$

3. Multiply the new fractions. Change the answer to a whole number.

   $\frac{4}{1} \times \frac{6}{1} = \frac{24}{1} = 24$

Divide. Reduce if possible.

1.

2			
$\frac{1}{2}$	$\frac{1}{2}$	$\frac{1}{2}$	$\frac{1}{2}$

$2 \div \frac{1}{2} = \frac{2}{1} \times \frac{2}{1} = \frac{4}{1} = 4$

2.

1		
$\frac{1}{3}$	$\frac{1}{3}$	$\frac{1}{3}$

$1 \div \frac{1}{3} =$

3. $2 \div \frac{1}{4} =$

4. $3 \div \frac{1}{6} =$

5. $4 \div \frac{1}{4} =$

6. $5 \div \frac{1}{5} =$

7. $5 \div \frac{1}{4} =$

8. $8 \div \frac{1}{3} =$

9. $6 \div \frac{1}{9} =$

10. $7 \div \frac{1}{2} =$

11. $15 \div \frac{1}{3} =$

12. $12 \div \frac{1}{4} =$

13. $20 \div \frac{1}{5} =$

14. $5 \div \frac{1}{8} =$

Dividing Whole Numbers by Fractions

Remember to invert only the fraction to the right of the division sign and then multiply.

Use These Steps

Divide $2 \div \frac{3}{4}$

1. Change the whole number, 2, to an improper fraction with a denominator of 1.

$$2 = \frac{2}{1}$$

2. Invert the fraction to the right of the division sign.

$$\frac{3}{4} \diagup \frac{4}{3}$$

3. Multiply the new fractions. Change the answer to a mixed number.

$$\frac{2}{1} \times \frac{4}{3} = \frac{8}{3} = 2\frac{2}{3}$$

Divide. Cancel and reduce if possible.

1.
$$3 \div \frac{2}{5} =$$
$$\frac{3}{1} \times \frac{5}{2} = \frac{15}{2} = 7\frac{1}{2}$$

2.
$$5 \div \frac{3}{4} =$$

3.
$$10 \div \frac{2}{3} =$$

4.
$$9 \div \frac{5}{6} =$$

5.
$$12 \div \frac{3}{7} =$$

6.
$$7 \div \frac{4}{9} =$$

7.
$$15 \div \frac{3}{5} =$$

8.
$$13 \div \frac{7}{8} =$$

9.
$$6 \div \frac{3}{10} =$$

10.
$$20 \div \frac{1}{3} =$$

11.
$$18 \div \frac{2}{9} =$$

12.
$$21 \div \frac{7}{11} =$$

13.
$$7 \div \frac{1}{3} =$$

14.
$$6 \div \frac{5}{8} =$$

15.
$$10 \div \frac{1}{5} =$$

16.
$$13 \div \frac{3}{4} =$$

17. Jana bought two pieces of plastic sheeting. If she cuts each piece of plastic into twelfths, how many pieces will she get?
(Hint: Divide 2 by $\frac{1}{12}$.)

18. If Jana cut both pieces of plastic into ninths, how many pieces will she get?

Answer_____

Answer_____

Dividing Mixed Numbers by Fractions

To divide a mixed number by a fraction, first change the mixed number to an improper fraction. Then invert the fraction to the right of the division sign and multiply.

For example, if you have $1\frac{1}{2}$ pounds of ground beef, how many $\frac{1}{4}$-pound hamburgers can you make?

$1\frac{1}{2}$					
$\frac{1}{4}$	$\frac{1}{4}$	$\frac{1}{4}$	$\frac{1}{4}$	$\frac{1}{4}$	$\frac{1}{4}$

$1\frac{1}{2} \div \frac{1}{4} = \frac{3}{\cancel{2}} \times \frac{\cancel{4}^{2}}{1} = \frac{6}{1} = 6$ hamburgers

Use These Steps

Divide $2\frac{3}{4} \div \frac{1}{8}$

1. **Change the mixed number, $2\frac{3}{4}$, to an improper fraction.**

   $2\frac{3}{4} = \frac{11}{4}$

2. **Invert the fraction to the right of the division sign.**

   $\frac{1}{8} \times \frac{8}{1}$

3. **Multiply the new fractions. Cancel. Change the answer to a whole number.**

   $\frac{11}{\cancel{4}_{1}} \times \frac{\cancel{8}^{2}}{1} = \frac{22}{1} = 22$

Divide. Cancel and reduce if possible.

1.

$1\frac{1}{3}$			
$\frac{1}{3}$	$\frac{1}{3}$	$\frac{1}{3}$	$\frac{1}{3}$

$1\frac{1}{3} \div \frac{1}{3} = \frac{4}{\cancel{3}} \times \frac{\cancel{3}}{1} = \frac{4}{1} = 4$

2.

$2\frac{1}{2}$									
$\frac{1}{4}$	$\frac{1}{4}$	$\frac{1}{4}$	$\frac{1}{4}$	$\frac{1}{4}$	$\frac{1}{4}$	$\frac{1}{4}$	$\frac{1}{4}$	$\frac{1}{4}$	$\frac{1}{4}$

$2\frac{1}{2} \div \frac{1}{4} =$

3. $1\frac{2}{5} \div \frac{1}{10} =$

4. $3\frac{3}{4} \div \frac{1}{4} =$

5. $2\frac{5}{8} \div \frac{1}{8} =$

6. $1\frac{2}{3} \div \frac{1}{6} =$

7. $3\frac{2}{7} \div \frac{1}{7} =$

8. $4\frac{1}{4} \div \frac{1}{16} =$

9. $5\frac{4}{9} \div \frac{1}{9} =$

10. $6\frac{3}{10} \div \frac{1}{20} =$

11. $2\frac{2}{5} \div \frac{1}{15} =$

Dividing Mixed Numbers by Fractions

When you divide a mixed number by a fraction, the answer may be an improper fraction. Change the improper fraction to a whole number or a mixed number.

Use These Steps

Divide $3\frac{1}{8} \div \frac{1}{4}$

1. Change $3\frac{1}{8}$ to an improper fraction.

$$3\frac{1}{8} = \frac{25}{8}$$

2. Invert the fraction to the right of the division sign.

$$\frac{1}{4} \times \frac{4}{1}$$

3. Multiply the new fractions. Cancel. Change the answer to a mixed number.

$$\frac{25}{\cancel{8}_2} \times \frac{\cancel{4}^1}{1} = \frac{25}{2} = 12\frac{1}{2}$$

Divide. Cancel and reduce if possible.

1.
$$4\frac{1}{2} \div \frac{2}{3} =$$
$$\frac{9}{2} \times \frac{3}{2} = \frac{27}{4} = 6\frac{3}{4}$$

2.
$$5\frac{2}{5} \div \frac{1}{8} =$$

3.
$$2\frac{7}{8} \div \frac{3}{4} =$$

4.
$$6\frac{1}{9} \div \frac{1}{3} =$$

5.
$$7\frac{5}{7} \div \frac{1}{6} =$$

6.
$$10\frac{4}{5} \div \frac{2}{9} =$$

7.
$$8\frac{3}{4} \div \frac{1}{2} =$$

8.
$$1\frac{5}{8} \div \frac{4}{5} =$$

9.
$$3\frac{6}{11} \div \frac{2}{3} =$$

10.
$$9\frac{1}{14} \div \frac{2}{7} =$$

11.
$$12\frac{5}{6} \div \frac{5}{18} =$$

12.
$$15\frac{7}{20} \div \frac{1}{10} =$$

13.
$$3\frac{1}{3} \div \frac{5}{7} =$$

14.
$$8\frac{1}{4} \div \frac{9}{10} =$$

15.
$$5\frac{2}{9} \div \frac{2}{3} =$$

16.
$$2\frac{5}{6} \div \frac{15}{16} =$$

17. At Edna's Cooking School, Joe, one of her students, prepared $3\frac{1}{2}$ pounds of dough to make bread. He used $\frac{3}{4}$ pound of dough for each loaf of bread. How many loaves of bread did he make?

18. Another student, Betty, is making pecan cookies. She has $5\frac{1}{3}$ cups of pecans. If she needs $\frac{1}{2}$ cup for each dozen, how many dozen cookies can she make?

Answer_____

Answer_____

Application

The Smithville Food Co-op buys some items in large packages. Gracie's job is to divide the large packages into smaller packages of equal size. Then she puts the packages out for sale.

Example The co-op buys granola in 20-pound bags. If Gracie divides one 20-pound bag into $\frac{3}{4}$-pound bags, how many of the smaller bags can she get? How much granola will be left over?

$$20 \div \frac{3}{4} = \frac{20}{1} \times \frac{4}{3} = \frac{80}{3} = 26\frac{2}{3}$$

Gracie will get 26 whole bags. She will have $\frac{2}{3}$ pound of granola left over.

Solve.

1. The co-op buys cheddar cheese in 10-pound blocks. If Gracie divides one block into $\frac{1}{2}$-pound pieces, how many pieces can she get?

   Answer_____

2. The co-op bought a box of mixed nuts weighing 18 pounds. How many $\frac{1}{4}$-pound packages can Gracie get from the whole box?

   Answer_____

3. The co-op buys some spices in $\frac{1}{2}$-pound packages. If Gracie divides the spices into $\frac{1}{16}$-pound packages, how many smaller packages can she get from each $\frac{1}{2}$-pound package?

   Answer_____

4. The co-op bought a can of pepper weighing 1 pound. How many $\frac{1}{8}$-pound packages can Gracie make from the can?

   Answer_____

5. The co-op buys popcorn in 5-pound bags. One bag weighed only $4\frac{9}{10}$ pounds. How many $\frac{2}{3}$-pound packages can Gracie get from that bag? How much popcorn is left over?

   Answer_____

6. The co-op bought a bushel of corn from a farmer. The corn weighed $25\frac{3}{4}$ pounds. How many $\frac{3}{4}$-pound packages can Gracie get from the bushel? How much corn is left over?

   Answer_____

Mixed Review

Add, subtract, multiply, or divide. Cancel and reduce if possible.

1. $\frac{2}{3} \div \frac{1}{6} =$

2. $\frac{1}{2} + \frac{1}{3} =$

3. $\frac{2}{5} - \frac{1}{4} =$

4. $\frac{1}{2} \div \frac{1}{8} =$

5. $\frac{9}{10} \div \frac{3}{5} =$

6. $\frac{5}{7} - \frac{3}{8} =$

7. $\frac{1}{4} \times \frac{1}{3} =$

8. $\frac{2}{5} \times \frac{10}{12} =$

9. $\frac{4}{9} - \frac{1}{3} =$

10. $\frac{4}{10} \div \frac{2}{5} =$

11. $\frac{7}{12} + \frac{3}{10} =$

12. $\frac{3}{4} \times \frac{1}{2} =$

13. $4 \times \frac{2}{3} =$

14. $3 \div \frac{1}{2} =$

15. $2 + \frac{8}{9} =$

16. $9 \div \frac{1}{3} =$

17. $7 - \frac{4}{5} =$

18. $6 + \frac{3}{7} =$

19. $4 \div \frac{5}{8} =$

20. $10 \times \frac{5}{6} =$

21. $8 \div \frac{1}{4} =$

22. $12 \div \frac{7}{10} =$

23. $15 \times \frac{11}{30} =$

24. $20 \div \frac{5}{12} =$

25. $2\frac{5}{8} \div \frac{1}{8} =$

26. $1\frac{1}{2} \div \frac{3}{4} =$

27. $4\frac{2}{3} \times \frac{1}{3} =$

28. $7\frac{6}{10} \div \frac{1}{5} =$

29. $5\frac{3}{16} \times \frac{1}{2} =$

30. $1\frac{3}{10} \div \frac{4}{5} =$

31. $8\frac{2}{9} \div \frac{2}{3} =$

32. $12\frac{1}{5} \div \frac{3}{8} =$

33. $3\frac{3}{4} \div \frac{5}{16} =$

34. $6\frac{6}{7} \times \frac{2}{6} =$

35. $20\frac{9}{10} \div \frac{3}{4} =$

36. $7\frac{2}{3} \times \frac{5}{6} =$

Dividing Fractions by Whole Numbers

To divide a fraction by a whole number, change the whole number to an improper fraction with a denominator of 1. Invert and multiply.

For example, if you have $\frac{1}{2}$ a cake and want to divide it evenly among 3 people, how much of the cake does each person get?

 $\frac{1}{2} \div 3 = \frac{1}{2} \div \frac{3}{1} = \frac{1}{2} \times \frac{1}{3} = \frac{1}{6}$ of the cake

Use These Steps

Divide $\frac{3}{4} \div 2$

1. Change the whole number, 2, to an improper fraction with a denominator of 1.

$$2 = \frac{2}{1}$$

2. Invert the improper fraction, $\frac{2}{1}$.

$$\frac{2}{1} \times \frac{1}{2}$$

3. Multiply $\frac{3}{4}$ by the new fraction.

$$\frac{3}{4} \times \frac{1}{2} = \frac{3}{8}$$

Divide. Cancel and reduce if possible.

1.

$\frac{1}{4} \div 2 = \frac{1}{4} \div \frac{2}{1} = \frac{1}{4} \times \frac{1}{2} = \frac{1}{8}$

2.

$\frac{3}{5} \div 2 =$

3. $\frac{2}{3} \div 4 =$

4. $\frac{1}{2} \div 5 =$

5. $\frac{1}{7} \div 2 =$

6. $\frac{1}{8} \div 6 =$

7. $\frac{2}{5} \div 4 =$

8. $\frac{2}{9} \div 7 =$

9. $\frac{3}{8} \div 3 =$

10. $\frac{7}{10} \div 3 =$

11. $\frac{8}{9} \div 16 =$

12. $\frac{5}{6} \div 3 =$

13. $\frac{4}{5} \div 5 =$

14. $\frac{1}{3} \div 12 =$

Dividing Fractions by Whole Numbers

Remember, first change the whole number to an improper fraction. Then invert and multiply. Reduce to lowest terms if possible.

Use These Steps

Divide $\frac{5}{7} \div 9$

1. Change the whole number, 9, to an improper fraction with a denominator of 1.

$$9 = \frac{9}{1}$$

2. Invert the improper fraction, $\frac{9}{1}$.

$$\frac{9}{1} \diagdown \frac{1}{9}$$

3. Multiply $\frac{5}{7}$ by the new fraction.

$$\frac{5}{7} \times \frac{1}{9} = \frac{5}{63}$$

Divide. Cancel and reduce if possible.

1.
$$\frac{2}{3} \div 2 =$$

$$\frac{2}{3} \div \frac{2}{1} = \frac{\overset{1}{\cancel{2}}}{3} \times \frac{1}{\underset{1}{\cancel{2}}} = \frac{1}{3}$$

2.
$$\frac{3}{4} \div 6 =$$

3.
$$\frac{7}{8} \div 5 =$$

4.
$$\frac{1}{6} \div 3 =$$

5.
$$\frac{6}{7} \div 6 =$$

6.
$$\frac{9}{10} \div 4 =$$

7.
$$\frac{5}{12} \div 10 =$$

8.
$$\frac{15}{16} \div 5 =$$

9.
$$\frac{7}{11} \div 7 =$$

10.
$$\frac{3}{10} \div 6 =$$

11.
$$\frac{5}{14} \div 15 =$$

12.
$$\frac{1}{8} \div 3 =$$

13. Maxine needs to divide $\frac{3}{4}$ pound of mocha coffee into two packages for a customer. If she divides the coffee evenly, how much will each package weigh?

14. Marie makes scarves for Madeline's Accessories. She used $\frac{7}{8}$ yard of fabric to make 3 scarves. How much fabric did she use for each scarf?

Answer_____

Answer_____

Dividing Mixed Numbers by Whole Numbers

To divide a mixed number by a whole number, change both the mixed number and the whole number to improper fractions. Then invert and multiply.

Use These Steps

Divide $4\frac{3}{4} \div 2$

1. Change the mixed number, $4\frac{3}{4}$, and the whole number, 2, to improper fractions.

$$4\frac{3}{4} = \frac{19}{4} \qquad 2 = \frac{2}{1}$$

2. Invert the improper fraction, $\frac{2}{1}$.

$$\frac{2}{1} \diagup \frac{1}{2}$$

3. Multiply the new fractions. Change the answer to a mixed number.

$$\frac{19}{4} \times \frac{1}{2} = \frac{19}{8} = 2\frac{3}{8}$$

Divide. Cancel and reduce if possible.

1.
$$6\frac{5}{8} \div 3 =$$
$$\frac{53}{8} \div \frac{3}{1} = \frac{53}{8} \times \frac{1}{3} = \frac{53}{24} = 2\frac{5}{24}$$

2.
$$5\frac{2}{3} \div 2 =$$

3.
$$8\frac{1}{5} \div 5 =$$

4.
$$7\frac{3}{7} \div 6 =$$

5.
$$3\frac{1}{2} \div 4 =$$

6.
$$2\frac{5}{6} \div 7 =$$

7.
$$1\frac{2}{9} \div 2 =$$

8.
$$9\frac{7}{12} \div 10 =$$

9.
$$10\frac{9}{11} \div 5 =$$

10.
$$7\frac{13}{16} \div 6 =$$

11. Greg has to lose weight. If he loses 2 pounds each week, how many weeks will it take him to lose $10\frac{1}{2}$ pounds?

12. Carla needs to gain weight. If she gains 3 pounds each week, how many weeks will it take her to gain $12\frac{3}{4}$ pounds?

Answer_____

Answer_____

Dividing Mixed Numbers by Mixed Numbers

To divide a mixed number by a mixed number, change both mixed numbers to improper fractions. Invert and multiply.

Use These Steps

Divide $5\frac{1}{3} \div 2\frac{1}{2}$

1. **Change the mixed numbers to improper fractions.**

$5\frac{1}{3} = \frac{16}{3}$ $2\frac{1}{2} = \frac{5}{2}$

2. **Invert the number to the right of the division sign.**

$\frac{5}{2} \diagdown \frac{2}{5}$

3. **Multiply the new fractions. Change the answer to a mixed number.**

$\frac{16}{3} \div \frac{5}{2} = \frac{16}{3} \times \frac{2}{5} = \frac{32}{15} = 2\frac{2}{15}$

Divide. Cancel and reduce if possible.

1.
$6\frac{1}{2} \div 1\frac{3}{4} =$

$\frac{13}{2} \div \frac{7}{4} = \frac{13}{\underset{1}{\cancel{2}}} \times \frac{\overset{2}{\cancel{4}}}{7} = \frac{26}{7} = 3\frac{5}{7}$

2.
$7\frac{2}{3} \div 5\frac{1}{6} =$

3.
$8\frac{3}{5} \div 3\frac{3}{10} =$

4.
$10\frac{6}{7} \div 2\frac{8}{14} =$

5.
$2\frac{5}{6} \div 3\frac{1}{10} =$

6.
$4\frac{2}{7} \div 5\frac{1}{14} =$

7.
$3\frac{5}{9} \div 4\frac{2}{27} =$

8.
$12\frac{2}{5} \div 2\frac{1}{10} =$

9.
$5\frac{1}{3} \div 5\frac{1}{3} =$

10.
$20\frac{7}{10} \div 10\frac{1}{2} =$

11. Chris needs $3\frac{3}{4}$ yards of material to make curtains for one window in a client's living room. If he has $18\frac{3}{4}$ yards of material, how many windows can he make curtains for?

12. Isabel wants the students in her exercise class to run $7\frac{1}{2}$ miles every other day. If every lap around the track is $2\frac{1}{2}$ miles, how many laps do they need to make to run $7\frac{1}{2}$ miles?

Answer _____

Answer _____

Problem Solving: Using a Sketch

Sometimes using a sketch or drawing helps you work with fractions. Hector is a carpenter. He needs to make drawings to help him remember measurements. This helps him cut the correct size pieces of wood.

Example   Hector is measuring a living room wall so that he can make bookcases to fit along that wall. He made this sketch and wrote in the measurements.

Hector wants 3 bookcases of equal size along the wall. How wide can each bookcase be?

▶ **Step 1.**   Look at the drawing to find out how wide the wall is.

$$10 \frac{1}{2} \text{ feet}$$

▶ **Step 2.**   Divide by 3.

$$10 \frac{1}{2} \div 3 = \frac{\overset{7}{\cancel{21}}}{2} \times \frac{1}{\underset{1}{\cancel{3}}} = \frac{7}{2} = 3 \frac{1}{2} \text{ feet}$$

Each bookcase can be no more than $3 \frac{1}{2}$ feet wide.

Solve using the sketch above.

1. Hector wants one bookcase under the window. The shelves in this bookcase are about $11 \frac{1}{2}$ inches apart. How many whole shelves will Hector be able to put in this bookcase?
(Hint: 4 feet = 48 inches)

2. Hector wants one bookcase on each side of the window. Each bookcase is $6 \frac{2}{3}$ feet tall. If there are 8 shelves in each bookcase, how far apart will the shelves be?

Answer_____

Answer_____

Use Hector's drawing to answer the questions.

3. If Hector buys one 12-foot long board, how many whole bookcase tops can he cut from this piece?

Answer_____

4. He buys one 14-foot long board to make the long sides of the bookcases. How many complete sides $6\frac{2}{3}$ feet long can he cut from this piece of board?

Answer_____

5. To fit inside the two tall bookcases, the shelves must be $3\frac{5}{12}$ feet long. How many whole shelves can be cut from a 24-foot long board?

Answer_____

6. Hector may decide to make glass doors for the middle bookcase. How wide would one of the doors be?
(Hint: The width of the two doors together will equal $3\frac{1}{2}$ feet.)

Answer_____

Unit 5 *Review*

Divide. Cancel and reduce if possible.

1. $\frac{2}{3} \div \frac{1}{2} =$

2. $\frac{3}{10} \div \frac{3}{5} =$

3. $\frac{2}{7} \div \frac{4}{9} =$

4. $\frac{5}{6} \div \frac{3}{4} =$

5. $\frac{9}{11} \div \frac{2}{3} =$

6. $\frac{5}{8} \div \frac{1}{6} =$

7. $\frac{4}{5} \div \frac{1}{5} =$

8. $\frac{2}{9} \div \frac{4}{9} =$

9. $4 \div \frac{1}{2} =$

10. $9 \div \frac{1}{3} =$

11. $7 \div \frac{3}{4} =$

12. $5 \div \frac{2}{5} =$

13. $8 \div \frac{3}{8} =$

14. $3 \div \frac{1}{7} =$

15. $6 \div \frac{5}{12} =$

16. $10 \div \frac{5}{6} =$

17. $5\frac{1}{2} \div \frac{1}{2} =$

18. $4\frac{3}{8} \div \frac{1}{4} =$

19. $6\frac{5}{9} \div \frac{2}{3} =$

20. $2\frac{2}{5} \div \frac{3}{7} =$

21. $9\frac{5}{6} \div \frac{1}{3} =$

22. $8\frac{3}{4} \div \frac{1}{2} =$

23. $10\frac{7}{10} \div \frac{1}{10} =$

24. $7\frac{2}{3} \div \frac{5}{6} =$

25. $\frac{1}{9} \div 3 =$

26. $\frac{3}{4} \div 2 =$

27. $\frac{5}{8} \div 5 =$

28. $\frac{2}{3} \div 6 =$

29. $\frac{9}{10} \div 10 =$

30. $\frac{5}{6} \div 4 =$

31. $\frac{1}{12} \div 2 =$

32. $\frac{1}{2} \div 7 =$

33. $\frac{22}{25} \div 11 =$

34. $\frac{2}{3} \div 9 =$

35. $\frac{16}{19} \div 4 =$

36. $\frac{3}{4} \div 8 =$

Divide. Cancel and reduce if possible.

37.
$$5\frac{1}{2} \div 4 =$$

38.
$$1\frac{2}{5} \div 7 =$$

39.
$$8\frac{5}{9} \div 3 =$$

40.
$$3\frac{2}{3} \div 5 =$$

41.
$$7\frac{3}{8} \div 2 =$$

42.
$$6\frac{3}{10} \div 6 =$$

43.
$$9\frac{3}{4} \div 10 =$$

44.
$$4\frac{1}{6} \div 8 =$$

45.
$$2\frac{7}{12} \div 5\frac{1}{8} =$$

46.
$$10\frac{7}{9} \div 4\frac{1}{3} =$$

47.
$$7\frac{4}{5} \div 5\frac{2}{7} =$$

48.
$$3\frac{1}{2} \div 1\frac{1}{2} =$$

49.
$$8\frac{5}{16} \div 2\frac{1}{16} =$$

50.
$$15\frac{1}{6} \div 2\frac{1}{2} =$$

51.
$$11\frac{3}{4} \div 1\frac{1}{3} =$$

52.
$$9\frac{11}{14} \div 2\frac{1}{7} =$$

53.
$$5\frac{1}{2} \div 3\frac{1}{4} =$$

Below is a list of the problems in this review and the pages on which the skills are taught. If you missed any problems, turn to the pages listed and practice the skills. Then correct the problems you missed in the Unit Review.

You have studied four operations with fractions—addition, subtraction, multiplication, and division. You have applied these skills to real-life problems, and you have learned techniques for solving word problems.

In this unit, you will study how to choose the correct operation needed to solve problems. You will also learn how to solve problems that require you to use more than one operation to find the answers.

Getting Ready

You should be familiar with the skills on this page and the next before you begin this unit. To check your answers, turn to page 203.

 To add fractions and mixed numbers, be sure the denominators are the same. Add the fractions. Add the whole numbers.

Add. Reduce if possible.

1.
$$\frac{3}{4} = \frac{9}{12}$$
$$+\frac{2}{3} = \frac{8}{12}$$
$$\frac{17}{12} = 1\frac{5}{12}$$

2.
$$1\frac{5}{8}$$
$$+ \quad \frac{4}{8}$$

3.
$$6\frac{2}{9}$$
$$+ 7\frac{17}{18}$$

4.
$$\frac{9}{10}$$
$$+ \frac{7}{8}$$

5.
$$\frac{15}{21}$$
$$+ 4\frac{2}{7}$$

6.
$$\frac{5}{6}$$
$$+\frac{1}{6}$$

7.
$$2\frac{3}{5}$$
$$+ \quad \frac{3}{4}$$

8.
$$\frac{1}{5}$$
$$+ 3\frac{2}{15}$$

9.
$$3\frac{5}{8}$$
$$+ 7\frac{1}{2}$$

10.
$$\frac{8}{9}$$
$$+ 2\frac{1}{3}$$

To subtract fractions and mixed numbers, be sure the denominators are the same. You may need to borrow from the whole number.

Subtract. Reduce if possible.

11.
$$\frac{3}{4}$$
$$-\frac{1}{4}$$
$$\frac{2}{4} = \frac{1}{2}$$

12.
$$1\frac{2}{3}$$
$$-\frac{1}{6}$$

13.
$$5\frac{9}{10}$$
$$-3\frac{3}{5}$$

14.
$$1$$
$$-\frac{3}{8}$$

15.
$$\frac{5}{7}$$
$$-\frac{1}{2}$$

16.
$$1\frac{1}{8}$$
$$-\frac{3}{8}$$

17.
$$7\frac{5}{12}$$
$$-\frac{5}{6}$$

18.
$$9$$
$$-3\frac{7}{10}$$

19.
$$2\frac{7}{15}$$
$$-\frac{2}{3}$$

20.
$$\frac{3}{4}$$
$$-\frac{2}{5}$$

For review, see Unit 3.

 To multiply fractions, multiply the numerators and then the denominators. Cancel before you multiply if possible.

Multiply. Reduce if possible.

21. $\frac{3}{\overset{4}{2}} \times \frac{\overset{1}{2}}{5} = \frac{3}{10}$

22. $1\frac{3}{8} \times \frac{8}{9} =$

23. $3\frac{2}{9} \times 3 =$

24. $6 \times \frac{1}{2} =$

25. $\frac{5}{9} \times \frac{3}{10} =$

26. $\frac{2}{3} \times 5\frac{1}{8} =$

27. $2\frac{1}{2} \times 8\frac{1}{5} =$

28. $\frac{1}{3} \times \frac{3}{4} \times \frac{5}{6} =$

For review, see Unit 4.

 To divide fractions, change any whole numbers and mixed numbers to improper fractions. Invert and multiply.

Divide. Reduce if possible.

29. $\frac{5}{6} \div \frac{1}{6} =$

$\frac{5}{\overset{6}{1}} \times \frac{\overset{1}{6}}{1} = \frac{5}{1} = 5$

30. $8 \div \frac{1}{5} =$

31. $1\frac{7}{11} \div \frac{2}{3} =$

32. $6\frac{3}{8} \div 13 =$

33. $\frac{9}{10} \div \frac{1}{4} =$

34. $\frac{2}{9} \div \frac{5}{12} =$

35. $10\frac{1}{2} \div 2\frac{1}{4} =$

36. $10 \div 5\frac{1}{10} =$

For review, see Unit 5.

Choose an Operation: Changing Units of Measurement

To change from one unit of measurement to another, remember that when you change a small unit to a larger unit, you divide. When you change a large unit to a smaller unit, you multiply.

12 inches	=	1 foot
3 feet	=	1 yard
1,760 yards	=	1 mile
5,280 feet	=	1 mile

Example Julian's workbench is $5\frac{5}{16}$ feet long. How many inches are in $5\frac{5}{16}$ feet?

Step 1. You are changing from a large unit (feet) to a smaller unit (inches). You will need to multiply.

Step 2. Use the chart to find out how many inches are in one foot.

$$12 \text{ inches} = 1 \text{ foot}$$

Step 3. Multiply.

$$5\frac{5}{16} \times 12 = \frac{85}{16} \times \frac{\overset{3}{\cancel{12}}}{1} = \frac{255}{4} = 63\frac{3}{4}$$

The bench is $63\frac{3}{4}$ inches long.

Solve.

1. Casey cut $1\frac{1}{2}$ feet from a piece of chain. How many inches are in $1\frac{1}{2}$ feet?

   Answer_____

2. Susan is putting a fence around a garden. The fence will be $\frac{1}{4}$ mile long. How many yards are in $\frac{1}{4}$ mile?

   Answer_____

3. A sports coach jogs every morning for $2\frac{1}{4}$ miles. Circle the expression you would use to find how many feet he jogs.

   a. $2\frac{1}{4} + 5,280$
   b. $2\frac{1}{4} \times 1,760$
   c. $2\frac{1}{4} \times 5,280$
   d. $2\frac{1}{4} \div 1,760$

   Solve for the answer.

   Answer_____

4. Circle the expression you would use to find how many yards he jogs.

   a. $2\frac{1}{4} \times 5,280$
   b. $2\frac{1}{4} \times 1,760$
   c. $2\frac{1}{4} \div 5,280$
   d. $2\frac{1}{4} - 1,760$

   Solve for the answer.

   Answer_____

Choose an Operation: Being a Consumer

Comparing unit costs is one way to find out which of two brands is less expensive to buy. To find the unit cost, write a fraction for each brand.

Example Tasty green beans are 2 cans for 43 cents. Flavorite green beans are 3 cans for 65 cents. Which is less expensive?

Step 1. Find the unit cost for each brand by writing a fraction for each. Write the cost as the numerator and the unit as the denominator. Change each to a mixed number. Find a common denominator for the fractions.

Tasty: $\frac{43}{2} = 21\frac{1}{2} = 21\frac{3}{6}$ Flavorite: $\frac{65}{3} = 21\frac{2}{3} = 21\frac{4}{6}$

Step 2. Compare the costs.

$21\frac{4}{6} > 21\frac{3}{6}$, so $21\frac{2}{3} > 21\frac{1}{2}$
Tasty is less expensive.

Solve.

1. Crispy Apple Bites cost 79 cents for the 10-ounce package. Crispy Cherry Bites cost 89 cents for the 11-ounce package. Which costs more?

Answer_____

2. Yellow apples are 4 for 99 cents. Red apples are 3 for 69 cents. Which cost less?

Answer_____

3. Beefy hot dogs are 7 packages for 6 dollars. Meaty hot dogs are 6 packages for 5 dollars. Which cost less?

Answer_____

4. Softy tissues are on sale 3 boxes for 2 dollars. Squeezy tissues are on sale 8 boxes for 6 dollars. Which cost more?

Answer_____

Choose an Operation: Using a Line Graph

Carl has worked for A-Mart for five years and is eligible to buy stock in the company. He decided to watch how the stock was doing on the stock market for a week before he made up his mind whether to buy any. He learned that stocks are sold in shares and prices are given in units called points.

A–MART

	MON	TUES	WED	THURS	FRI
	$10\frac{7}{8}$	$13\frac{1}{4}$	$11\frac{1}{2}$	$12\frac{3}{8}$	$14\frac{3}{4}$

Example How much did the price of a share of stock go up from Monday to Tuesday?

▷ **Step 1.** Find the price of the stock on Monday, $10\frac{7}{8}$. Find the price of the stock on Tuesday, $13\frac{1}{4}$.

▷ **Step 2.** Subtract to find the difference.

$$13\frac{1}{4} = 13\frac{2}{8} = 12\frac{10}{8}$$
$$- 10\frac{7}{8} = 10\frac{7}{8} = 10\ \frac{7}{8}$$
$$\overline{\hspace{2cm} 2\ \frac{3}{8}}$$

The price of one share of stock went up $2\frac{3}{8}$ points from Monday to Tuesday.

Solve.

1. How many points did a share of stock go down from Tuesday to Wednesday?

   Answer_____

2. How much higher was the stock on Thursday than it was on Monday?

   Answer_____

3. Circle the expression you would use to find the price of 20 shares of stock if you bought them on Tuesday.

   a. $20 + 13\frac{1}{4}$ Solve for the answer.
   b. $20 - 13\frac{1}{4}$
   c. $20 \times 13\frac{1}{4}$
   d. $20 \div 13\frac{1}{4}$

   Answer_____

4. Circle the expression you would use to find the price of one share of stock if the price went up $1\frac{1}{8}$ points from the price it was on Friday.

   a. $14\frac{3}{4} + 1\frac{1}{8}$ Solve for the answer.
   b. $14\frac{3}{4} - 1\frac{1}{8}$
   c. $14\frac{3}{4} \times 1\frac{1}{8}$
   d. $14\frac{3}{4} \div 1\frac{1}{8}$

   Answer_____

Multi-Step Problems: Using Measurement

You may need to use two or more operations to solve a problem. When working with measurement, you may need to add, subtract, multiply, or divide. You may also need to change from one unit to another unit.

1 cup	=	8 ounces
1 pint	=	2 cups
1 quart	=	2 pints
1 gallon	=	4 quarts

Example Lucy works at Speedy Lube. She needs 6 quarts of oil to change the oil in a customer's car. She has $\frac{3}{4}$ gallon of oil. How many more quarts does she need?

Step 1. Change $\frac{3}{4}$ gallon to quarts. To change from a large unit to a smaller unit, multiply.

$$\frac{3}{4} \times 4 = \frac{3}{\underset{1}{\cancel{4}}} \times \frac{\overset{1}{\cancel{4}}}{1} = \frac{3}{1} = 3$$

Lucy has 3 quarts.

Step 2. To find out how many more quarts she needs, subtract.

$$6 - 3 = 3$$

Lucy needs 3 more quarts.

Solve.

1. Pete is a furniture refinisher. To paint a chest of drawers, he needs $\frac{1}{2}$ gallon of paint. He has 1 quart. How many more quarts does he need?

Answer_____

2. Tony works for a lawn maintenance company. He needs $3\frac{1}{2}$ gallons of liquid fertilizer for a small yard. If he makes 12 quarts of fertilizer from concentrate, how many more quarts will he need?

Answer_____

3. Dawn is making cheese puffs for a party she is catering. She needs 3 cups of milk. She has $\frac{1}{2}$ pint. How many more cups does she need?

4. Norm is a contractor. He is planning to buy some wood sealer to seal a deck. He has $\frac{1}{2}$ gallon in one can and a full quart can. How many quarts of sealer does he have all together?

Answer_____

Answer_____

Solve.

5. Danielle filled 12 pint containers and 20 half-pint containers with green beans for the produce department of Gene's Grocery. How many pints did she fill all together?

Answer_____

6. A chef is using a recipe that calls for 24 ounces of sour cream. She has $1\frac{1}{2}$ cups of sour cream in her refrigerator. How many more cups does she need to buy?

Answer_____

7. David is making 3 pecan pies for the restaurant where he works. He needs $1\frac{1}{2}$ cups of pecans for each pie. How many ounces of pecans does he need for all 3 pies?

Answer_____

8. Randi had two 8-ounce packages of cream cheese. She used $1\frac{3}{4}$ cups to make sandwiches for the children at the daycare center. How much cream cheese does she have left?

Answer_____

9. Delores makes 32 ounces of orange juice from each can of frozen concentrate. If each serving of juice at her diner is $\frac{1}{2}$ cup, how many servings will Delores get from 32 ounces?

Answer_____

10. Frank is painting a house. He needs $1\frac{2}{3}$ quarts of paint for trim for each room in the house. If he buys $2\frac{1}{2}$ gallons of paint, for how many rooms can he expect to paint the trim?

Answer_____

11. Gwen buys coffee beans for The Coffee Cafe in 22-ounce packages. She uses $\frac{1}{4}$ cup of beans to make each pot of coffee. How many pots of coffee can she make from one 22-ounce package?

Answer_____

12. Liz works as a dietary aide in a nursing home. She gives patients fresh fruit salad in $\frac{1}{2}$-cup servings. How many servings will she get from $1\frac{1}{2}$ quarts of fruit salad?

Answer_____

Multi-Step Problems: Being a Consumer

If you buy 3 packs of gum for a dollar, you can write this as a fraction, $\frac{3}{1}$. If you buy 3 pounds of fish for $5, the fraction is $\frac{3}{5}$. These fractions are called ratios.

Ratios are useful for solving some kinds of problems.

Example   Bert's Roadside Stand sells walnuts in 10-pound bags for $25. How many pounds will you get for $5?

▷ **Step 1.**   Write a ratio (fraction) to show 10 pounds for $25.

$$\frac{10 \text{ pounds}}{25 \text{ dollars}}$$

▷ **Step 2.**   Write a second ratio (fraction) to show the unknown number of pounds for $5.

$$\frac{? \text{ pounds}}{5 \text{ dollars}}$$

▷ **Step 3.**   Write the two ratios as equal fractions. This is called a proportion.

$$\frac{10}{25} = \frac{?}{5}$$

▷ **Step 4.**   Find the numerator of the second fraction. Since $25 \div 5 = 5$, divide the numerator by 5.

$$\frac{10}{25} = \frac{10 \div 5}{25 \div 5} = \frac{2}{5}$$

You can get 2 pounds of walnuts for $5.

Solve.

1. Bert's Roadside Stand sells 20 pounds of potatoes for $4. How many pounds can you get for $2?

   Answer_____

2. If onions cost $2 for 4 pounds, how many pounds can you get for a dollar?

   Answer_____

3. Bert's Roadside Stand sells 2 jars of strawberry jam for $3. How much will it cost to buy 4 jars?
   (Hint: Find the denominator.)

   Answer_____

4. Apple cider costs $5 for 2 half-gallons. How much do 6 half-gallons cost?

   Answer_____

5. If oranges are 5 pounds for $4, how much do 15 pounds cost?

   Answer_____

6. Homemade cherry pies are 3 for $10. How many pies will you get for $20?

   Answer_____

7. Asparagus is $2 a pound. How many pounds can you get for $8?

   Answer_____

8. Homemade pickles cost $5 for 3 jars. How much will 6 jars cost?

   Answer_____

9. Bert's sells 6 dozen fresh eggs for $4. How much would 3 dozen eggs cost?

   Answer_____

10. Honey costs $4 for 3 pints. How many pints will you get for $12?

    Answer_____

11. Carrots are 3 bunches for a dollar. How much will 6 bunches of carrots cost?

    Answer_____

12. Fresh corn costs a dollar for 6 ears. How much would 3 dozen ears cost?
    (Hint: 1 dozen = 12)

    Answer_____

Multi-Step Problems: Using a Time Record

Augusta offers child care in her own home on a drop-in basis. She must keep a record of how much time each child spends in her care. She charges parents based on these records.

Child	Mon.	Tues.	Wed.	Thurs.	Fri.
1 Teddy	7:30-11:45	8-11:30	Sick	Sick	
2 Peter H.	1-3:45	12:30-6:30	1:15-5:30	2-6:30	—
3 Susie	5:30-10:45	—	6-11:30	—	5:45-10:45
4 Peter W.					
5 Hannah					
6					
7					
8					
9					

Example On Monday, Teddy's mother dropped him off at 7:30 and picked him up at 11:45. How many hours did Teddy spend at Augusta's on Monday?

Step 1. To find the number of hours Teddy spent at Augusta's on Monday, subtract the time he arrived from the time he left.

$$
\begin{array}{rl}
11 \text{ hours} & 45 \text{ minutes} \\
-\ 7 \text{ hours} & 30 \text{ minutes} \\
\hline
4 \text{ hours} & 15 \text{ minutes}
\end{array}
$$

Step 2. Write the time as a mixed number with 60 minutes as the denominator of the fraction. Reduce.

$$4 \text{ hours } 15 \text{ minutes} = 4\frac{15}{60} = 4\frac{1}{4}$$

Teddy spent $4\frac{1}{4}$ hours at Augusta's on Monday.

Solve. Put your answers in the correct space on the time record.

1. How many hours did Teddy spend at Augusta's on Tuesday?

   Answer_____

2. Teddy stayed at Augusta's from 8:00 to 12:30 on Friday morning. Write these times in the chart. How many hours did Teddy stay on Friday morning?

   Answer_____

3. Peter W. stayed at Augusta's only on Thursday from 1:30 to 3:45. Fill in the weekly record for Peter W. on the chart. How much time did Peter W. spend at Augusta's on Thursday?

   Answer_____

4. Susie's mother works Monday, Wednesday, and Friday mornings. Susie stays at Augusta's only on these days. How many hours did Susie stay on Wednesday?

   Answer_____

5. Hannah's dad dropped her off at Augusta's on Monday at 3:15 and her mom picked her up at 6:45. Write these times in the chart. How many hours did Hannah spend at Augusta's on Monday?

   Answer_____

6. Hannah was dropped off at Augusta's again on Friday at 3:30 and she was picked up at 6:30. Write these times in the chart. How many hours did Hannah stay on Friday?

   Answer_____

7. Augusta charges $4 for each hour of child care. Peter H. stayed $4\frac{1}{4}$ hours on Wednesday. How much did Augusta charge Peter's parents for Wednesday?

   Answer_____

8. How many hours did Peter H. stay at Augusta's on Monday? How much did Augusta charge his parents for Monday?

   Answer_____

Fractions Skills Inventory

Reduce to lowest terms. If the fraction is in lowest terms, write LT.

1. $\dfrac{3}{6} =$

2. $\dfrac{3}{12} =$

3. $\dfrac{3}{20} =$

4. $\dfrac{30}{40} =$

5. $\dfrac{24}{36} =$

Raise to higher terms with the given denominator.

6. $\dfrac{1}{3} = \dfrac{}{12}$

7. $\dfrac{2}{7} = \dfrac{}{21}$

8. $\dfrac{1}{2} = \dfrac{}{10}$

9. $\dfrac{4}{5} = \dfrac{}{20}$

10. $\dfrac{5}{8} = \dfrac{}{32}$

Change to a whole or mixed number.

11. $\dfrac{5}{4} =$

12. $\dfrac{10}{5} =$

13. $\dfrac{15}{7} =$

14. $\dfrac{4}{1} =$

15. $\dfrac{21}{10} =$

Change to an improper fraction.

16. $2\dfrac{2}{5} =$

17. $3\dfrac{1}{3} =$

18. $5\dfrac{3}{4} =$

19. $1\dfrac{2}{9} =$

20. $8\dfrac{1}{12} =$

Add. Reduce if possible.

21. $\dfrac{1}{4} + \dfrac{1}{4} =$

22. $\dfrac{3}{5} + \dfrac{2}{5} =$

23. $\dfrac{5}{6} + \dfrac{4}{6} =$

24. $\dfrac{3}{8} + \dfrac{1}{8} + \dfrac{5}{8} =$

25. $3\dfrac{5}{7}$
    $+ 1\dfrac{1}{7}$

26. $4\dfrac{1}{10}$
    $+ 6\dfrac{3}{10}$

27. $9\dfrac{2}{3}$
    $+ 3\dfrac{2}{3}$

28. $\dfrac{2}{9}$
    $+ 5\dfrac{7}{9}$

29. 1
    $+ 6\dfrac{3}{4}$

30. $\dfrac{1}{3}$
    $+ \dfrac{1}{6}$

31. $\dfrac{1}{4}$
    $+ \dfrac{3}{5}$

32. $\dfrac{2}{7}$
    $+ \dfrac{9}{21}$

33. $\dfrac{5}{8}$
    $+ \dfrac{3}{10}$

34. $\dfrac{5}{9}$
    $+ \dfrac{3}{4}$

Add. Reduce if possible.

35.
$$5\frac{5}{7}$$
$$+2\frac{1}{3}$$

36.
$$8$$
$$+2\frac{3}{8}$$

37.
$$10\frac{9}{14}$$
$$+\ 3\frac{1}{2}$$

38.
$$12\frac{4}{5}$$
$$+\ 3\frac{3}{20}$$

39.
$$\frac{5}{6}$$
$$+5\frac{1}{8}$$

Subtract. Reduce if possible.

40. $\frac{7}{8} - \frac{3}{8} =$

41. $\frac{5}{9} - \frac{1}{9} =$

42. $\frac{3}{7} - \frac{3}{7} =$

43. $\frac{7}{10} - \frac{1}{10} =$

44.
$$8\frac{5}{6}$$
$$-2\frac{1}{6}$$

45.
$$6\frac{4}{5}$$
$$-\ \frac{2}{5}$$

46.
$$7\frac{3}{4}$$
$$-3\frac{1}{4}$$

47.
$$2\frac{13}{15}$$
$$-\ \frac{7}{15}$$

48.
$$9\frac{10}{21}$$
$$-\ 3$$

49.
$$1$$
$$-\ \frac{2}{7}$$

50.
$$5$$
$$-\ \frac{2}{9}$$

51.
$$7\frac{3}{10}$$
$$-\ \frac{9}{10}$$

52.
$$6\frac{1}{8}$$
$$-4\frac{3}{8}$$

53.
$$1\frac{5}{12}$$
$$-\ \frac{7}{12}$$

54.
$$\frac{2}{3}$$
$$-\ \frac{1}{6}$$

55.
$$\frac{5}{12}$$
$$-\ \frac{1}{4}$$

56.
$$\frac{7}{8}$$
$$-\ \frac{3}{10}$$

57.
$$\frac{3}{4}$$
$$-\ \frac{1}{7}$$

58.
$$\frac{4}{5}$$
$$-\ \frac{2}{3}$$

59.
$$5\frac{1}{3}$$
$$-2\frac{2}{9}$$

60.
$$9\frac{2}{7}$$
$$-\ \frac{2}{5}$$

61.
$$8\frac{3}{16}$$
$$-4\frac{5}{8}$$

62.
$$1\frac{1}{6}$$
$$-\ \frac{1}{4}$$

Multiply. Reduce if possible.

63.
$$\frac{2}{5} \times \frac{1}{2} =$$

64.
$$\frac{5}{6} \times \frac{3}{10} =$$

65.
$$\frac{3}{8} \times \frac{4}{7} =$$

66.
$$\frac{2}{9} \times \frac{6}{8} \times \frac{4}{5} =$$

67.
$$8 \times \frac{1}{4} =$$

68.
$$\frac{4}{9} \times 6 =$$

69.
$$3\frac{1}{5} \times 10 =$$

70.
$$5 \times 1\frac{2}{7} =$$

71.
$$4\frac{9}{10} \times \frac{5}{7} =$$

72.
$$\frac{3}{5} \times 3\frac{3}{4} =$$

73.
$$2\frac{1}{3} \times 5\frac{4}{7} =$$

74.
$$1\frac{1}{5} \times 6\frac{1}{2} =$$

Divide. Reduce if possible.

75.
$$\frac{3}{4} \div \frac{1}{4} =$$

76.
$$\frac{1}{2} \div \frac{3}{8} =$$

77.
$$\frac{5}{9} \div \frac{9}{10} =$$

78.
$$\frac{2}{3} \div \frac{2}{7} =$$

79.
$$8 \div \frac{1}{2} =$$

80.
$$7 \div \frac{1}{6} =$$

81.
$$4\frac{3}{7} \div \frac{5}{14} =$$

82.
$$3\frac{2}{5} \div \frac{2}{5} =$$

83.
$$\frac{2}{3} \div 2 =$$

84.
$$\frac{1}{5} \div 5 =$$

85.
$$1\frac{8}{9} \div 3 =$$

86.
$$4\frac{1}{6} \div 2 =$$

87.
$$10\frac{1}{2} \div 5 =$$

88.
$$4\frac{2}{3} \div 2\frac{1}{3} =$$

89.
$$1\frac{7}{8} \div 4\frac{3}{8} =$$

90.
$$25\frac{1}{2} \div 3\frac{1}{4} =$$

Below is a list of the problems in this Skills Inventory and the pages on which the skills are taught. If you missed any problems, turn to the pages listed and practice the skills. Then correct the problems you missed in the Skills Inventory.

addition (page 39) - Putting numbers together to find a total. The symbol + is used in addition.

$$\begin{array}{r} \frac{1}{5} \\ + \frac{2}{5} \\ \hline \frac{3}{5} \end{array}$$

borrowing (page 87) - Taking an amount from the whole number and adding it to the fraction part of a mixed number.

$$4\frac{1}{3} = 3\frac{1}{3} + \frac{3}{3} = 3\frac{4}{3}$$
$$- 1\frac{2}{3} = \qquad\quad 1\frac{2}{3}$$
$$\rule{4cm}{0.4pt}$$
$$2\frac{2}{3}$$

cancellation (page 113) - Dividing a numerator and a denominator by the same number when you multiply or divide fractions.

$$\overset{2}{\cancel{\frac{4}{5}}} \times \frac{1}{\underset{1}{\cancel{2}}} = \frac{2}{5}$$

chart (page 43) - Information arranged in rows and columns.

ITEM	NUMBER SOLD	FRACTION OF TOTAL
Rulers	8	$\frac{1}{6}$
Scissors	2	$\frac{1}{24}$
Pencils	16	$\frac{1}{3}$
Staplers	4	$\frac{1}{12}$
Pens	12	$\frac{1}{4}$
Notepads	6	$\frac{1}{8}$
TOTAL ITEMS SOLD	48	

circle graph (page 17) - A circle cut into sections to show the parts that make a total. Each part is a fraction of the total.

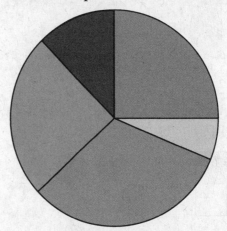

common denominator (page 25) - A number that all denominators you're working with divide into evenly.

$$\frac{1}{2} = \frac{3}{6}$$
$$\frac{1}{3} = \frac{2}{6}$$

comparing (page 23) - Deciding if a fraction is equal to, greater than, or less than another fraction.

denominator (page 11) - The bottom number in a fraction. The number of equal parts in the whole.

$$\frac{2}{3}$$

difference (page 73) - The answer to a subtraction problem.

$$\begin{array}{r} \frac{3}{8} \\ - \frac{2}{8} \\ \hline \frac{1}{8} \end{array}$$

division (page 127) - Splitting an amount into equal groups. The symbol ÷ is used in division.

$$\frac{1}{4} \div \frac{2}{3} = \frac{1}{4} \times \frac{3}{2} = \frac{3}{8}$$

equal (page 11) - The same in value. The symbol = means *equal*.

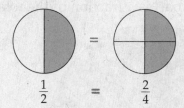

$$\frac{1}{2} \quad = \quad \frac{2}{4}$$

fraction (page 11) - Part of a whole or a group.

or ... $= \frac{3}{4}$

fraction bar (page 11) - The line that separates the numerator and denominator of a fraction.

$\frac{2}{3}$

greater than (page 23) - More than. The symbol > means *greater than*.

$\frac{2}{7} > \frac{1}{7}$ means $\frac{2}{7}$ is greater than $\frac{1}{7}$

horizontal (page 42) - Side-to-side.

---

higher terms (page 19) - A fraction is in higher terms when you multiply the numerator and denominator by the same number.

$\frac{1}{2} = \frac{1 \times 2}{2 \times 2} = \frac{2}{4}$

improper fraction (page 31) - A fraction with the numerator equal to or larger than the denominator.

$\frac{3}{3} \quad \frac{4}{3}$

invert (page 129) - Turn upside down.

$\frac{1}{2} \quad \frac{2}{1}$

less than (page 23) - Smaller than. The symbol < means *less than*.

$\frac{6}{9} < \frac{8}{9}$ means $\frac{6}{9}$ is less than $\frac{8}{9}$.

line graph (page 149) - A graph with lines connecting points that show different amounts.

	MON	TUES	WED	THURS	FRI
	$10\frac{7}{8}$	$13\frac{1}{4}$	$11\frac{1}{2}$	$12\frac{3}{8}$	$14\frac{3}{4}$

lowest common denominator (LCD) (page 65) - The smallest number that the denominators of fractions being added or subtracted divide into evenly.

$\frac{1}{4} = \frac{3}{12}$

$\frac{1}{3} = \frac{4}{12}$

lowest terms (page 15) - A fraction is in lowest terms when 1 is the only number that divides evenly into both the numerator and denominator.

$\frac{4}{8} = \frac{4 \div 4}{8 \div 4} = \frac{1}{2}$

mixed number (page 26) -A number with a whole number part and a fraction part.

$3\frac{1}{10}$

multiple (page 65) - Number found when you multiply a whole number by 0, 1, 2, 3, and so on.

$3 \times 1 = 3 \qquad 3 \times 2 = 6$

$3 \times 3 = 9 \qquad 3 \times 4 = 12$

multiplication (page 107) - Combining equal numbers two or more times to get a total. The symbol $\times$ is used in multiplication.

$\frac{2}{3} \times \frac{1}{3} = \frac{2}{9}$

number line (page 23) - A line with equally spaced points that are labeled with fractions, whole numbers, or mixed numbers.

numerator (page 11) - The top number in a fraction. The number of parts being considered.

$\frac{5}{9}$

of (page 109) - *Of* means to multiply or find part of something.

$\frac{1}{2}$ of $\frac{9}{10} = \frac{1}{2} \times \frac{9}{10}$

operation (page 145) - The process you use to solve a math problem. The basic operations are addition, subtraction, multiplication, and division.

proper fraction (page 31) - A fraction with a numerator that is smaller than the denominator.

$\frac{2}{3}$

proportion (page 152) - Two equal ratios or fractions.

$\frac{2}{3} = \frac{4}{9}$

ratio (page 152) - A fraction showing the relationship of two numbers.

$\frac{4}{6}$ pounds dollars

reducing (page 15) - Dividing both the numerator and denominator of a fraction by the same number.

$\frac{3}{9} = \frac{3 \div 3}{9 \div 3} = \frac{1}{3}$

remainder (page 27) - The numerator of a fraction when the amount left over in a division problem is shown as a fraction.

$$6 \overline{)37} \quad 6 \text{ R } 1 = 6\frac{1}{6}$$
$$\underline{-36}$$
$$1$$

subtraction (page 73) - Taking away a certain amount from another amount to find a difference. The symbol $-$ is used in subtraction.

$$\frac{5}{9}$$
$$-\frac{2}{9}$$
$$\overline{\frac{3}{9}}$$

sum (page 35) - The answer to an addition problem.

$$\frac{2}{7}$$
$$+\frac{3}{7}$$
$$\overline{\frac{5}{7}}$$

table (page 18) - Information arranged in rows and columns.

ITEM	NUMBER SOLD	FRACTION OF TOTAL
Rulers	8	$\frac{1}{6}$
Scissors	2	$\frac{1}{24}$
Pencils	16	$\frac{1}{3}$
Staplers	4	$\frac{1}{12}$
Pens	12	$\frac{1}{4}$
Notepads	6	$\frac{1}{8}$
TOTAL ITEMS SOLD	48	

vertical (page 42) - Up-and-down.

whole number (page 26) - A number that shows a whole amount.

$6 \frac{5}{8}$

Answers & Explanations

The answer to the problem that was worked out for you in the lesson is written here in color. The next answer has an explanation written beneath it. The answers to the rest of the problems in the lesson follow in order.

Skills Inventory

Page 6

1. $\frac{1}{2}$
2. $\frac{3}{4}$
3. LT
4. $\frac{1}{3}$
5. $\frac{2}{3}$
6. $\frac{3}{9}$
7. $\frac{4}{10}$
8. $\frac{9}{21}$
9. $\frac{21}{30}$
10. $\frac{16}{36}$
11. $1\frac{1}{3}$
12. 4
13. $2\frac{2}{5}$
14. 3
15. $1\frac{4}{5}$
16. $\frac{23}{4}$
17. $\frac{5}{2}$
18. $\frac{14}{3}$
19. $\frac{39}{5}$
20. $\frac{97}{10}$
21. $\frac{3}{5}$
22. $\frac{3}{4}$
23. $1\frac{3}{5}$
24. 1
25. $7\frac{5}{9}$
26. $9\frac{1}{2}$
27. $8\frac{2}{3}$
28. 10
29. $15\frac{11}{15}$
30. $1\frac{1}{4}$
31. $1\frac{5}{21}$
32. $\frac{20}{27}$
33. $\frac{13}{24}$
34. $1\frac{11}{20}$

Page 7

35. $3\frac{25}{42}$
36. $13\frac{1}{2}$
37. $16\frac{2}{15}$
38. 11
39. $7\frac{11}{15}$
40. $\frac{2}{5}$
41. $\frac{2}{3}$
42. 0
43. $\frac{1}{2}$
44. $7\frac{2}{11}$
45. $8\frac{1}{5}$
46. $1\frac{2}{3}$
47. $9\frac{2}{3}$
48. $7\frac{17}{25}$
49. $\frac{2}{5}$
50. $3\frac{1}{8}$
51. $6\frac{2}{3}$
52. $\frac{4}{7}$
53. $\frac{5}{9}$
54. $\frac{1}{4}$
55. $\frac{1}{10}$
56. $\frac{7}{24}$
57. $\frac{1}{12}$
58. $\frac{11}{42}$
59. $2\frac{1}{2}$
60. $4\frac{13}{20}$
61. $\frac{43}{60}$
62. $\frac{11}{18}$

Page 8

63. $\frac{1}{3}$
64. $\frac{1}{6}$
65. $\frac{5}{8}$
66. $\frac{1}{10}$
67. $\frac{2}{3}$
68. $1\frac{1}{2}$
69. 34
70. $25\frac{2}{3}$
71. $\frac{7}{9}$
72. $1\frac{3}{5}$
73. 6
74. $22\frac{1}{2}$
75. $2\frac{2}{3}$
76. 5
77. $1\frac{1}{9}$
78. 2
79. 27
80. 16
81. $31\frac{1}{2}$
82. 12
83. $\frac{1}{6}$
84. $\frac{2}{21}$
85. $\frac{19}{32}$
86. $3\frac{1}{10}$
87. $1\frac{4}{5}$
88. 3
89. $2\frac{11}{12}$
90. $6\frac{4}{21}$

Unit 1

Page 9

1. 70
2. 51
   $$\begin{array}{r} 19 \\ + 32 \\ \hline 51 \end{array}$$
3. 162
4. 143

163

5. 925   **6.** 395
7. 520   **8.** 840

Page 10
9. 27
10. 25

$$\begin{array}{r} 41 \\ -16 \\ \hline 25 \end{array}$$

11. 35   **12.** 68
13. 66
14. 276

$$\begin{array}{r} 46 \\ \times\ 6 \\ \hline 276 \end{array}$$

15. 122   **16.** 415
17. 13 R1
18. 19

$$\begin{array}{r} 19 \\ 2\overline{)38} \\ -2 \\ \hline 18 \\ -18 \\ \hline 0 \end{array}$$

19. 5 R4   **20.** 7

Page 11
1. $\frac{4}{8}$

2. $\frac{2}{4}$

2 of the 4 parts are shaded.

3. $\frac{2}{5}$ **4.** $\frac{1}{3}$

5. $\frac{5}{9}$ **6.** $\frac{7}{10}$

7. $\frac{8}{10}$ **8.** $\frac{3}{4}$

9.

10.–12. Shading should be similar to this.

10.

2 of the 3 parts are shaded.

11.

12.

Page 12
1. one half
2. five sixths

There are 6 circles in the whole. 5 of them are shaded.

3. one third   **4.** one fifth
5. two thirds   **6.** four ninths
7. three sevenths   **8.** seven tenths
9. one half   **10.** three eighths
11. five eighths   **12.** four fourths

Page 13
1. $\frac{3}{12}$

2. $\frac{25}{36}$

Write the parts in a whole yard, 36 inches, as the denominator. Write the number of parts given, 25 inches, as the numerator.

3. $\frac{1}{4}$ **4.** $\frac{2}{3}$

5. $\frac{9}{10}$ **6.** $\frac{42}{60}$

7. $\frac{17}{24}$ **8.** $\frac{12}{12}$

Page 14
1. Cake C
$\frac{3}{5}$

2. Cake A
$\frac{3}{8}$

Cake A is cut into 8 equal parts (eighths). 5 of the 8 parts are still on the plate. 3 of the 8 parts have been sold. $\frac{3}{8}$ of the cake has been sold.

3. $\frac{3}{6}$ **4.** $\frac{1}{4}$

5. $\frac{6}{10}$ **6.** $\frac{5}{8}$

Page 15
1. $\frac{2}{3}$

2. $\frac{3}{7}$

Divide each number by 3. The fraction is reduced to $\frac{3}{7}$. Only 1 divides into 3 and 7 evenly. $\frac{3}{7}$ is in lowest terms.

$$\frac{9}{21} = \frac{9 \div 3}{21 \div 3} = \frac{3}{7}$$

3. $\frac{7}{10}$ **4.** $\frac{3}{4}$

5. $\frac{5}{8}$ **6.** $\frac{4}{5}$

7. $\frac{3}{4}$ **8.** $\frac{5}{6}$

9. $\frac{3}{4}$ **10.** $\frac{9}{10}$

11. $\frac{4}{5}$ **12.** $\frac{2}{3}$

13. $\frac{1}{3}$ **14.** $\frac{5}{6}$

15. $\frac{1}{2}$ **16.** $\frac{3}{5}$

17. $\frac{1}{2}$ **18.** $\frac{1}{3}$

Page 16

1. $\frac{3}{5}$

2. LT

Only 1 divides evenly into 9 and 25.

3. $\frac{2}{3}$ **4.** $\frac{1}{4}$

5. $\frac{3}{7}$ **6.** $\frac{1}{10}$

7. LT   **8.** $\frac{30}{73}$

9. LT

10. $\frac{1}{3}$

$\frac{8}{24} = \frac{8 \div 8}{24 \div 8} = \frac{1}{3}$

11. $\frac{2}{3}$ **12.** LT

13. LT   **14.** $\frac{1}{7}$

15. LT   **16.** $\frac{3}{5}$

17. $\frac{1}{2}$

Set up a fraction with the total gallons the gas tank will hold, 20, as the denominator. The number of gallons of gas Jack put into the tank, 10, is the numerator. Reduce the fraction to lowest terms by crossing out the zeros on the top and the bottom.

$\frac{1\cancel{0}}{2\cancel{0}} = \frac{1}{2}$

18. $\frac{3}{4}$

Reduce to lowest terms by dividing the numerator and the denominator by 2.

$\frac{6}{8} = \frac{6 \div 2}{8 \div 2} = \frac{3}{4}$

Page 17

1. $\frac{1}{4}$

Set up a fraction with the total expenses, $1,200, as the denominator. The amount

spent for employees' salaries, $300, is the numerator. Cross out the same number of zeros on the end of the numerator and the denominator. Reduce to lowest terms by dividing the numerator and denominator by 3.

$\frac{3\cancel{0}\cancel{0}}{12\cancel{0}\cancel{0}} = \frac{3}{12} = \frac{3 \div 3}{12 \div 3} = \frac{1}{4}$

2. $\frac{1}{2}$

$\frac{6\cancel{0}\cancel{0}}{12\cancel{0}\cancel{0}} = \frac{6 \div 6}{12 \div 6} = \frac{1}{2}$

Page 18

3. $\frac{1}{12}$

$\frac{1\cancel{0}\cancel{0}}{12\cancel{0}\cancel{0}} = \frac{1}{12}$

4. $\frac{7}{12}$

Add the amount spent on car parts, $100, and the amount spent on gas and oil, $600. $100 + $600 = $700. Set up a fraction with the total, $700, as the numerator. Manuel's total expenses, $1,200, is the denominator. Reduce by crossing out the same number of zeros on the end of the numerator and the denominator.

$\frac{7\cancel{0}\cancel{0}}{12\cancel{0}\cancel{0}} = \frac{7}{12}$

5. $\frac{5}{12}$

Rent ($200) + Salaries ($300) = $500

$\frac{5\cancel{0}\cancel{0}}{12\cancel{0}\cancel{0}} = \frac{5}{12}$

6. $\frac{12}{12} = 1$

Rent	$ 200
Salaries	300
Car parts	100
Gas and oil	600
	$1,200

$\frac{12\cancel{0}\cancel{0}}{12\cancel{0}\cancel{0}} = \frac{12}{12} = 1$

7. $\frac{1}{2}$

$\frac{150}{300}$ mechanic's salary / total salary expense

$\frac{15\cancel{0}}{30\cancel{0}} = \frac{15}{30} = \frac{1}{2}$

8. $\frac{1}{5}$

$\frac{250}{1250}$ rent / total expenses

$\frac{25\cancel{0}}{125\cancel{0}} = \frac{25}{125} = \frac{1}{5}$

9.

Expense	Amount	Fraction
rent	$200	$\frac{200}{1200} = \frac{1}{6}$
salaries	$300	$\frac{300}{1200} = \frac{1}{4}$
car parts	$100	$\frac{100}{1200} = \frac{1}{12}$
gas and oil	$600	$\frac{600}{1200} = \frac{1}{2}$

Page 19

1. $\frac{2}{3} = \frac{4}{6}$

2. $\frac{1}{2} = \frac{3}{6}$

$\frac{1}{2} = \frac{1 \times 3}{2 \times 3} = \frac{3}{6}$

3. $\frac{1}{6} = \frac{2}{12}$ **4.** $\frac{1}{2} = \frac{5}{10}$

5. $\frac{7}{8} = \frac{14}{16}$ **6.** $\frac{3}{4} = \frac{6}{8}$

7. $\frac{8}{20}$ **8.** $\frac{12}{32}$

$\frac{3}{8} = \frac{3 \times 4}{8 \times 4} = \frac{12}{32}$

9. $\frac{4}{24}$ **10.** $\frac{16}{20}$

11. $\frac{15}{20}$ **12.** $\frac{20}{35}$

$\frac{4}{7} = \frac{4 \times 5}{7 \times 5} = \frac{20}{35}$

13. $\frac{10}{15}$ **14.** $\frac{5}{45}$

Page 20

1. 3

2. 4

Both the numerator, 3, and the denominator, 4, were multiplied by 4.

3. 3   **4.** 6

5. 3   **6.** 4

7. 5   **8.** 5

9. $\frac{9}{21}$

10. $\frac{8}{56}$

The denominator, 14, was multiplied by 4 to get 56. Multiply 2 by 4 to get 8.

11. $\frac{60}{100}$ **12.** $\frac{27}{48}$

13. $\frac{36}{90}$ **14.** $\frac{72}{90}$

15. $\frac{6}{54}$ **16.** $\frac{49}{77}$

17. $\frac{42}{84}$ **18.** $\frac{20}{96}$

19. $\frac{9}{63}$ **20.** $\frac{48}{72}$

21. 20 pages

Write a fraction with the number of pages Kevin read, 10, as the numerator. The total number of pages in the report, 25, is the denominator. Raise this fraction, $\frac{10}{25}$, to higher terms. Use the total number of pages in the report Beverly read, 50, as the denominator.

$\frac{10}{25} = \frac{}{50}$

25 multiplied by 2 is 50.
10 multiplied by 2 is 20.

$\frac{10}{25} = \frac{20}{50}$

22. 28 pages

Set up a fraction with the number of pages Carmen input, 14, as the numerator. The total number of pages in the manual, 30, is the denominator. This fraction, $\frac{14}{30}$, equals the fraction set up with the total number of pages in the manual Scott input, 60, as the denominator.

$\frac{14}{30} = \frac{}{60}$

30 multiplied by 2 is 60.
14 multiplied by 2 is 28.

$\frac{14}{30} = \frac{28}{60}$

Page 21

1. $\frac{1}{2}$ ton   **2.** $\frac{7}{20}$ ton

$\frac{1000}{2000} = \frac{1}{2}$ ton $\frac{700}{2000} = \frac{7}{20}$ ton

3. $\frac{7}{8}$ pound   **4.** $\frac{1}{2}$ pound

$\frac{14}{16} = \frac{7}{8}$ pound $\frac{8}{16} = \frac{1}{2}$ pound

5. $\frac{1}{20}$ ton   **6.** $\frac{3}{4}$ pound

$\frac{100}{2000} = \frac{1}{20}$ ton $\frac{12}{16} = \frac{3}{4}$ pound

Page 22

1. $\frac{3}{8}$ three eighths   **2.** $\frac{5}{6}$ five sixths

3. $\frac{3}{4}$ three fourths   **4.** $\frac{7}{10}$ seven tenths

5. $\frac{5}{12}$ **6.** $\frac{2}{7}$

7. $\frac{13}{24}$ **8.** $\frac{3}{52}$

9. $\frac{3}{5}$ **10.** $\frac{3}{7}$

11. $\frac{2}{3}$ **12.** $\frac{9}{10}$

13. LT   **14.** $\frac{1}{5}$

15. $\frac{1}{2}$ **16.** $\frac{1}{3}$

17. $\frac{1}{2}$ **18.** $\frac{1}{8}$

19. $\frac{2}{4}$ **20.** $\frac{6}{9}$

21. $\frac{12}{15}$ **22.** $\frac{9}{21}$

23. $\frac{25}{30}$ **24.** $\frac{12}{16}$

25. $\frac{15}{24}$ **26.** $\frac{35}{50}$

Page 23

1. $\frac{3}{8} > \frac{2}{10}$ **2.** $\frac{5}{8} < \frac{7}{8}$

3. $\frac{5}{10} = \frac{4}{8}$

4. $\frac{3}{8} < \frac{5}{8}$

$\frac{5}{8}$ is to the right of $\frac{3}{8}$ on the number line.

5. $\frac{3}{4} > \frac{7}{10}$ **6.** $\frac{4}{10} < \frac{5}{8}$

7. $\frac{1}{8} > \frac{1}{10}$ **8.** $\frac{3}{8} > \frac{3}{10}$

9. $\frac{1}{2} = \frac{5}{10}$ **10.** $\frac{7}{10} < \frac{7}{8}$

11. $\frac{9}{10} > \frac{3}{4}$ **12.** $\frac{1}{4} > \frac{1}{10}$

Page 24

1. $\frac{2}{5} = \frac{6}{15}$

2. $\frac{3}{8} < \frac{1}{2}$

Raise $\frac{1}{2}$ to higher terms with 8 as the denominator.

$\frac{1}{2} = \frac{1 \times 4}{2 \times 4} = \frac{4}{8}$

Compare the numerators.
3 is less than 4.

$\frac{3}{8} < \frac{4}{8}$, so $\frac{3}{8} < \frac{1}{2}$

3. $\frac{2}{4} > \frac{3}{8}$ **4.** $\frac{4}{5} > \frac{2}{10}$

5. $\frac{1}{2} < \frac{6}{10}$ **6.** $\frac{4}{9} < \frac{2}{3}$

7. $\frac{1}{4} < \frac{4}{12}$ **8.** $\frac{5}{6} > \frac{2}{3}$

9. $\frac{1}{4} < \frac{3}{8}$ **10.** $\frac{2}{7} < \frac{5}{14}$

11. $\frac{3}{4} > \frac{7}{16}$ **12.** $\frac{4}{7} > \frac{10}{21}$

13. $\frac{5}{8} < \frac{13}{16}$ **14.** $\frac{7}{12} > \frac{1}{2}$

15. $\frac{2}{5} < \frac{10}{15}$ **16.** $\frac{3}{4} < \frac{16}{20}$

17. $\frac{7}{9} < \frac{15}{18}$ **18.** $\frac{3}{10} < \frac{10}{20}$

19. $\frac{5}{8} = \frac{15}{24}$ **20.** $\frac{5}{10} = \frac{1}{2}$

21. Pat had completed more work.

$\frac{2}{3} = \frac{2 \times 3}{3 \times 3} = \frac{6}{9}$

6 is more than 5.

$\frac{6}{9} > \frac{5}{9}$, so $\frac{2}{3} > \frac{5}{9}$

22. It's more time.

$\frac{1}{2} = \frac{1 \times 4}{2 \times 4} = \frac{4}{8}$

5 is more than 4.

$\frac{5}{8} > \frac{4}{8}$, so $\frac{5}{8} > \frac{1}{2}$

Page 25

1. $\frac{1}{5} > \frac{1}{6}$

2. $\frac{2}{3} < \frac{3}{4}$

Multiply the two denominators to find a common denominator. Write each fraction in higher terms with the new denominator.

$\frac{2}{3} = \frac{2 \times 4}{3 \times 4} = \frac{8}{12}$

$\frac{3}{4} = \frac{3 \times 3}{4 \times 3} = \frac{9}{12}$

Compare the numerators.

$\frac{8}{12} < \frac{9}{12}$, so $\frac{2}{3} < \frac{3}{4}$

3. $\frac{1}{2} < \frac{3}{5}$ **4.** $\frac{5}{6} > \frac{4}{7}$

5. $\frac{3}{4} > \frac{3}{5}$ **6.** $\frac{4}{5} > \frac{4}{7}$

7. $\frac{3}{8} < \frac{2}{3}$ **8.** $\frac{7}{10} > \frac{1}{3}$

9. $\frac{1}{2} = \frac{5}{10}$ **10.** $\frac{3}{4} < \frac{9}{10}$

11. $\frac{1}{3} > \frac{1}{4}$ **12.** $\frac{2}{4} = \frac{3}{6}$

13. Miami

$\frac{3}{10} = \frac{3 \times 4}{4 \times 10} = \frac{12}{40}$

$\frac{3}{4} = \frac{3 \times 10}{4 \times 10} = \frac{30}{40}$

$\frac{30}{40} > \frac{12}{40}$, so $\frac{3}{4} > \frac{3}{10}$

14. Peterboro

$\frac{3}{4} = \frac{3}{4}$

$\frac{1}{2} = \frac{1 \times 2}{1 \times 2} = \frac{2}{4}$

$\frac{3}{4} > \frac{2}{4}$, so $\frac{3}{4} > \frac{1}{2}$

Page 26

1. $1\frac{1}{2}$

2. $2\frac{1}{3}$

2 whole figures are shaded. $\frac{1}{3}$ of the remaining figure is shaded.

3. $4\frac{2}{4}$ or $4\frac{1}{2}$ **4.** $2\frac{4}{6}$ or $2\frac{2}{3}$

5. $3\frac{5}{8}$　　　　**6.** $5\frac{1}{2}$

7. $4\frac{1}{8}$ gallons　　**8.** $3\frac{1}{2}$ gallons

Page 27

1. $2\frac{1}{2}$

2. $2\frac{1}{4}$

Divide. Write the remainder as a fraction.
The remainder, 1, is the numerator of the
fraction. The number you divided by, 4, is
the denominator.

$$\begin{array}{r} 2 \text{ R1} = 2\frac{1}{4} \\ 4\overline{)9} \\ \underline{-8} \\ 1 \end{array}$$

3. $1\frac{3}{7}$　　　　**4.** $2\frac{2}{5}$

5. $6\frac{2}{3}$　　　　**6.** $2\frac{1}{4}$

7. $8\frac{1}{2}$　　　　**8.** $2\frac{1}{5}$

9. $2\frac{4}{7}$　　　　**10.** $2\frac{1}{2}$

11. $2\frac{2}{5}$　　　　**12.** $6\frac{2}{3}$

Page 28

1. $2\frac{3}{8} > 2\frac{1}{4}$

2. $3\frac{1}{3} < 4\frac{1}{8}$

Compare the whole number parts. 3 is less
than 4.

3. $4\frac{1}{5} = 4\frac{2}{10}$　　**4.** $5\frac{3}{4} < 5\frac{7}{8}$

5. $11\frac{1}{2} > 11\frac{1}{10}$　　**6.** $7 < 7\frac{1}{5}$

7. $\frac{1}{5} < 1\frac{1}{5}$　　　**8.** $12\frac{3}{4} < 12\frac{15}{16}$

9. $2\frac{1}{2} > 2\frac{1}{12}$　　**10.** $8\frac{7}{8} > 8\frac{9}{16}$

11. $5\frac{1}{3} = 5\frac{5}{15}$　　**12.** $\frac{9}{10} < 10\frac{1}{10}$

Page 29

1. $4\frac{1}{8}$ inches　　**2.** $4\frac{9}{16}$ inches

3. 5 inches　　　　**4.** $5\frac{1}{2}$ inches

Page 30

5.–16.

168

17. $3\frac{3}{8}$ inches　　**18.** $1\frac{1}{2}$ inches

19. $\frac{3}{4}$ inch　　　**20.** LT

21. $5\frac{1}{2}$ inches　　**22.** $2\frac{1}{4}$ inches

Page 31

1. $\frac{8}{4}$

2. $\frac{14}{6}$

Count the number of equal parts in each
figure. Write this number, 6, as the
denominator. Count the number of shaded
pieces. Write this number, 14, as the
numerator.

3. $\frac{11}{2}$　　　　**4.** $\frac{11}{3}$

5. $\frac{12}{8}$　　　　**6.** $\frac{15}{10}$

7. $\frac{18}{12}$　　　　**8.** $\frac{7}{4}$

9. $\frac{13}{8}$

Page 32

1. M
2. P

The numerator, 2, is smaller than the
denominator, 5.

3. I　　　　**4.** I

5. M　　　　**6.** W

7. I　　　　**8.** I

9. W　　　　**10.** I

11. P　　　　**12.** P

13. M　　　　**14.** I

15. W　　　　**16.** M

17. M　　　　**18.** I

19. I　　　　**20.** I

21. $\frac{11}{8}$

One whole container $= \frac{8}{8}$. Three quarts
of the second $= \frac{3}{8}$. Add the numerators. $\frac{11}{8}$
is an improper fraction.

22. $1\frac{3}{8}$

Walter used 1 whole container. He used 3
of the 8 quarts of the second. Write 1 for the
whole number and $\frac{3}{8}$ for the fraction.

Page 33

1. $\frac{17}{6} = 2\frac{5}{6}$

2. $\frac{9}{2} = 4\frac{1}{2}$

The number of equal parts in each whole, 2,
is the denominator. The total number of

shaded parts, 9, is the numerator. Divide the denominator into the numerator to change $\frac{9}{2}$ to a mixed number.

$$2\overline{)9} \quad \begin{array}{r} 4 \ \text{R1} = 4\frac{1}{2} \\ \underline{-8} \\ 1 \end{array}$$

3. $\frac{14}{9} = 1\frac{5}{9}$ 4. $\frac{6}{3} = 2$

5. $\frac{6}{5} = 1\frac{1}{5}$ 6. $\frac{11}{4} = 2\frac{3}{4}$

7. $2\frac{1}{4}$ 8. $1\frac{4}{9}$

$$9\overline{)13} \quad \begin{array}{r} 1 \ \text{R4} = 1\frac{4}{9} \\ \underline{-9} \\ 4 \end{array}$$

9. 2   10. $1\frac{3}{5}$

11. 3

12. $1\frac{5}{8}$

$$\frac{13}{8} = \quad 8\overline{)13} \quad \begin{array}{r} 1 \ \text{R5} = 1\frac{5}{8} \\ \underline{-8} \\ 5 \end{array}$$

13. $2\frac{2}{9}$ 14. $2\frac{2}{7}$

Page 34

1. $5\frac{1}{6}$

2. 2

Divide the denominator, 3, into the numerator, 6. 3 goes evenly into 6. The answer is a whole number, 2.

$$3\overline{)6} \quad \begin{array}{r} 2 \\ \underline{-6} \\ 0 \end{array}$$

3. 5   4. $8\frac{3}{8}$

5. $2\frac{2}{5}$ 6. $1\frac{8}{9}$

7. $6\frac{1}{9}$ 8. $9\frac{1}{3}$

9. $2\frac{2}{9}$ 10. $3\frac{3}{5}$

11. 5   12. $2\frac{8}{15}$

13. $2\frac{8}{15}$ 14. 6

15. $7\frac{1}{9}$ 16. $7\frac{4}{11}$

17. $23\frac{1}{3}$ 18. 4

19. $5\frac{1}{4}$ 20. $1\frac{1}{7}$

21. $4\frac{1}{3}$ pies

The number of pieces in each pie, 6, is the denominator. The total number of pieces sold, 26, is the numerator. Divide to find the number of pies sold. Reduce to lowest terms.

$$\frac{26}{6} = \quad 6\overline{)26} \quad \begin{array}{r} 4 \ \text{R2} = 4\frac{2}{6} = 4\frac{1}{3} \\ \underline{-24} \\ 2 \end{array}$$

22. $3\frac{1}{2}$ dozen

The number of eggs in a dozen, 12, is the denominator. The total number of eggs used, 42, is the numerator. Divide to find how many dozen are used. Reduce to lowest terms.

$$12\overline{)42} \quad \begin{array}{r} 3 \ \text{R6} = 3\frac{6}{12} = 3\frac{1}{2} \\ \underline{-36} \\ 6 \end{array}$$

Page 35

1. $1\frac{1}{2} = \frac{3}{2}$

2. $2\frac{2}{3} = \frac{8}{3}$

2 whole circles are shaded. 2 of the 3 parts in the third circle are shaded. Write as a mixed number, $2\frac{2}{3}$. Multiply the denominator, 3, by the whole number, 2. $3 \times 2 = 6$. Add 6 to the numerator, 2. $6 + 2 = 8$. Write 8 over 3. $\frac{8}{3}$ is an improper fraction.

3. $2\frac{2}{6} = \frac{14}{6}$ 4. $1\frac{4}{8} = \frac{12}{8}$

5. $1\frac{2}{5} = \frac{7}{5}$ 6. $3\frac{3}{4} = \frac{15}{4}$

7. $4\frac{2}{4} = \frac{18}{4}$ 8. $1\frac{1}{4} = \frac{5}{4}$

9. $2\frac{3}{8} = \frac{19}{8}$

Page 36

1. $\frac{10}{3}$

2. $\frac{32}{5}$

Write the denominator, 5, for the improper fraction. Multiply the denominator, 5, by the whole number, 6. $5 \times 6 = 30$. Add the numerator of the fraction, 2, to the answer 30. $30 + 2 = 32$. Write the sum over the denominator, 5.

3. $\frac{105}{8}$ 4. $\frac{98}{8}$

5. $\frac{15}{2}$

6. $\frac{26}{3}$

7. $\frac{107}{10}$

8. $\frac{59}{6}$

9. $\frac{36}{5}$

10. $\frac{111}{7}$

11. $\frac{13}{12}$

12. $\frac{37}{9}$

13. $\frac{10}{2}$

Write the length of each piece, 2, as the denominator. Write the total length of the plank, 10, as the numerator.

14. $\frac{9}{2}$

$4\frac{1}{2} = \frac{9}{2}$
$2 \times 4 = 8$
$8 + 1 = 9$

Unit 1 Review, page 37

1. $\frac{1}{3}$

2. $\frac{2}{5}$

3. $\frac{5}{6}$

4. $\frac{7}{4} = 1\frac{3}{4}$

5. $\frac{9}{3} = 3$

6. $\frac{13}{6} = 2\frac{1}{6}$

7. $\frac{15}{6} = 2\frac{3}{6} = 2\frac{1}{2}$

8.–10. Shading should be similar to this.

8.

9.

10.

11. $\frac{3}{4}$

12. LT

13. $\frac{3}{7}$

14. $\frac{2}{3}$

15. $\frac{4}{7}$

16. $\frac{3}{4}$

17. LT

18. $\frac{2}{3}$

19. $\frac{2}{3}$

20. $\frac{1}{2}$

Page 38

21. $\frac{4}{6}$

22. $\frac{3}{24}$

23. $\frac{4}{18}$

24. $\frac{20}{28}$

25. $\frac{5}{10}$

26. $\frac{9}{15}$

27. $\frac{15}{20}$

28. $\frac{27}{30}$

29. $\frac{1}{2} > \frac{2}{5}$

30. $\frac{2}{3} < \frac{15}{20}$

31. $\frac{4}{7} < \frac{7}{10}$

32. $4\frac{1}{9} < 4\frac{1}{3}$

33. $\frac{5}{8} = \frac{10}{16}$

34. $7\frac{3}{9} > 7\frac{1}{4}$

35. $\frac{4}{10} < \frac{2}{4}$

36. $\frac{6}{8} = \frac{3}{4}$

37. $1\frac{1}{2}$

38. $3\frac{3}{4}$

39. 4

40. $1\frac{1}{2}$

41. $6\frac{3}{7}$

42. $8\frac{7}{8}$

43. $3\frac{2}{9}$

44. 4

45. $\frac{25}{6}$

46. $\frac{27}{5}$

47. $\frac{40}{3}$

48. $\frac{13}{8}$

Unit 2

Page 39

1. $\frac{1}{3} < \frac{2}{3}$

2. $\frac{7}{10} > \frac{3}{5}$

Change $\frac{3}{5}$ to an equal fraction with a denominator of 10.
$\frac{3}{5} = \frac{3 \times 2}{5 \times 2} = \frac{6}{10}$
Compare the numerators. 7 is larger than 6.
$\frac{7}{10} > \frac{6}{10}$, so $\frac{7}{10} > \frac{3}{5}$

3. $\frac{9}{12} < \frac{5}{6}$

4. $\frac{2}{3} < \frac{3}{4}$

5. $\frac{2}{9} < \frac{1}{3}$

6. $\frac{3}{8} = \frac{6}{16}$

7. $\frac{8}{11} > \frac{5}{11}$

8. $\frac{1}{2} < \frac{2}{3}$

Page 40

9. $\frac{2}{3}$

10. $\frac{3}{4}$

$\frac{15}{20} = \frac{15 \div 5}{20 \div 5} = \frac{3}{4}$

11. $\frac{1}{2}$

12. $3\frac{3}{4}$

13. $1\frac{2}{3}$

14. $\frac{2}{3}$

15. $\frac{4}{5}$

16. $4\frac{1}{2}$

17. $5\frac{1}{2}$

18. $10\frac{3}{4}$

19. $\frac{8}{12}$

20. $\frac{9}{12}$

$\frac{3}{4} = \frac{3 \times 3}{4 \times 3} = \frac{9}{12}$

21. $\frac{6}{12}$　　　**22.** $2\frac{10}{12}$

23. $5\frac{3}{12}$　　　**24.** $\frac{10}{12}$

25. $\frac{4}{12}$　　　**26.** $9\frac{6}{12}$

27. $3\frac{8}{12}$　　　**28.** $1\frac{8}{12}$

29. $2\frac{1}{5}$

30. $6\frac{2}{3}$

$$3\overline{)20} \quad \frac{6}{} \; R2 = 6\frac{2}{3}$$
$$\underline{-18}$$
$$2$$

31. $5\frac{4}{9}$　　　**32.** 3

33. 5　　　**34.** $3\frac{1}{2}$

35. $1\frac{3}{5}$　　　**36.** 2

37. $2\frac{1}{2}$　　　**38.** $1\frac{1}{4}$

Page 41

1. $\frac{2}{3}$

2.–4. and 6. Shading should be similar to this.

2. $\frac{3}{4}$

Add the numerators.
$1 + 3 = 4$. Write the sum over the denominator, 4. Shade in 3 of the 4 squares in the final figure.

3. $\frac{4}{5}$

4. $\frac{5}{6}$

5.

$\frac{3}{8}$

6.

$\frac{7}{9}$

Shade in 2 squares in the first figure. Shade in 5 squares in the second figure. Add $2 + 5$. The sum, 7, is the numerator over the denominator, 9. Shade in 7 of the 9 squares in the final figure.

Page 42

1. $\frac{5}{6}$

2. $\frac{7}{12}$

The denominators are the same, 12. Add the numerators. $6 + 1 = 7$. Write the sum over the denominator.

$$\frac{6}{12} + \frac{1}{12} = \frac{7}{12}$$

3. $\frac{13}{15}$　　　**4.** $\frac{11}{20}$

5. $\frac{9}{10}$　　　**6.** $\frac{13}{14}$

7. $\frac{31}{35}$

The denominators are the same, 35. Add the numerators. $10 + 15 + 6 = 31$. Write the sum over the denominator.

$$\frac{10}{35} + \frac{15}{35} + \frac{6}{35} = \frac{31}{35}$$

8. $\frac{21}{40}$　　　**9.** $\frac{31}{50}$

10. $\frac{33}{100}$　　　**11.** $\frac{14}{25}$

12. $\frac{7}{9}$　　　**13.** $\frac{5}{7}$

14. $\frac{4}{5}$

Add $\frac{2}{5} + \frac{2}{5}$. The denominators are the same, 5. Add the numerators. $2 + 2 = 4$. Write the sum over the denominator.

$$\frac{2}{5} + \frac{2}{5} = \frac{4}{5}$$

15. $\frac{5}{8}$ gallon

Add $\frac{2}{8} + \frac{3}{8}$. The denominators are the same, 8. Add the numerators. $2 + 3 = 5$. Write the sum over the denominator.

$\frac{2}{8} + \frac{3}{8} = \frac{5}{8}$

Page 43

1. $\frac{1}{2}$ hour

Ann spent $\frac{1}{4}$ hour on the rowing machine. Otis spent $\frac{1}{4}$ hour on the rowing machine. Petra did not spend any time on the rowing machine. Add $\frac{1}{4} + \frac{1}{4}$. Reduce to lowest terms.

$\frac{1}{4} + \frac{1}{4} = \frac{2}{4} = \frac{2 \div 2}{4 \div 2} = \frac{1}{2}$

2. 1 hour

Ann spent $\frac{2}{4}$ hour on the exercise bike, $\frac{1}{4}$ hour on the treadmill, and $\frac{1}{4}$ hour on the rowing machine. Add $\frac{2}{4} + \frac{1}{4} + \frac{1}{4}$. Reduce to lowest terms.

$\frac{2}{4} + \frac{1}{4} + \frac{1}{4} = \frac{4}{4} = 1$

3. $1\frac{1}{2}$ hours

Otis spent $\frac{3}{4}$ hour on the exercise bike, $\frac{2}{4}$ hour on the treadmill, and $\frac{1}{4}$ hour on the rowing machine. Add $\frac{3}{4} + \frac{2}{4} + \frac{1}{4}$. Reduce to lowest terms.

$\frac{3}{4} + \frac{2}{4} + \frac{1}{4} = \frac{6}{4} = 1\frac{2}{4} = 1\frac{1}{2}$

4. $\frac{3}{4}$ hour

Otis spent $\frac{2}{4}$ hour on the treadmill. Ann spent $\frac{1}{4}$ hour. Add $\frac{2}{4} + \frac{1}{4}$.

$\frac{2}{4} + \frac{1}{4} = \frac{3}{4}$

Page 44

1. $\frac{1}{2}$

2. $\frac{2}{3}$

The denominators are the same, 6. Add the numerators. $3 + 1 = 4$. Write the sum over the denominator. Reduce to lowest terms.

$\frac{4}{6} = \frac{4 \div 2}{6 \div 2} = \frac{2}{3}$

3. $\frac{4}{5}$ **4.** $\frac{2}{3}$

5. $\frac{2}{3}$ **6.** $\frac{3}{5}$

7. $\frac{2}{3}$ **8.** $\frac{1}{4}$

9. $\frac{17}{22}$ **10.** $\frac{7}{8}$

11. $\frac{9}{10}$ **12.** $\frac{7}{9}$

13. $\frac{5}{6}$ **14.** $\frac{1}{3}$

15. $\frac{2}{3}$ **16.** $\frac{5}{6}$

17. $\frac{4}{5}$ **18.** $\frac{3}{4}$

19. $\frac{7}{10}$

20. $\frac{4}{5}$ mile

Add how far it is from the depot to the gas station, $\frac{2}{10}$, to how far it is from the gas station to Luis' first stop, $\frac{6}{10}$. Reduce to lowest terms.

$\frac{2}{10} + \frac{6}{10} = \frac{8}{10} = \frac{8 \div 2}{10 \div 2} = \frac{4}{5}$

21. $\frac{1}{2}$ inch

Add the widths of the two ribbons. Reduce to lowest terms.

$\frac{2}{16} + \frac{6}{16} = \frac{8}{16} = \frac{8 \div 8}{16 \div 8} = \frac{1}{2}$

Page 45

1. 1

2. 1

The denominators are the same. Add the numerators. The sum is an improper fraction. Divide the numerator by the denominator.

$\frac{5}{6} + \frac{1}{6} = \frac{6}{6}$

$$6 \overline{)6} \quad \begin{array}{r} 1 \\ -6 \\ \hline 0 \end{array}$$

3. 1   **4.** 1

5. 3

6. 2

Add the numerators. The answer is an improper fraction. Divide the numerator by the denominator.

$\frac{6}{4} + \frac{2}{4} = \frac{8}{4}$

$$4 \overline{)8} \quad \begin{array}{r} 2 \\ -8 \\ \hline 0 \end{array}$$

7. 3   **8.** 2

9. 2   **10.** 3

11. 3   **12.** 1

13. 3   **14.** 4

15. 1   **16.** 5

17. 2 feet

Add the 3 lengths of pipe.

$$\frac{9}{12} + \frac{9}{12} + \frac{6}{12} = \frac{24}{12}$$

Change the improper fraction to a whole number.

$$12\overline{)24} \quad \begin{array}{r} 2 \\ -24 \\ \hline 0 \end{array}$$

18. 1 inch

Add the rainfall for all 3 days last week.

$$\frac{2}{10} + \frac{1}{10} + \frac{7}{10} = \frac{10}{10}$$

Change the improper fraction to a whole number.

$$10\overline{)10} \quad \begin{array}{r} 1 \\ -10 \\ \hline 0 \end{array}$$

Page 46

1. $1\frac{1}{3}$

2. $3\frac{1}{2}$

The denominators are the same. Add the numerators. The answer is an improper fraction. Change to a mixed number. Reduce.

$$\frac{6}{4} + \frac{8}{4} = \frac{14}{4}$$

$$4\overline{)14} \quad \begin{array}{r} 3\frac{2}{4} = 3\frac{1}{2} \\ -12 \\ \hline 2 \end{array}$$

3. $1\frac{2}{5}$ **4.** $1\frac{2}{3}$

5. $2\frac{1}{5}$

6. $4\frac{1}{3}$

The denominators are the same. Add the numerators. The answer is an improper fraction. Change to a mixed number.

$$\frac{11}{3} + \frac{1}{3} + \frac{1}{3} = \frac{13}{3}$$

$$3\overline{)13} \quad \begin{array}{r} 4\frac{1}{3} \\ -12 \\ \hline 1 \end{array}$$

7. $1\frac{8}{9}$ **8.** $2\frac{1}{2}$

---

9. $1\frac{8}{15}$ **10.** $1\frac{3}{20}$

11. $1\frac{3}{7}$ **12.** $1\frac{1}{5}$

13. $1\frac{1}{2}$ hours

Add the amounts of time Anita spent in the park. Change to a mixed number. Reduce.

$$\frac{3}{4} + \frac{3}{4} = \frac{6}{4}$$

$$4\overline{)6} \quad \begin{array}{r} 1\frac{2}{4} = 1\frac{1}{2} \\ -4 \\ \hline 2 \end{array}$$

14. $1\frac{7}{10}$ miles

Add the distance from Adams to Bailey, $\frac{8}{10}$, to the distance from Bailey to Carter, $\frac{9}{10}$. Change to a mixed number.

$$\frac{8}{10} + \frac{9}{10} = \frac{17}{10}$$

$$10\overline{)17} \quad \begin{array}{r} 1\frac{7}{10} \\ -10 \\ \hline 7 \end{array}$$

Page 47

1. $\frac{1}{2}$ **2.** 3

3. $4\frac{1}{3}$ **4.** $\frac{1}{4}$

5. $3\frac{3}{4}$ **6.** $12\frac{1}{2}$

7. $3\frac{1}{4}$ **8.** 1

9. $\frac{1}{7}$ **10.** LT

11. $1\frac{4}{7}$ **12.** $1\frac{8}{11}$

13. $1\frac{1}{5}$ **14.** $1\frac{1}{6}$

15. $\frac{2}{5}$ **16.** $\frac{9}{10}$

17. $\frac{22}{25}$ **18.** $\frac{71}{100}$

19. $\frac{4}{5}$ **20.** $\frac{2}{3}$

21. $\frac{5}{6}$ **22.** $\frac{4}{5}$

23. 1   **24.** 2

25. 3   **26.** 1

27. $1\frac{7}{9}$ **28.** $1\frac{1}{3}$

29. $2\frac{11}{25}$ **30.** $1\frac{1}{6}$

31. $\frac{7}{8}$ **32.** $1\frac{5}{7}$

33. $\frac{2}{3}$ **34.** $1\frac{2}{5}$

35. $1\frac{1}{3}$

Page 48

1. 3 sections were used for a retail store.
$\frac{3}{12} = \frac{1}{4}$

2. 7 sections; $\frac{7}{12}$

3. 1 section; $\frac{1}{12}$

4. $\frac{2}{12} = \frac{1}{6}$ **5.** $\frac{9}{12} = \frac{3}{4}$

6. 1
$\frac{3}{12} + \frac{4}{12} + \frac{2}{12} + \frac{2}{12} + \frac{1}{12} = \frac{12}{12} = 1$

Page 49

1. $9\frac{1}{2}$

2. $8\frac{1}{2}$

Add the fractions. Add the whole numbers. Reduce.

$1\frac{1}{4}$
$+ 7\frac{1}{4}$
_____
$8\frac{2}{4} = 8\frac{1}{2}$

3. $7\frac{7}{8}$ **4.** $9\frac{4}{5}$

5. $21\frac{19}{20}$ **6.** $41\frac{4}{5}$

7. $63\frac{7}{10}$ **8.** $79\frac{3}{5}$

9. $17\frac{1}{2}$

10. $45\frac{5}{7}$

Line up the fractions and the whole numbers in columns. Add the fractions. Add the whole numbers.

$10\frac{2}{7}$
$13\frac{1}{7}$
$+ 22\frac{2}{7}$
_____
$45\frac{5}{7}$

11. $16\frac{1}{2}$

Page 50

1. 7

2. $11\frac{1}{2}$

Line up the mixed numbers. Add the fractions. Add the whole numbers.

$5\frac{3}{4}$
$+ 5\frac{3}{4}$
_____
$10\frac{6}{4}$

Change $\frac{6}{4}$ to a mixed number, $1\frac{2}{4}$. Add the whole numbers. Reduce the fraction.

$10\frac{6}{4} = 10 + 1\frac{2}{4} = 11\frac{2}{4} = 11\frac{1}{2}$

3. $25\frac{2}{5}$ **4.** $27\frac{1}{9}$

5. 41   **6.** $110\frac{3}{10}$

7. 159   **8.** 46

9. $5\frac{1}{2}$ hours

Add the amounts of time Phil made sales calls on the 3 days given. Change the fraction to a mixed number. Add it to the whole number.

$1\frac{1}{2}$
$2\frac{1}{2}$
$+ 1\frac{1}{2}$
_____
$4\frac{3}{2} = 4 + 1\frac{1}{2} = 5\frac{1}{2}$

10. $11\frac{1}{10}$ miles

Add all the distances. Change the answer to a mixed number.

$3\frac{7}{10}$
$1\frac{3}{10}$
$+ 6\frac{1}{10}$
_____
$10\frac{11}{10} = 10 + 1\frac{1}{10} = 11\frac{1}{10}$

Page 51

1. $7\frac{1}{4}$

2. $11\frac{1}{5}$

Add the fractions. Add the whole numbers. Change the improper fraction to a mixed number. Add it to the whole number.

$$\begin{array}{r} 3\frac{2}{5} \\ 7 \\ + \ \ \frac{4}{5} \\ \hline 10\frac{6}{5} = 10 + 1\frac{1}{5} = 11\frac{1}{5} \end{array}$$

3. $16\frac{3}{10}$ **4.** 16

5. $34\frac{5}{9}$ **6.** $18\frac{1}{4}$

7. $7\frac{3}{4}$ yards

Add the amounts of material given. Line up the whole numbers and fractions. Add the fractions. Add the whole numbers. Reduce to lowest terms.

$$\begin{array}{r} 3\frac{1}{8} \\ 4 \\ + \ \ \frac{5}{8} \\ \hline 7\frac{6}{8} = 7\frac{3}{4} \end{array}$$

8. $4\frac{3}{4}$ yards

Add the amounts of material given. Add the fractions. Add the whole numbers. Reduce to lowest terms.

$$\begin{array}{r} 2\frac{3}{8} \\ 2 \\ + \ \ \frac{3}{8} \\ \hline 4\frac{6}{8} = 4\frac{3}{4} \end{array}$$

Page 52

1. LT   **2.** $4\frac{1}{2}$

3. 5   **4.** LT

5. LT   **6.** $\frac{3}{4}$

7. $8\frac{1}{4}$ **8.** LT

9. 3   **10.** 1

11. $\frac{5}{9}$ **12.** $\frac{3}{4}$

13. $1\frac{2}{5}$ **14.** $1\frac{5}{14}$

15. $12\frac{1}{4}$ **16.** 10

17. $11\frac{1}{4}$ **18.** $33\frac{1}{2}$

19. $13\frac{7}{8}$ **20.** $17\frac{1}{2}$

21. $1\frac{3}{4}$ **22.** $25\frac{5}{8}$

23. $72\frac{4}{25}$

24. $63\frac{1}{2}$ inches

$$\begin{array}{r} 62\frac{3}{4} \\ + \ \ \frac{3}{4} \\ \hline 62\frac{6}{4} = 62 + 1\frac{2}{4} = 63\frac{2}{4} = 63\frac{1}{2} \end{array}$$

25. $64\frac{3}{4}$ inches

$$\begin{array}{r} 63\frac{1}{2} = 63\frac{2}{4} \\ + \ 1\frac{1}{4} = \ 1\frac{1}{4} \\ \hline 64\frac{3}{4} \end{array}$$

Page 53

1. $1\frac{3}{4}$ inches

Add the measures. Draw an arrow pointing to the answer and label it B.

$$\begin{array}{r} 1\frac{1}{2} = 1\frac{2}{4} \\ + \ \ \frac{1}{4} = \ \ \frac{1}{4} \\ \hline 1\frac{3}{4} \end{array}$$

2. $3\frac{5}{8}$ inches   **3.** $5\frac{3}{4}$ inches

4. $5\frac{9}{16}$ inches

Page 54

5. $3\frac{3}{4}$ inches   **6.** $4\frac{1}{8}$ inches

7. $3\frac{1}{2}$ inches   **8.** $4\frac{9}{16}$ inches

9. $2\frac{3}{4}$ inches   **10.** $5\frac{1}{4}$ inches

11. $4\frac{3}{8}$ inches   **12.** 6 inches

Page 55

1. $\frac{1}{2} = \frac{5}{10}$

$\frac{3}{10} = \frac{3}{10}$

2. $\frac{4}{5} = \frac{12}{15}$

$\frac{7}{15} = \frac{7}{15}$

Compare the denominators. 5 divides evenly into 15. Raise $\frac{4}{5}$ to higher terms with 15 as the denominator.

$\frac{4}{5} = \frac{4 \times 3}{5 \times 3} = \frac{12}{15}$

3. $\frac{2}{3} = \frac{6}{9}$

$\frac{4}{9} = \frac{4}{9}$

4. $\frac{7}{12} = \frac{7}{12}$

$\frac{5}{6} = \frac{10}{12}$

5. $\frac{3}{4} = \frac{6}{8}$

$\frac{5}{8} = \frac{5}{8}$

6. $\frac{1}{2} = \frac{3}{6}$

$\frac{5}{6} = \frac{5}{6}$

7. $\frac{7}{21} = \frac{7}{21}$

$\frac{3}{7} = \frac{9}{21}$

8. $\frac{1}{5} = \frac{5}{25}$

$\frac{3}{25} = \frac{3}{25}$

9. $\frac{3}{14} = \frac{3}{14}$

$\frac{2}{7} = \frac{4}{14}$

10. $\frac{5}{8} = \frac{15}{24}$

$\frac{7}{24} = \frac{7}{24}$

11. $\frac{9}{20} = \frac{9}{20}$

$\frac{3}{10} = \frac{6}{20}$

12. $\frac{2}{9} = \frac{6}{27}$

$\frac{5}{27} = \frac{5}{27}$

13. $\frac{1}{2} = \frac{4}{8}$

$\frac{3}{4} = \frac{6}{8}$

$\frac{7}{8} = \frac{7}{8}$

14. $\frac{2}{3} = \frac{12}{18}$

$\frac{5}{6} = \frac{15}{18}$

$\frac{1}{18} = \frac{1}{18}$

Compare the denominators. The two smaller denominators, 3 and 6, will divide evenly into the largest denominator, 18. Raise $\frac{2}{3}$ and $\frac{5}{6}$ to higher terms with 18 as the denominator.

$\frac{2}{3} = \frac{2 \times 6}{3 \times 6} = \frac{12}{18}$

$\frac{5}{6} = \frac{5 \times 3}{6 \times 3} = \frac{15}{18}$

15. $\frac{1}{3} = \frac{5}{15}$

$\frac{3}{5} = \frac{9}{15}$

$\frac{7}{15} = \frac{7}{15}$

Page 56

1. $\frac{7}{10}$

2. $\frac{5}{6}$

Compare the denominators. 2 divides evenly into 6. Raise $\frac{1}{2}$ to higher terms with 6 as the denominator.

$\frac{1}{2} = \frac{1 \times 3}{2 \times 3} = \frac{3}{6}$

Add the fractions.

$\frac{2}{6} = \frac{2}{6}$

$+ \frac{1}{2} = \frac{3}{6}$

$\frac{5}{6}$

3. $\frac{5}{14}$

4. $\frac{3}{4}$

5. $\frac{7}{8}$

6. $\frac{8}{9}$

7. $\frac{7}{10}$

8. $\frac{4}{15}$

9. $\frac{7}{20}$

Page 57

1. $1\frac{1}{5}$

2. $\frac{9}{16}$

Compare the denominators. The two smaller denominators, 4 and 8, will divide evenly into the largest denominator, 16. Raise $\frac{1}{4}$ and $\frac{1}{8}$ to higher terms with 16 as the denominator.

$\frac{1}{4} = \frac{1 \times 4}{4 \times 4} = \frac{4}{16}$

$\frac{1}{8} = \frac{1 \times 2}{8 \times 2} = \frac{2}{16}$

Add the fractions.

$\frac{1}{4} = \frac{4}{16}$

$\frac{1}{8} = \frac{2}{16}$

$+ \frac{3}{16} = \frac{3}{16}$

$\frac{9}{16}$

3. $1\frac{5}{18}$

4. $\frac{13}{18}$

5. $\frac{13}{16}$

6. $\frac{9}{10}$

7. $\frac{19}{20}$

8. $\frac{19}{45}$

9. $\frac{41}{60}$

10. $\frac{27}{52}$

11. $\frac{99}{100}$

Page 58

1. $\frac{1}{2}$

2. $\frac{1}{3}$

Raise $\frac{1}{5}$ to higher terms with 15 as the denominator.

$\frac{1}{5} = \frac{1 \times 3}{5 \times 3} = \frac{3}{15}$

Add the fractions. Reduce to lowest terms.

$\begin{array}{r} \frac{2}{15} = \frac{2}{15} \\ + \frac{1}{5} = \frac{3}{15} \\ \hline \frac{5}{15} = \frac{1}{3} \end{array}$

3. $\frac{2}{5}$ **4.** $\frac{24}{25}$

5. $\frac{1}{2}$ **6.** $\frac{5}{6}$

7. $\frac{4}{5}$ **8.** $\frac{33}{50}$

9. $\frac{1}{4}$ **10.** $\frac{7}{8}$

11. $\frac{9}{10}$ **12.** $\frac{5}{6}$

13. $\frac{3}{4}$ day

Add the amounts of time Joan helped patients. Raise $\frac{1}{2}$ to higher terms with 4 as the denominator.

$\frac{1}{2} = \frac{1 \times 2}{2 \times 2} = \frac{2}{4}$

Add the fractions.

$\begin{array}{r} \frac{1}{2} = \frac{2}{4} \\ + \frac{1}{4} = \frac{1}{4} \\ \hline \frac{3}{4} \end{array}$

14. $\frac{1}{2}$

Add the parts of his paycheck that Chris spent. Raise $\frac{1}{3}$ to higher terms with 6 as the denominator.

$\frac{1}{3} = \frac{1 \times 2}{3 \times 2} = \frac{2}{6}$

Add the fractions. Reduce to lowest terms.

$\begin{array}{r} \frac{1}{6} = \frac{1}{6} \\ + \frac{1}{3} = \frac{2}{6} \\ \hline \frac{3}{6} = \frac{1}{2} \end{array}$

Page 59

1. $1\frac{1}{6}$

2. $1\frac{5}{8}$

Raise $\frac{3}{4}$ to higher terms with 8 as the denominator.

$\frac{3}{4} = \frac{3 \times 2}{4 \times 2} = \frac{6}{8}$

Add the fractions. Change the improper fraction to a mixed number.

$\begin{array}{r} \frac{7}{8} = \frac{7}{8} \\ + \frac{3}{4} = \frac{6}{8} \\ \hline \frac{13}{8} = 1\frac{5}{8} \end{array}$

3. $1\frac{1}{3}$ **4.** $1\frac{5}{16}$

5. $1\frac{1}{6}$ **6.** 2

7. $1\frac{2}{3}$ **8.** $1\frac{3}{8}$

9. $1\frac{5}{14}$ **10.** $1\frac{7}{12}$

11. $1\frac{8}{15}$ **12.** 1

13. $2\frac{1}{4}$ pounds

Add the weights of the three boxes to find the total weight.

$\begin{array}{r} \frac{12}{16} = \frac{12}{16} \\ \frac{3}{4} = \frac{12}{16} \\ + \frac{6}{8} = \frac{12}{16} \\ \hline \frac{36}{16} = 2\frac{4}{16} = 2\frac{1}{4} \end{array}$

14. $1\frac{3}{5}$ yards

Add the three lengths of ribbon to find the combined length.

$\begin{array}{r} \frac{4}{5} = \frac{8}{10} \\ \frac{3}{10} = \frac{3}{10} \\ + \frac{1}{2} = \frac{5}{10} \\ \hline \frac{16}{10} = 1\frac{6}{10} = 1\frac{3}{5} \end{array}$

Page 60

1. $\frac{2}{8}$ **2.** $\frac{9}{12}$

3. $\frac{6}{9}$ **4.** $\frac{15}{18}$

5. $\frac{12}{20}$ **6.** $\frac{2}{3}$

7. $\frac{3}{5}$ **8.** $\frac{1}{6}$

9. LT   **10.** $\frac{1}{2}$

11. 1 **12.** $1\frac{1}{4}$

13. 3 **14.** $3\frac{1}{7}$

15. $2\frac{1}{4}$ **16.** $\frac{1}{2}$

17. 1 **18.** $1\frac{4}{9}$

19. $\frac{1}{2}$ **20.** $\frac{7}{16}$

21. $\frac{5}{8}$

22. $1\frac{9}{14}$

23. $1\frac{7}{12}$

24. $2\frac{1}{18}$

25. $\frac{3}{5}$

26. $5\frac{6}{7}$

27. $14\frac{5}{6}$

28. $\frac{21}{25}$

29. $10\frac{1}{2}$

Page 61

1. $2\frac{1}{8}$ pounds

   Add the amounts of weight Theresa lost. Raise $\frac{1}{2}$ and $\frac{3}{4}$ to higher terms with 16 as the denominator. Add the fractions. Change the improper fraction to a mixed number. Reduce.

   $$\frac{1}{2} = \frac{8}{16}$$
   $$\frac{3}{4} = \frac{12}{16}$$
   $$\frac{9}{16} = \frac{9}{16}$$
   $$+\frac{5}{16} = \frac{5}{16}$$
   $$\overline{\qquad\quad \frac{34}{16} = 2\frac{2}{16} = 2\frac{1}{8}}$$

2. $2\frac{9}{16}$ pounds

   Add the amounts of weight Lisa lost.

   $$\frac{3}{4} = \frac{12}{16}$$
   $$\frac{15}{16} = \frac{15}{16}$$
   $$\frac{1}{2} = \frac{8}{16}$$
   $$+\frac{3}{8} = \frac{6}{16}$$
   $$\overline{\qquad\quad \frac{41}{16} = 2\frac{9}{16}}$$

3. $1\frac{11}{16}$ pounds

   Add the amounts of weight Janet lost.

   $$\frac{3}{8} = \frac{6}{16}$$
   $$\frac{1}{4} = \frac{4}{16}$$
   $$\frac{7}{8} = \frac{14}{16}$$
   $$+\frac{3}{16} = \frac{3}{16}$$
   $$\overline{\qquad\quad \frac{27}{16} = 1\frac{11}{16}}$$

4. Mona and Lisa lost the same amount of weight, $2\frac{9}{16}$ pounds, so they tied.

Page 62

1. $\frac{1}{5} = \frac{3}{15}$

   $\frac{2}{3} = \frac{10}{15}$

2. $\frac{2}{5} = \frac{8}{20}$

   $\frac{1}{4} = \frac{5}{20}$

   Compare the denominators. 4 will not divide evenly into 5. Multiply the denominators of the two fractions to get the common denominator, 20. Raise each fraction to higher terms with 20 as the denominator.

   $$\frac{2}{5} = \frac{2 \times 4}{5 \times 4} = \frac{8}{20}$$
   $$\frac{1}{4} = \frac{1 \times 5}{4 \times 5} = \frac{5}{20}$$

3. $\frac{1}{6} = \frac{5}{30}$

   $\frac{3}{5} = \frac{18}{30}$

4. $\frac{3}{7} = \frac{6}{14}$

   $\frac{1}{2} = \frac{7}{14}$

5. $\frac{1}{3} = \frac{4}{12}$

   $\frac{1}{4} = \frac{3}{12}$

   $\frac{1}{6} = \frac{2}{12}$

6. $\frac{1}{2} = \frac{35}{70}$

   $\frac{2}{5} = \frac{28}{70}$

   $\frac{3}{7} = \frac{30}{70}$

   Compare the two larger denominators. 5 will not divide evenly into 7. Multiply 5×7. $5 \times 7 = 35$. The third denominator, 2, will not divide evenly into 35. Multiply 35×2. $35 \times 2 = 70$. The common denominator is 70. Raise all three fractions to higher terms with 70 as the denominator.

7. $\frac{4}{9} = \frac{28}{63}$

   $\frac{1}{3} = \frac{21}{63}$

   $\frac{2}{7} = \frac{18}{63}$

8. $\frac{5}{9} = \frac{20}{36}$

   $\frac{1}{4} = \frac{9}{36}$

9. $\frac{2}{3} = \frac{28}{42}$

   $\frac{2}{7} = \frac{12}{42}$

   $\frac{5}{6} = \frac{35}{42}$

10. $\frac{3}{4} = \frac{27}{36}$

    $\frac{2}{9} = \frac{8}{36}$

11. $\frac{3}{8} = \frac{45}{120}$

$\frac{3}{5} = \frac{72}{120}$

$\frac{2}{3} = \frac{80}{120}$

Page 63

1. $\frac{5}{6}$

2. $\frac{7}{12}$

Multiply the denominators to find the common denominator, 24. Raise each fraction to higher terms with 24 as the denominator. Add the fractions. Reduce.

$$\frac{2}{6} = \frac{8}{24}$$
$$+\frac{1}{4} = \frac{6}{24}$$
$$\frac{14}{24} = \frac{7}{12}$$

3. $\frac{17}{24}$ **4.** $\frac{15}{28}$

5. $\frac{13}{20}$

6. $\frac{5}{6}$

Multiply the denominators to find the common denominator, 18. Raise each fraction to higher terms with 18 as the denominator. Add the fractions. Reduce.

$$\frac{2}{3} = \frac{12}{18}$$
$$+\frac{1}{6} = \frac{3}{18}$$
$$\frac{15}{18} = \frac{15 \div 3}{18 \div 3} = \frac{5}{6}$$

7. $\frac{5}{9}$ **8.** $\frac{8}{15}$

9. $\frac{11}{12}$ **10.** $\frac{9}{14}$

11. $\frac{33}{40}$ **12.** $\frac{19}{30}$

Page 64

1. $1\frac{13}{24}$

2. $1\frac{11}{20}$

Multiply the two denominators to find the common denominator, 20. Raise each fraction to higher terms with 20 as the denominator. Add the fractions. Change the improper fraction to a mixed number.

$$\frac{4}{5} = \frac{16}{20}$$
$$+\frac{3}{4} = \frac{15}{20}$$
$$\frac{31}{20} = 1\frac{11}{20}$$

3. $1\frac{7}{30}$ **4.** $1\frac{5}{42}$

5. $1\frac{9}{20}$

6. $2\frac{7}{24}$

Multiply 3×8 to find a common denominator, 24. 4 will divide evenly into 24. Raise each fraction to higher terms. Add. Change the improper fraction to a mixed number.

$$\frac{7}{8} = \frac{21}{24}$$
$$\frac{3}{4} = \frac{18}{24}$$
$$+\frac{2}{3} = \frac{16}{24}$$
$$\frac{55}{24} = 2\frac{7}{24}$$

7. $1\frac{19}{140}$

8. $2\frac{1}{12}$ pounds

Add the weights of the sandwich meat. Multiply the two larger denominators to find the common denominator, 24. Raise each fraction to higher terms. Add. Reduce to lowest terms.

$$\frac{5}{6} = \frac{20}{24}$$
$$\frac{3}{4} = \frac{18}{24}$$
$$+\frac{1}{2} = \frac{12}{24}$$
$$\frac{50}{24} = 2\frac{2}{24} = 2\frac{1}{12}$$

9. $1\frac{11}{12}$ pounds

Add the weights of the fruit.

$$\frac{2}{3} = \frac{8}{12}$$
$$\frac{3}{4} = \frac{9}{12}$$
$$+\frac{1}{2} = \frac{6}{12}$$
$$\frac{23}{12} = 1\frac{11}{12}$$

Page 65

1. $\frac{5}{18}$

2. $1\frac{1}{12}$

List the multiples of each denominator. The smallest number on both lists is 12. 12 is the LCD. Raise each fraction to higher terms with 12 as the LCD. Add the fractions. Change the improper fraction to a mixed number.

$\frac{5}{6}$　　6　⑫　18

$\frac{1}{4}$　　4　8　⑫

$$\frac{5}{6} = \frac{10}{12}$$
$$+\frac{1}{4} = \frac{3}{12}$$
$$\frac{13}{12} = 1\frac{1}{12}$$

3. $\frac{37}{40}$

$\frac{5}{8}$　　8　16　32　㊵

$\frac{3}{10}$　　10　20　30　㊵

4. $\frac{13}{48}$

$\frac{1}{12}$　　12　24　36　㊽

$\frac{3}{16}$　　16　32　㊽

5. $\frac{13}{15}$

$\frac{1}{6}$　　6　12　18　24　㉚

$\frac{7}{10}$　　10　20　㉚

6. $1\frac{13}{36}$

$\frac{5}{12}$　　12　24　�36

$\frac{17}{18}$　　18　�36

7. $1\frac{1}{36}$

$\frac{4}{9}$　　9　18　27　�36

$\frac{7}{12}$　　12　24　�36

8. $1\frac{5}{24}$

$\frac{3}{8}$　　8　16　㉔

$\frac{5}{6}$　　6　12　18　㉔

Page 66

1. $\frac{1}{2} = \frac{2}{4}$
$\frac{1}{4} = \frac{1}{4}$

2. $\frac{1}{3} = \frac{5}{15}$
$\frac{2}{5} = \frac{6}{15}$

---

3. $\frac{6}{7} = \frac{18}{21}$
$\frac{2}{21} = \frac{2}{21}$

4. $\frac{1}{6} = \frac{4}{24}$
$\frac{5}{8} = \frac{15}{24}$

5. $\frac{5}{9} = \frac{50}{90}$
$\frac{3}{10} = \frac{27}{90}$

6. $\frac{1}{2}$

7. $\frac{5}{8}$

8. $\frac{8}{9}$

9. $1\frac{3}{16}$

10. $1\frac{5}{12}$

11. $1\frac{13}{30}$

12. $\frac{17}{20}$

13. $1\frac{5}{18}$

14. $1\frac{1}{2}$

15. $1\frac{1}{8}$

16. $\frac{15}{28}$

17. $\frac{8}{15}$

18. $1\frac{5}{12}$

19. $1\frac{3}{5}$

20. $1\frac{5}{16}$

21. $1\frac{7}{18}$

22. $1\frac{5}{6}$

23. $1\frac{1}{6}$

24. $\frac{20}{21}$

25. $2\frac{1}{12}$

26. $1\frac{7}{18}$

Page 67

1. $5\frac{3}{8}$

2. $7\frac{7}{9}$

Raise $\frac{2}{3}$ to higher terms with 9 as the denominator. Add the fractions. Add the whole numbers.

$$3\frac{2}{3} = 3\frac{6}{9}$$
$$+4\frac{1}{9} = 4\frac{1}{9}$$
$$7\frac{7}{9}$$

3. $12\frac{3}{14}$

4. $20\frac{1}{3}$

5. $7\frac{11}{12}$

6. $5\frac{19}{24}$

7. $17\frac{31}{35}$

8. $14\frac{19}{30}$

9. $14\frac{11}{18}$

10. $11\frac{1}{12}$

Find the LCD for the fractions. List multiples of each denominator. The smallest number on each list is 12, the LCD. Raise each fraction to higher terms with 12 as the LCD. Add the fractions. Add the whole numbers. Change the improper fraction to a mixed number.

$\frac{1}{2}$ 2 4 6 8 10 ⑫

$\frac{3}{4}$ 4 8 ⑫

$\frac{5}{6}$ 6 ⑫

$$1\frac{1}{2} = 1\frac{6}{12}$$

$$6\frac{3}{4} = 6\frac{9}{12}$$

$$+\ 2\frac{5}{6} = 2\frac{10}{12}$$

$$9\frac{25}{12} = 9 + 2\frac{1}{12} = 11\frac{1}{12}$$

11. $19\frac{2}{5}$

Page 68

1. $10\frac{5}{24}$

2. $11\frac{1}{2}$

Line up the whole numbers. Bring down the fraction. Add the whole numbers.

$$4\frac{1}{2}$$
$$+\ 7$$
$$11\frac{1}{2}$$

3. $9\frac{7}{12}$ **4.** $9\frac{31}{56}$

5. $24\frac{1}{10}$ **6.** $6\frac{7}{12}$

7. $6\frac{1}{3}$ **8.** $24\frac{3}{4}$

9. $17\frac{13}{30}$ **10.** $9\frac{1}{2}$

11. $54\frac{19}{30}$

Page 69

1. Jorge worked 25 hours.

$$3\frac{3}{4} = 3\frac{9}{12}$$
$$5\frac{1}{2} = 5\frac{6}{12}$$
$$6\frac{1}{3} = 6\frac{4}{12}$$
$$3\frac{3}{4} = 3\frac{9}{12}$$
$$+\ 5\frac{2}{3} = 5\frac{8}{12}$$
$$22\frac{36}{12} = 25 \text{ hours}$$

2. Sue worked 30 hours.

$$6\frac{1}{3} = 6\frac{2}{6}$$
$$7\ \ = 7$$
$$6\frac{1}{2} = 6\frac{3}{6}$$
$$4\frac{1}{2} = 4\frac{3}{6}$$
$$+\ 5\frac{2}{3} = 5\frac{4}{6}$$
$$28\frac{12}{6} = 30 \text{ hours}$$

3. Rachel worked 29 hours.

$$6\frac{2}{3} = 6\frac{4}{6}$$
$$5\frac{2}{3} = 5\frac{4}{6}$$
$$5\frac{1}{2} = 5\frac{3}{6}$$
$$5\frac{1}{2} = 5\frac{3}{6}$$
$$+\ 5\frac{2}{3} = 5\frac{4}{6}$$
$$26\frac{18}{6} = 29 \text{ hours}$$

4. 100 hours grand total

$$16$$
$$25$$
$$30$$
$$+\ 29$$
$$100 \text{ hours}$$

Aide	November 5					Hours Worked
	M	Tu	W	Th	F	Total
Tim	$2\frac{2}{3}$	$2\frac{1}{3}$	3	$4\frac{3}{4}$	$3\frac{1}{4}$	16
Jorge	$3\frac{3}{4}$	$5\frac{1}{2}$	$6\frac{1}{3}$	$3\frac{3}{4}$	$5\frac{2}{3}$	25
Sue	$6\frac{1}{3}$	7	$6\frac{1}{2}$	$4\frac{1}{2}$	$5\frac{2}{3}$	30
Rachel	$6\frac{2}{3}$	$5\frac{2}{3}$	$5\frac{1}{2}$	$5\frac{1}{2}$	$5\frac{2}{3}$	29

Page 70

5. $\frac{3}{10}$

Set up a fraction with the number of hours June worked, 15, as the numerator. The grand total, 50, is the denominator. Reduce the fraction to lowest terms.

$$\frac{15}{50} = \frac{3}{10}$$

6. $\frac{1}{3}$ **7.** $\frac{1}{5}$

8. $\frac{1}{12}$

Unit 2 Review, page 71

1. $\frac{2}{3}$
2. $\frac{3}{4}$
3. $\frac{5}{8}$
4. $\frac{14}{15}$
5. $\frac{13}{16}$
6. $\frac{9}{10}$
7. $\frac{17}{25}$
8. $\frac{29}{50}$
9. $\frac{41}{100}$
10. $\frac{1}{2}$
11. $1\frac{1}{9}$
12. $1\frac{1}{11}$
13. $2\frac{1}{5}$
14. 1
15. $1\frac{1}{2}$
16. $1\frac{1}{6}$
17. $\frac{3}{5}$
18. 1
19. 6
20. $27\frac{1}{4}$
21. $50\frac{2}{3}$
22. $4\frac{3}{5}$
23. $11\frac{1}{2}$
24. $23\frac{1}{2}$
25. $24\frac{4}{5}$
26. $22\frac{1}{9}$
27. $11\frac{3}{5}$
28. $\frac{7}{10}$
29. $\frac{11}{16}$
30. $\frac{11}{18}$
31. $\frac{7}{8}$
32. $\frac{5}{14}$
33. $\frac{11}{12}$
34. $\frac{3}{10}$
35. $\frac{14}{15}$
36. $\frac{24}{25}$

Page 72

37. $\frac{1}{2}$
38. 1
39. $1\frac{1}{12}$
40. 2
41. $\frac{5}{8}$
42. $1\frac{1}{12}$
43. 1
44. $1\frac{1}{6}$
45. $1\frac{2}{5}$
46. $\frac{7}{12}$
47. $1\frac{7}{24}$
48. $\frac{25}{28}$
49. $1\frac{7}{15}$
50. $1\frac{1}{6}$
51. $1\frac{7}{12}$
52. $\frac{11}{15}$
53. $1\frac{1}{18}$
54. $1\frac{5}{24}$
55. $10\frac{1}{6}$
56. $14\frac{17}{20}$
57. $17\frac{11}{24}$
58. $11\frac{7}{12}$
59. $11\frac{3}{20}$
60. $15\frac{11}{15}$
61. $17\frac{11}{18}$
62. $46\frac{23}{24}$

Unit 3

Page 73

1. 8
2. 53

$$\begin{array}{r} 92 \\ -\,39 \\ \hline 53 \end{array}$$

3. 22
4. 674
5. 208
6. 575
7. 90
8. $2,178$
9. $1,759$
10. $16,395$

Page 74

11. $\frac{6}{8}$
12. $\frac{5}{10}$

$$\frac{1\times 5}{2\times 5} = \frac{5}{10}$$

13. $\frac{8}{12}$
14. $\frac{9}{15}$
15. $\frac{9}{21}$
16. $\frac{12}{27}$
17. $\frac{3}{30}$
18. $\frac{25}{40}$
19. $\frac{28}{48}$
20. $\frac{20}{60}$
21. $\frac{1}{4} = \frac{1}{4}$

$\frac{1}{2} = \frac{2}{4}$

22. $\frac{2}{3} = \frac{8}{12}$

$\frac{3}{4} = \frac{9}{12}$

$$\frac{2\times 4}{3\times 4} = \frac{8}{12}$$

$$\frac{3\times 3}{4\times 3} = \frac{9}{12}$$

23. $\frac{5}{7} = \frac{25}{35}$

$\frac{3}{5} = \frac{21}{35}$

24. $3\frac{3}{12} = 3\frac{3}{12}$

$1\frac{1}{4} = 1\frac{3}{12}$

25. $2\frac{1}{10} = 2\frac{1}{10}$

$6\frac{3}{5} = 6\frac{6}{10}$

26. $\frac{3}{8} = \frac{9}{24}$

$\frac{5}{6} = \frac{20}{24}$

27. $2\frac{4}{9} = 2\frac{8}{18}$

$5\frac{1}{18} = 5\frac{1}{18}$

28. $\frac{3}{10} = \frac{15}{50}$

$\frac{3}{25} = \frac{6}{50}$

29. $\frac{2}{3} = \frac{6}{9}$

$\frac{2}{9} = \frac{2}{9}$

30. $\frac{1}{6} = \frac{2}{12}$

$\frac{1}{4} = \frac{3}{12}$

31. $\frac{1}{2}$

32. LT

Both fractions can be divided evenly only by 1.

33. $\frac{2}{3}$ **34.** $2\frac{3}{5}$

35. LT   **36.** LT

37. $\frac{1}{2}$ **38.** $\frac{1}{4}$

39. $2\frac{1}{3}$ **40.** $\frac{2}{7}$

Page 75

1. $\frac{3}{8}$

2.–4. Shading should be similar to this.

2. $\frac{2}{5}$

The denominators are the same. Write the denominator under the fraction bar. Subtract the numerators. Write the difference over the denominator. Shade in 2 of the 5 parts in the final figure.

$3 - 1 = 2$

$\frac{3}{5} - \frac{1}{5} = \frac{2}{5}$

3. $\frac{4}{9}$

4. $\frac{1}{6}$

5. $\frac{2}{9}$

6. $\frac{1}{6}$

The denominators are the same. Subtract the numerators.

$4 - 3 = 1$

$\frac{4}{6} - \frac{3}{6} = \frac{1}{6}$

7. $\frac{3}{7}$ **8.** $\frac{2}{5}$

Page 76

1. $\frac{3}{14}$

2. $\frac{7}{16}$

The denominators are the same Subtract the numerators.

$$\begin{array}{r} \frac{9}{16} \\ -\frac{2}{16} \\ \hline \frac{7}{16} \end{array}$$

3. $\frac{6}{25}$ **4.** $\frac{7}{12}$

5. $\frac{2}{7}$ **6.** $\frac{4}{9}$

7. $\frac{7}{10}$ **8.** $\frac{8}{15}$

9. $\frac{7}{20}$ **10.** $\frac{11}{30}$

11. $\frac{3}{50}$ **12.** $\frac{19}{42}$

13. $\frac{3}{11}$ **14.** $\frac{31}{100}$

15. $\frac{23}{75}$ **16.** $\frac{25}{63}$

17. $\frac{9}{35}$ **18.** $\frac{5}{18}$

19. $\frac{1}{4}$ pound

Subtract to find how much is left.

$\frac{3}{4} - \frac{2}{4} = \frac{1}{4}$

20. $\frac{3}{8}$ yard

$\frac{7}{8} - \frac{4}{8} = \frac{3}{8}$

Page 77

1. $\frac{1}{3}$

2. $\frac{3}{4}$

The denominators are the same. Subtract the numerators. Reduce the answer to lowest terms.

$\frac{10}{12} - \frac{1}{12} = \frac{9}{12}$

$\frac{9}{12} = \frac{9 \div 3}{12 \div 3} = \frac{3}{4}$

3. $\frac{1}{4}$ **4.** $\frac{1}{2}$

5. $\frac{1}{2}$ **6.** $\frac{1}{3}$

7. $\frac{3}{7}$ **8.** $\frac{2}{3}$

9. $\frac{1}{2}$ 10. $\frac{3}{4}$

11. $\frac{1}{5}$ 12. $\frac{3}{4}$

13. $\frac{2}{3}$ 14. $\frac{2}{3}$

15. $\frac{1}{6}$ 16. $\frac{2}{5}$

17. $\frac{1}{2}$ 18. $\frac{3}{4}$

19. $\frac{1}{2}$ ton

Subtract to find how much topsoil is left.

$\frac{3}{4} - \frac{1}{4} = \frac{2}{4} = \frac{2 \div 2}{4 \div 2} = \frac{1}{2}$

20. $\frac{1}{8}$ bushel

$\frac{9}{16} - \frac{7}{16} = \frac{2}{16} = \frac{2 \div 2}{16 \div 2} = \frac{1}{8}$

Page 78

1. $4\frac{1}{2}$

2. $5\frac{1}{4}$

Line up the fractions and whole numbers in columns. Subtract the fractions. Subtract the whole numbers. Reduce the fraction to lowest terms.

$$\begin{array}{r} 10\frac{7}{8} \\ - 5\frac{5}{8} \\ \hline 5\frac{2}{8} = 5\frac{1}{4} \end{array}$$

3. $6\frac{1}{2}$ 4. $7\frac{1}{4}$

5. $3\frac{3}{4}$ 6. $11\frac{1}{7}$

7. $7\frac{1}{2}$ 8. $4\frac{1}{5}$

9. $4\frac{1}{10}$ 10. $3\frac{3}{5}$

11. $11\frac{3}{16}$ 12. $6\frac{1}{5}$

13. $14\frac{2}{3}$

14. $1\frac{1}{2}$ yards

Subtract to find how many yards are left.

$$\begin{array}{r} 2\frac{7}{8} \\ - 1\frac{3}{8} \\ \hline 1\frac{4}{8} = 1\frac{1}{2} \end{array}$$

15. $6\frac{1}{2}$ yards

$$\begin{array}{r} 12\frac{3}{4} \\ - 6\frac{1}{4} \\ \hline 6\frac{2}{4} = 6\frac{1}{2} \end{array}$$

Page 79

1. $2\frac{1}{2}$ pounds

Subtract how much puppy food she has from how much she needs.

$$\begin{array}{r} 12\frac{7}{8} \\ - 10\frac{3}{8} \\ \hline 2\frac{4}{8} = 2\frac{1}{2} \end{array}$$

2. $4\frac{1}{4}$ pounds

Subtract to find how much is left.

$$\begin{array}{r} 14\frac{9}{16} \\ - 10\frac{5}{16} \\ \hline 4\frac{4}{16} = 4\frac{1}{4} \end{array}$$

3. $5\frac{1}{3}$ cups   4. $22\frac{1}{2}$ pounds

$$\begin{array}{r} 15\frac{2}{3} \\ - 10\frac{1}{3} \\ \hline 5\frac{1}{3} \end{array} \qquad \begin{array}{r} 50\frac{3}{4} \\ - 28\frac{1}{4} \\ \hline 22\frac{2}{4} = 22\frac{1}{2} \end{array}$$

Page 80

1. $3\frac{1}{8}$

2. $9\frac{1}{2}$

Line up the fractions. Subtract the fractions. Bring down the whole number. Reduce the fraction to lowest terms.

$$\begin{array}{r} 9\frac{7}{12} \\ - \frac{1}{12} \\ \hline 9\frac{6}{12} = 9\frac{1}{2} \end{array}$$

3. $11\frac{1}{3}$ 4. $4\frac{1}{3}$

5. $36\frac{3}{5}$ 6. $42\frac{1}{3}$

7. $50\frac{5}{16}$ 8. $61\frac{2}{7}$

9. $79\frac{9}{100}$ 10. $12\frac{3}{5}$

11. $20\frac{1}{6}$ **12.** $14\frac{1}{2}$

13. $22\frac{7}{17}$ **14.** $59\frac{2}{15}$

15. $32\frac{1}{4}$ **16.** $44\frac{2}{3}$

17. $95\frac{1}{2}$ **18.** $102\frac{3}{5}$

Page 81

1. $3\frac{5}{11}$

2. $8\frac{2}{3}$
Line up the whole numbers. Bring down the fraction. Subtract the whole numbers.

$$15\frac{2}{3}$$
$$\frac{-\ 7\quad}{8\frac{2}{3}}$$

3. $6\frac{1}{7}$ **4.** $2\frac{2}{9}$

5. $25\frac{9}{16}$ **6.** $65\frac{22}{35}$

7. $19\frac{9}{10}$ **8.** $23\frac{27}{50}$

9. $79\frac{73}{100}$ **10.** $9\frac{7}{13}$

11. $15\frac{10}{21}$ **12.** $7\frac{9}{20}$

13. $4\frac{12}{25}$

14. $1\frac{1}{2}$ pounds
Subtract to find how much he has left.

$$3\frac{1}{2}$$
$$\frac{-\ 2\quad}{1\frac{1}{2}}$$

15. $\frac{3}{4}$ gallon

$$1\frac{3}{4}$$
$$\frac{-\ 1\quad}{\frac{3}{4}}$$

Page 82

1. $\frac{3}{4}$ **2.** $\frac{1}{5}$

3. $\frac{2}{3}$ **4.** $\frac{1}{2}$

5. $\frac{8}{9}$ **6.** $\frac{4}{5}$

7. $3\frac{1}{3}$ **8.** $\frac{1}{2}$

9. $6\frac{3}{4}$ **10.** $\frac{4}{7}$

11. $6\frac{3}{5}$ **12.** $4\frac{1}{2}$

13. $\frac{1}{3}$ **14.** $32\frac{1}{4}$

---

15. $1\frac{2}{3}$ **16.** $\frac{1}{5}$

17. $10\frac{10}{13}$ **18.** $\frac{2}{7}$

19. $\frac{27}{35}$ **20.** $\frac{1}{9}$

21. $11\frac{2}{3}$ **22.** $9\frac{1}{7}$

23. $\frac{1}{7}$ **24.** $5\frac{9}{10}$

25. $\frac{1}{4}$ **26.** $13\frac{1}{2}$

27. $\frac{3}{7}$ **28.** $16\frac{3}{5}$

29. $4\frac{41}{49}$ **30.** $\frac{2}{3}$

31. $8\frac{1}{8}$ **32.** $50\frac{99}{100}$

33. $8\frac{2}{3}$ **34.** $\frac{9}{20}$

35. $\frac{1}{5}$ **36.** $3\frac{1}{3}$

Page 83

1. $4\frac{1}{4}$ inches
Point B is $\frac{5}{8}$ inch from 0. Point I is $4\frac{7}{8}$ inches from 0. Subtract. Reduce to lowest terms.

$$4\frac{7}{8}$$
$$\frac{-\ \ \frac{5}{8}}{4\frac{2}{8}=4\frac{1}{4}}$$

2. $5\frac{1}{2}$ inches

$$5\frac{3}{4}$$
$$\frac{-\ \ \frac{1}{4}}{5\frac{2}{4}=5\frac{1}{2}}$$

3. $3\frac{1}{4}$ inches   **4.** $\frac{1}{2}$ inch

$$3\frac{7}{8}\qquad\qquad 1\frac{1}{2}$$
$$\frac{-\ \ \frac{5}{8}}{3\frac{2}{8}=3\frac{1}{4}}\qquad \frac{-\ 1\quad}{\frac{1}{2}}$$

Page 84

5. 1 inch   **6.** 3 inches

$$2\frac{1}{2}\qquad\qquad 5\frac{3}{4}$$
$$\frac{-\ 1\frac{1}{2}}{1}\qquad\quad \frac{-\ 2\frac{3}{4}}{3}$$

7. $1\frac{3}{4}$ inches

$$2\frac{3}{4}$$
$$\underline{-1\phantom{\frac{3}{4}}}$$
$$1\frac{3}{4}$$

8. 1 inch

$$4\frac{7}{8}$$
$$\underline{-3\frac{7}{8}}$$
$$1$$

9. $1\frac{1}{2}$ inches

$$5\frac{3}{4}$$
$$\underline{-4\frac{1}{4}}$$
$$1\frac{2}{4}=1\frac{1}{2}$$

10. 4 inches

$$4\frac{1}{4}$$
$$\underline{-\frac{1}{4}}$$
$$4$$

11. 1 inch

Subtract to find how much molding is left.

$$4\frac{1}{2}$$
$$\underline{-3\frac{1}{2}}$$
$$1$$

12. $3\frac{1}{2}$ inches

$$9\frac{3}{4}$$
$$\underline{-6\frac{1}{4}}$$
$$3\frac{2}{4}=3\frac{1}{2}$$

13. $2\frac{1}{2}$ inches

Subtract to find the difference.

$$36\frac{3}{4}$$
$$\underline{-34\frac{1}{4}}$$
$$2\frac{2}{4}=2\frac{1}{2}$$

14. $3\frac{1}{2}$ inches

$$52\frac{5}{8}$$
$$\underline{-49\frac{1}{8}}$$
$$3\frac{4}{8}=3\frac{1}{2}$$

Page 85

1. $\frac{3}{3}$

2. $\frac{5}{5}$

Change 1 to an improper fraction with 5 as the denominator and the numerator.

3. $\frac{10}{10}$

4. $\frac{7}{7}$

5. $1\frac{2}{2}$

6. $2\frac{5}{5}$

Borrow 1 from 3. $3 - 1 = 2$. Change 1 to an improper fraction with 5 as the denominator. Write $\frac{5}{5}$ next to the 2.

7. $6\frac{10}{10}$

8. $8\frac{12}{12}$

9. $5\frac{7}{7}$

10. $3\frac{6}{6}$

11. $4\frac{4}{4}$

12. $7\frac{9}{9}$

13. $11\frac{3}{3}$

14. $14\frac{16}{16}$

15. $9\frac{14}{14}$

16. $16\frac{15}{15}$

17. $26\frac{5}{5}$

18. $98\frac{12}{12}$

Borrow 1 from 99. $99 - 1 = 98$. Change 1 to an improper fraction with 12 as the denominator. Write $\frac{12}{12}$ next to the 98.

19. $13\frac{17}{17}$

20. $18\frac{20}{20}$

21. $120\frac{8}{8}$

22. $135\frac{11}{11}$

23. $139\frac{18}{18}$

24. $58\frac{21}{21}$

25. $99\frac{25}{25}$

26. $89\frac{30}{30}$

27. $100\frac{49}{49}$

28. $127\frac{100}{100}$

Page 86

1. $\frac{9}{9}$

2. $\frac{6}{6}$

Change 1 to an improper fraction with 6 as the denominator and the numerator.

3. $\frac{10}{10}$

4. $\frac{15}{15}$

5. $\frac{50}{50}$

6. $\frac{4}{7}$

7. $\frac{5}{12}$

Change 1 to an improper fraction with 12 as the denominator. Subtract the fractions.

$$\frac{12}{12} - \frac{7}{12} = \frac{5}{12}$$

8. $\frac{4}{15}$

9. $\frac{13}{25}$

10. $\frac{1}{6}$

11. $\frac{9}{19}$

12. $\frac{5}{11}$

13. $\frac{3}{17}$

14. $\frac{1}{30}$ **15.** $\frac{1}{3}$

16. $\frac{1}{10}$ **17.** $\frac{5}{8}$

18. $\frac{13}{20}$

11. $\frac{20}{21}$ **12.** $\frac{51}{76}$

13. $\frac{89}{100}$ **14.** $\frac{6}{7}$

15. $\frac{4}{5}$ **16.** $\frac{3}{4}$

17. $\frac{3}{5}$ **18.** $\frac{37}{54}$

Page 87

1. $1\frac{1}{3}$

2. $4\frac{1}{4}$

Borrow 1 from 5. $5-1=4$. Change 1 to a fraction with 4 as the denominator. Subtract the fractions. Bring down the whole number.

$$5 \quad = 4\frac{4}{4}$$
$$-\frac{3}{4} = \frac{3}{4}$$
$$\overline{\qquad 4\frac{1}{4}}$$

3. $3\frac{7}{10}$ **4.** $7\frac{5}{9}$

5. $29\frac{7}{18}$ **6.** $25\frac{1}{20}$

7. $36\frac{8}{21}$ **8.** $39\frac{22}{25}$

9. $52\frac{23}{35}$ **10.** $9\frac{2}{5}$

11. $12\frac{1}{6}$ **12.** $14\frac{5}{12}$

13. $20\frac{13}{15}$ **14.** $93\frac{39}{49}$

15. $29\frac{11}{29}$ **16.** $75\frac{47}{50}$

17. $80\frac{38}{75}$ **18.** $24\frac{19}{100}$

Page 88

1. $\frac{2}{3}$

2. $\frac{4}{7}$

Change 1 to an improper fraction with 7 as the denominator. Add $\frac{7}{7}+\frac{2}{7}=\frac{9}{7}$. Subtract.

$$1\frac{2}{7} = \frac{9}{7}$$
$$-\frac{5}{7} = \frac{5}{7}$$
$$\overline{\qquad \frac{4}{7}}$$

3. $\frac{1}{2}$ **4.** $\frac{8}{11}$

5. $\frac{14}{15}$ **6.** $\frac{11}{21}$

7. $\frac{7}{8}$ **8.** $\frac{17}{25}$

9. $\frac{16}{21}$ **10.** $\frac{2}{3}$

Page 89

1. $10\frac{10}{11}$

2. $30\frac{5}{8}$

Since $\frac{5}{8}$ is greater than $\frac{2}{8}$, borrow 1 from 31. Change the borrowed 1 to an improper fraction with 8 as the denominator. $1 = \frac{8}{8}$. Add the mixed number and the fraction. $30\frac{2}{8}+\frac{8}{8} = 30\frac{10}{8}$. Subtract the fractions. Bring down the whole number. Reduce.

$$31\frac{2}{8} = 30\frac{10}{8}$$
$$-\frac{5}{8} = \frac{5}{8}$$
$$\overline{\qquad 30\frac{5}{8}}$$

3. $11\frac{1}{3}$ **4.** $19\frac{3}{4}$

5. $44\frac{7}{15}$ **6.** $6\frac{7}{9}$

7. $3\frac{3}{5}$

Since $\frac{7}{10}$ is greater than $\frac{3}{10}$, borrow 1 from 4. Change the borrowed 1 to an improper fraction with 10 as the denominator. $1 = \frac{10}{10}$. Add the mixed number and the fraction. $3\frac{3}{10}+\frac{10}{10} = 3\frac{13}{10}$. Subtract the fractions. Bring down the whole number. Reduce to lowest terms.

$$4\frac{3}{10} = 3\frac{13}{10}$$
$$-\frac{7}{10} = \frac{7}{10}$$
$$\overline{\qquad 3\frac{6}{10} = 3\frac{3}{5}}$$

8. $5\frac{1}{2}$ **9.** $1\frac{4}{7}$

10. $16\frac{20}{21}$ **11.** $39\frac{7}{9}$

12. $12\frac{13}{15}$ **13.** $71\frac{47}{50}$

14. $17\frac{61}{63}$ **15.** $24\frac{7}{8}$

16. $30\frac{2}{5}$ **17.** $5\frac{5}{9}$

18. $11\frac{1}{5}$

1. $3\frac{2}{3}$

2. $1\frac{1}{2}$

   Since $\frac{3}{4}$ is greater than $\frac{1}{4}$, borrow 1 from the 5. Change the borrowed 1 to an improper fraction with 4 as the denominator. Add the mixed number and the fraction. $4\frac{1}{4}+\frac{4}{4}=4\frac{5}{4}$. Subtract the fractions. Subtract the whole numbers. Reduce.

   $$5\frac{1}{4}=4\frac{5}{4}$$
   $$-3\frac{3}{4}=3\frac{3}{4}$$
   $$\overline{\phantom{-3\frac{3}{4}=}1\frac{2}{4}=1\frac{1}{2}}$$

3. $4\frac{6}{7}$ 4. $1\frac{4}{5}$

5. $4\frac{1}{2}$ 6. $\frac{2}{3}$

7. $9\frac{9}{10}$ 8. $9\frac{4}{5}$

9. $5\frac{15}{19}$

10. $1\frac{1}{2}$ gallons

    Subtract to find how many gallons are left in the gas tank.

    $$18\frac{1}{4}=17\frac{5}{4}$$
    $$-16\frac{3}{4}=16\frac{3}{4}$$
    $$\overline{\phantom{-16\frac{3}{4}=}1\frac{2}{4}=1\frac{1}{2}}$$

11. $6\frac{3}{5}$ inches

    Subtract to find how much higher her record was this year than last year.

    $$59\frac{3}{10}=58\frac{13}{10}$$
    $$-52\frac{7}{10}=52\frac{7}{10}$$
    $$\overline{\phantom{-52\frac{7}{10}=}6\frac{6}{10}=6\frac{3}{5}}$$

1. 4 yards

   Subtract the length used for the back of the chair from $5\frac{1}{2}$ yards.

   $$5\frac{1}{2}$$
   $$-1\frac{1}{2}$$
   $$\overline{\phantom{-1\frac{1}{2}}4}$$

2. $\frac{2}{3}$ yard

   Subtract the length she cut off from $\frac{5}{6}$ yard. Reduce the answer.

   $$\frac{5}{6}$$
   $$-\frac{1}{6}$$
   $$\overline{\frac{4}{6}=\frac{2}{3}}$$

3. $\frac{1}{2}$ foot

   Since two pieces are needed, multiply 2 times 2 feet. Subtract the result from $4\frac{1}{2}$ feet.
   2 x 2 feet = 4 feet

   $$4\frac{1}{2}$$
   $$-4$$
   $$\overline{\frac{1}{2}}$$

4. $1\frac{5}{8}$ yards

   Subtract the amount she needs for the wings from the 3 yards.

   $$3\phantom{\frac{8}{8}}=2\frac{8}{8}$$
   $$-1\frac{3}{8}=1\frac{3}{8}$$
   $$\overline{\phantom{-1\frac{3}{8}=}1\frac{5}{8}}$$

1. 1   2. 7

3. $1\frac{1}{2}$ 4. $1\frac{1}{3}$

5. $4\frac{1}{2}$ 6. 13

7. $12\frac{3}{7}$ 8. 1

9. $\frac{3}{4}$ 10. $8\frac{2}{2}$

11. $5\frac{3}{3}$ 12. $17\frac{9}{9}$

13. $19\frac{10}{10}$ 14. $28\frac{35}{35}$

15. $\frac{1}{4}$ 16. $1\frac{3}{5}$

17. $14\frac{17}{20}$ 18. $19\frac{13}{16}$

19. $4\frac{3}{5}$ 20. 21

21. $4\frac{10}{11}$ 22. $2\frac{4}{5}$

23. $4\frac{4}{9}$ **24.** $30\frac{1}{2}$

25. $\frac{3}{4}$ **26.** 8

27. $18\frac{19}{21}$ **28.** $\frac{2}{3}$

29. $\frac{4}{5}$ **30.** $31\frac{3}{8}$

31. $1\frac{1}{8}$ **32.** $27\frac{3}{50}$

Page 93

1. $\frac{7}{10}$

2. $\frac{5}{12}$

The denominators are different. Since 4 divides evenly into 12, write 12 as the common denominator. Raise $\frac{1}{4}$ to higher terms with 12 as the denominator. Subtract the numerators. Write the difference over the denominator.

$$\begin{array}{r} \frac{8}{12} = \frac{8}{12} \\ -\frac{1}{4} = \frac{3}{12} \\ \hline \frac{5}{12} \end{array}$$

3. $\frac{4}{9}$ **4.** $\frac{9}{14}$

5. $\frac{4}{15}$ **6.** $\frac{5}{18}$

7. $\frac{11}{20}$ **8.** $\frac{3}{16}$

9. $\frac{3}{20}$ **10.** $\frac{1}{9}$

11. $\frac{1}{5}$ **12.** $\frac{1}{5}$

13. $\frac{2}{7}$

Page 94

1. $\frac{1}{4}$

2. $\frac{3}{8}$

Raise $\frac{1}{2}$ to higher terms with 8 as the denominator. Subtract. Reduce.

$$\begin{array}{r} \frac{1}{2} = \frac{4}{8} \\ -\frac{1}{8} = \frac{1}{8} \\ \hline \frac{3}{8} \end{array}$$

3. $\frac{5}{9}$ **4.** $\frac{1}{2}$

5. $\frac{9}{16}$ **6.** $\frac{3}{4}$

7. $\frac{5}{18}$ **8.** $\frac{1}{3}$

9. $\frac{5}{8}$ **10.** $\frac{13}{25}$

11. $\frac{2}{3}$ **12.** $\frac{2}{15}$

13. $\frac{9}{20}$

14. $\frac{1}{4}$ hour

Subtract to find how much more time Janie spent writing.

$$\begin{array}{r} \frac{1}{2} = \frac{2}{4} \\ -\frac{1}{4} = \frac{1}{4} \\ \hline \frac{1}{4} \end{array}$$

15. $\frac{1}{10}$ mile

Subtract to find how much farther Viola walked.

$$\begin{array}{r} \frac{4}{5} = \frac{8}{10} \\ -\frac{7}{10} = \frac{7}{10} \\ \hline \frac{1}{10} \end{array}$$

Page 95

1. $\frac{1}{10}$

2. $\frac{5}{12}$

Multiply to find the common denominator. $3 \times 4 = 12$. Raise each fraction to higher terms with 12 as the denominator. Subtract.

$$\begin{array}{r} \frac{3}{4} = \frac{9}{12} \\ -\frac{1}{3} = \frac{4}{12} \\ \hline \frac{5}{12} \end{array}$$

3. $\frac{1}{6}$ **4.** $\frac{2}{15}$

5. $\frac{19}{30}$ **6.** $\frac{1}{24}$

7. $\frac{1}{14}$ **8.** $\frac{11}{30}$

9. $\frac{7}{20}$ **10.** $\frac{11}{42}$

11. $\frac{8}{21}$ **12.** $\frac{3}{14}$

13. $\frac{5}{36}$ **14.** $\frac{6}{35}$

15. $\frac{5}{18}$ **16.** $\frac{11}{20}$

17. $\frac{7}{20}$ **18.** $\frac{7}{24}$

Page 96

1. $\frac{7}{12}$

2. $\frac{7}{18}$

List the multiples of each denominator. The smallest number on both lists is 18. Raise each fraction to higher terms with 18 as the LCD. Subtract.

$\frac{5}{6}$ 12   ⑱   24   30

$\frac{4}{9}$ ⑱   27   36

$$\begin{aligned} \frac{5}{6} &= \frac{15}{18} \\ -\frac{4}{9} &= \frac{8}{18} \\ \hline &\frac{7}{18} \end{aligned}$$

3. $\frac{9}{20}$ 4. $\frac{7}{24}$

5. $\frac{11}{36}$ 6. $\frac{7}{30}$

7. $\frac{7}{36}$ 8. $\frac{17}{45}$

9. $\frac{35}{48}$

Page 97

1. $\frac{17}{40}$ 2. $\frac{17}{24}$

3. $\frac{1}{8}$ 4. $\frac{9}{28}$

5. $\frac{11}{40}$ 6. $\frac{6}{35}$

7. $\frac{1}{10}$ 8. $\frac{13}{42}$

9. $\frac{5}{14}$ 10. $\frac{17}{39}$

11. $\frac{7}{24}$ 12. $\frac{5}{12}$

13. $\frac{5}{9}$ 14. $\frac{4}{9}$

15. $\frac{9}{20}$ 16. $\frac{7}{12}$

17. $\frac{1}{18}$ 18. $\frac{7}{30}$

19. $\frac{17}{45}$ 20. $\frac{11}{36}$

21. $\frac{1}{20}$ 22. $\frac{1}{5}$

23. $\frac{1}{12}$ 24. $\frac{17}{30}$

25. $\frac{17}{36}$ 26. $\frac{2}{3}$

Page 98

1. $\frac{2}{5}$ mile

Subtract to find how much farther Junction is from Fort Smith.

$$\begin{aligned} & 3\frac{7}{10} \\ -\ & 3\frac{3}{10} \\ \hline & \frac{4}{10} = \frac{2}{5} \end{aligned}$$

2. $8\frac{7}{10}$ miles

Subtract the distance from Fort Smith to Newton from the distance from Fort Smith to Keene.

$$\begin{aligned} 12 \quad\ &= 11\frac{10}{10} \\ -\ 3\frac{3}{10} &= 3\frac{3}{10} \\ \hline &\ 8\frac{7}{10} \end{aligned}$$

Page 99

3. $1\frac{1}{10}$ miles

Subtract to find how many more miles the distance is from Fort Smith to Keene.

$$\begin{aligned} 12 \quad\ &= 11\frac{10}{10} \\ -\ 10\frac{9}{10} &= 10\frac{9}{10} \\ \hline &\ 1\frac{1}{10} \end{aligned}$$

4. $7\frac{7}{10}$ miles

Add the distance from Fort Smith to Junction to the distance from Junction to Newton.

$$\begin{aligned} 4 \quad\ &= 3\frac{10}{10} \\ +\ 3\frac{7}{10} &= 3\frac{7}{10} \\ \hline 6\frac{17}{10} &= 7\frac{7}{10} \end{aligned}$$

5. $7\frac{9}{10}$ miles

Subtract to find how many miles he will save.

$$\begin{aligned} 15 \quad\ &= 14\frac{10}{10} \\ -\ 7\frac{1}{10} &= 7\frac{1}{10} \\ \hline &\ 7\frac{9}{10} \end{aligned}$$

6. $4\frac{1}{2}$ miles

Subtract to find how much shorter it is to cross the lake by boat.

$$10 \quad = 9\frac{2}{2}$$
$$-\ 5\frac{1}{2} = 5\frac{1}{2}$$
$$\overline{\qquad 4\frac{1}{2}}$$

7. $\frac{9}{10}$ mile

Subtract the distance from Wood to Keene from the distance from Wood to Newton.

$$6 \quad = 5\frac{10}{10}$$
$$-5\frac{1}{10} = 5\frac{1}{10}$$
$$\overline{\qquad \frac{9}{10}}$$

8. She lives closer to Keene.

Subtract the distance Bob's sister lives from Keene from the total distance between Wood and Keene. She lives 3 miles from Wood.

$$5\frac{1}{10}$$
$$-\ 2\frac{1}{10}$$
$$\overline{\qquad 3}$$

9. $2\frac{4}{5}$ miles

Subtract the distance at which Bob's car broke down from Keene from the total distance between Keene and Wood.

$$5\frac{1}{10} = 4\frac{11}{10}$$
$$-2\frac{3}{10} = 2\frac{3}{10}$$
$$\overline{\qquad 2\frac{8}{10} = 2\frac{4}{5}}$$

10. $38\frac{2}{5}$ miles

Subtract to find how many miles he drove this week.

$$42\frac{1}{10} = 41\frac{11}{10}$$
$$-\ 3\frac{7}{10} = \ 3\frac{7}{10}$$
$$\overline{\qquad 38\frac{4}{10} = 38\ \frac{2}{5}}$$

Page 100

1. $2\frac{1}{8}$

2. $4\frac{1}{2}$

Since 3 divides evenly into 6, use 6 as the common denominator. Raise $\frac{2}{3}$ to higher terms with 6 as the denominator. Subtract the fractions. Subtract the whole numbers. Reduce to lowest terms.

$$7\frac{2}{3} = 7\frac{4}{6}$$
$$-3\frac{1}{6} = 3\frac{1}{6}$$
$$\overline{\qquad 4\frac{3}{6} = 4\frac{1}{2}}$$

3. $3\frac{1}{4}$ **4.** $2\frac{1}{2}$

5. $10\frac{5}{12}$ **6.** $5\frac{7}{30}$

7. $12\frac{11}{30}$ **8.** $12\frac{1}{18}$

9. $7\frac{1}{8}$

10. $2\frac{1}{12}$ yards

Subtract the amount she will use for blocks from the total amount she has.

$$3\frac{3}{4} = 3\frac{9}{12}$$
$$-1\frac{2}{3} = 1\frac{8}{12}$$
$$\overline{\qquad 2\frac{1}{12}}$$

11. $3\frac{5}{24}$ yards

$$4\frac{7}{8} = 4\frac{21}{24}$$
$$-1\frac{2}{3} = 1\frac{16}{24}$$
$$\overline{\qquad 3\frac{5}{24}}$$

Page 101

1. $\frac{7}{9}$

2. $2\frac{5}{8}$

Since 2 will divide evenly into 8, use 8 as the common denominator. Raise $\frac{1}{2}$ to higher terms with 8 as the denominator. Since $\frac{7}{8}$ is greater than $\frac{4}{8}$, borrow 1 from the 9. Change it to $\frac{8}{8}$. Subtract.

$$9\frac{1}{2} = 9\frac{4}{8} = 8\frac{12}{8}$$
$$-6\frac{7}{8} = 6\frac{7}{8} = 6\frac{7}{8}$$
$$\overline{\qquad\qquad\qquad 2\frac{5}{8}}$$

3. $7\frac{19}{24}$ **4.** $8\frac{17}{36}$

5. $14\frac{1}{2}$ **6.** $7\frac{11}{24}$

7. $13\frac{15}{22}$ **8.** $15\frac{13}{15}$

9. $\frac{11}{20}$ **10.** $35\frac{14}{25}$

11. $36\frac{13}{18}$ **12.** $56\frac{7}{10}$

Page 102

1. $3\frac{14}{15}$

2. $2\frac{20}{21}$

Find a common denominator.
$7 \times 3 = 21$. Raise both fractions to higher terms with a denominator of 21. Since $\frac{7}{21}$ is

greater than $\frac{6}{21}$, borrow 1 from 4.
$4\frac{6}{21} = 3\frac{27}{21}$. Subtract the fractions.
Subtract the whole numbers.

$$4\frac{2}{7} = 4\frac{6}{21} = 3\frac{27}{21}$$
$$-1\frac{1}{3} = 1\frac{7}{21} = 1\frac{7}{21}$$
$$\overline{\hspace{2em} 2\frac{20}{21}}$$

3. $5\frac{9}{10}$ **4.** $6\frac{1}{4}$

5. $\frac{13}{24}$ **6.** $3\frac{7}{10}$

7. $12\frac{9}{10}$ **8.** $5\frac{20}{21}$

9. $5\frac{14}{15}$

Page 103

1. $\frac{4}{15}$

2. $2\frac{21}{40}$

Find a common denominator.
$5 \times 8 = 40$. Since $\frac{35}{40}$ is greater than $\frac{16}{40}$, borrow 1 from the 3. Add the mixed number and the fraction.
$2\frac{16}{40} + \frac{40}{40} = 2\frac{56}{40}$. Subtract the fractions.
Bring down the whole number.

$$3\frac{2}{5} = 3\frac{16}{40} = 2\frac{56}{40}$$
$$- \frac{7}{8} = \frac{35}{40} = \frac{35}{40}$$
$$\overline{\hspace{2em} 2\frac{21}{40}}$$

3. $\frac{19}{28}$ **4.** $3\frac{5}{6}$

5. $8\frac{7}{8}$ **6.** $\frac{17}{18}$

7. $4\frac{1}{2}$ **8.** $9\frac{7}{12}$

9. $1\frac{31}{33}$

Unit 3 Review, page 104

1. $\frac{9}{13}$ **2.** $\frac{3}{5}$

3. $\frac{1}{4}$ **4.** $\frac{1}{5}$

5. $\frac{1}{3}$ **6.** $\frac{1}{3}$

7. $\frac{2}{3}$ **8.** $\frac{1}{3}$

9. $\frac{1}{2}$ **10.** $8\frac{1}{5}$

11. $2\frac{1}{2}$ **12.** $14\frac{3}{8}$

13. $3\frac{2}{3}$ **14.** $6\frac{1}{5}$

15. $10\frac{1}{4}$ **16.** $1\frac{3}{5}$

17. $18\frac{12}{35}$ **18.** $2\frac{3}{8}$

19. $5\frac{1}{10}$ **20.** $8\frac{2}{3}$

21. $30\frac{47}{50}$ **22.** $5\frac{1}{6}$

23. $8\frac{10}{11}$ **24.** $\frac{1}{6}$

25. $\frac{3}{10}$ **26.** $\frac{1}{4}$

27. $\frac{2}{3}$

Page 105

28. $3\frac{1}{2}$ **29.** $5\frac{2}{3}$

30. $2\frac{1}{4}$ **31.** $5\frac{7}{9}$

32. $7\frac{7}{10}$ **33.** $9\frac{3}{5}$

34. $17\frac{5}{6}$ **35.** $10\frac{3}{7}$

36. $12\frac{7}{12}$ **37.** $3\frac{2}{3}$

38. $\frac{2}{3}$ **39.** $6\frac{1}{2}$

40. $8\frac{10}{11}$ **41.** $\frac{7}{9}$

42. $5\frac{3}{5}$ **43.** $1\frac{3}{5}$

44. $\frac{2}{3}$ **45.** $4\frac{4}{5}$

46. $\frac{1}{2}$ **47.** $\frac{1}{14}$

48. $\frac{1}{6}$ **49.** $\frac{2}{5}$

50. $\frac{1}{6}$ **51.** $\frac{3}{20}$

52. $\frac{7}{30}$ **53.** $\frac{11}{42}$

54. $\frac{5}{24}$ **55.** $\frac{7}{12}$

56. $\frac{1}{20}$ **57.** $\frac{13}{24}$

58. $\frac{13}{40}$

Page 106

59. $3\frac{1}{12}$ **60.** $3\frac{1}{2}$

61. $11\frac{7}{12}$ **62.** $1\frac{1}{4}$

63. $5\frac{1}{30}$ **64.** $19\frac{1}{20}$

65. $5\frac{4}{9}$ **66.** $5\frac{7}{12}$

67. $7\frac{1}{15}$ **68.** $8\frac{13}{14}$

69. $1\frac{7}{8}$ **70.** $12\frac{7}{20}$

71. $3\frac{13}{36}$ **72.** $12\frac{26}{33}$

73. $13\frac{17}{30}$ **74.** $\frac{35}{36}$

75. $4\frac{31}{40}$ **76.** $1\frac{47}{60}$

Unit 4

Page 107

1. 12 **2.** 12

$$\begin{array}{r} 6 \\ \times\, 2 \\ \hline 12 \end{array}$$

3. 5 **4.** 18

5. 21 **6.** 20

7. 6 **8.** 40

9. 27 **10.** 9

11. 42 **12.** 32

13. 63 **14.** 15

15. 10 **16.** 16

Page 108

17. $\frac{1}{6}$ **18.** $\frac{3}{10}$

$$\frac{6 \div 2}{20 \div 2} = \frac{3}{10}$$

19. LT **20.** $\frac{9}{16}$

21. $\frac{1}{3}$ **22.** $\frac{3}{7}$

23. LT **24.** $\frac{4}{5}$

25. $\frac{4}{15}$ **26.** $\frac{1}{3}$

27. $\frac{4}{5}$ **28.** LT

29. $\frac{1}{7}$ **30.** $\frac{1}{2}$

31. $\frac{1}{5}$ **32.** $5\frac{1}{2}$

33. $3\frac{1}{5}$

Divide the numerator, 16, by the denominator, 5. Write the remainder as a fraction.

$$5\overline{)16} \quad \begin{array}{r} 3 \\ \end{array} = 3\frac{1}{5}$$
$$\begin{array}{r} -\,15 \\ \hline 1 \end{array}$$

34. 18 **35.** $9\frac{2}{3}$

36. $8\frac{1}{2}$ **37.** $3\frac{1}{3}$

38. $3\frac{3}{8}$ **39.** 6

40. $5\frac{4}{9}$ **41.** $5\frac{3}{10}$

42. 6 **43.** 2

44. $6\frac{1}{4}$ **45.** $2\frac{1}{7}$

46. $1\frac{1}{20}$ **47.** $3\frac{1}{8}$

48. 4 **49.** $11\frac{1}{2}$

50. 3 **51.** $4\frac{2}{13}$

Page 109

1. $\frac{1}{6}$

2.–6. Shading should be similar to this.

2. $\frac{1}{8}$

Set up the problem. $\frac{1}{2} \times \frac{1}{4}$.
Multiply the numerators.
Multiply the denominators.

$$\frac{1}{2} \times \frac{1}{4} = \frac{1}{8}$$

3. $\frac{3}{8}$

4. $\frac{2}{9}$

5. $\frac{3}{10}$

6. $\frac{3}{12}$ or $\frac{1}{4}$ (lowest terms)

7. $\frac{3}{16}$ **8.** $\frac{7}{24}$

9. $\frac{1}{10}$

Page 110

1. $\frac{1}{10}$

2. $\frac{5}{12}$

Multiply the numerators.

Multiply the denominators.

$\frac{1}{2} \times \frac{5}{6} = \frac{5}{12}$

3. $\frac{1}{7}$ **4.** $\frac{1}{16}$

5. $\frac{1}{2}$ **6.** $\frac{4}{21}$

7. $\frac{9}{20}$ **8.** $\frac{4}{81}$

9. $\frac{12}{49}$ **10.** $\frac{5}{24}$

11. $\frac{4}{25}$ **12.** $\frac{1}{16}$

13. $\frac{5}{27}$ **14.** $\frac{1}{9}$

15. $\frac{2}{7}$ **16.** $\frac{21}{32}$

17. $\frac{5}{36}$ **18.** $\frac{1}{4}$

19. $\frac{30}{49}$ **20.** $\frac{1}{5}$

21. $\frac{9}{16}$ **22.** $\frac{1}{42}$

23. $\frac{2}{3}$ **24.** $\frac{15}{64}$

25. $\frac{3}{8}$ pound   **26.** $\frac{1}{6}$ quart

$\frac{3}{4} \times \frac{1}{2} = \frac{3}{8}$ $\frac{1}{2} \times \frac{1}{3} = \frac{1}{6}$

Page 111

1. $\frac{1}{10}$

Cassettes are $\frac{2}{5}$ of the total sales. $\frac{1}{4}$ of the cassettes sold are rap. Multiply.

$\frac{1}{4} \times \frac{2}{5} = \frac{2}{20} = \frac{2 \div 2}{20 \div 2} = \frac{1}{10}$

2. $\frac{1}{20}$

$\frac{1}{8} \times \frac{2}{5} = \frac{2}{40} = \frac{2 \div 2}{40 \div 2} = \frac{1}{20}$

3. $\frac{3}{100}$

$\frac{1}{5} \times \frac{3}{20} = \frac{3}{100}$

4. $\frac{9}{100}$

$\frac{3}{5} \times \frac{3}{20} = \frac{9}{100}$

5. $\frac{3}{20}$

$\frac{1}{3} \times \frac{9}{20} = \frac{9}{60} = \frac{9 \div 3}{60 \div 3} = \frac{3}{20}$

6. $\frac{1}{5}$

$\frac{4}{9} \times \frac{9}{20} = \frac{36}{180} = \frac{36 \div 36}{180 \div 36} = \frac{1}{5}$

Page 112

1. $\frac{1}{18}$

2. $\frac{1}{15}$

Multiply the first two numerators.
$1 \times 2 = 2$. Multiply 2 by the last numerator. $2 \times 1 = 2$. Multiply the first two denominators. $2 \times 5 = 10$. Multiply 10 by the last denominator. $10 \times 3 = 30$. Reduce the answer to lowest terms.

$\frac{1}{2} \times \frac{2}{5} \times \frac{1}{3} = \frac{2}{30} = \frac{2 \div 2}{30 \div 2} = \frac{1}{15}$

3. $\frac{3}{8}$ **4.** $\frac{1}{30}$

5. $\frac{4}{21}$ **6.** $\frac{5}{32}$

7. $\frac{3}{50}$ **8.** $\frac{1}{27}$

9. $\frac{4}{9}$ **10.** $\frac{2}{15}$

11. $\frac{1}{7}$ **12.** $\frac{1}{8}$

13. $\frac{6}{49}$ **14.** $\frac{7}{50}$

15. $\frac{3}{100}$ **16.** $\frac{5}{16}$

17. $\frac{1}{15}$ **18.** $\frac{1}{30}$

19. $\frac{1}{12}$ **20.** $\frac{3}{26}$

21. $\frac{3}{32}$

Page 113

1. $\frac{1}{15}$

2. $\frac{3}{14}$

Cancel by dividing the numerator of the second fraction, 4, and the denominator of the first fraction, 8, by 4. Multiply the numerators of the new fractions. Multiply the denominators of the new fractions.

$$\frac{3}{8} \times \frac{4}{7} = \frac{3}{\cancel{8}_{2}} \times \frac{\cancel{4}^{1}}{7} = \frac{3}{14}$$

3. $\frac{3}{7}$ **4.** $\frac{4}{7}$

5. $\frac{9}{14}$ **6.** $\frac{6}{49}$

7. $\frac{1}{6}$ **8.** $\frac{8}{39}$

9. $\frac{3}{32}$ **10.** $\frac{2}{17}$

11. $\frac{8}{63}$ **12.** $\frac{27}{50}$

13. $\frac{5}{54}$ **14.** $\frac{3}{28}$

15. $\frac{22}{75}$ **16.** $\frac{4}{33}$

17. $\frac{7}{55}$ **18.** $\frac{9}{28}$

19. $\frac{1}{36}$ **20.** $\frac{8}{105}$

21. $\frac{4}{45}$ **22.** $\frac{3}{35}$

23. $\frac{3}{10}$ **24.** $\frac{14}{19}$

Page 114

1. $\frac{1}{2}$

2. $\frac{1}{2}$

Cancel once by dividing the numerator of the first fraction, 4, and the denominator of the second fraction, 16, by 4. Write the new numbers. Cancel again by dividing the numerator of the second fraction, 10, and the denominator of the first fraction, 5, by 5. Multiply the new numerators and denominators.

$$\frac{\cancel{4}^{1}}{\cancel{5}_{1}} \times \frac{\cancel{10}^{2}}{\cancel{16}_{4}} = \frac{2}{4} = \frac{1}{2}$$

3. $\frac{3}{5}$ **4.** $\frac{3}{7}$

---

5. $\frac{7}{8}$ **6.** $\frac{2}{9}$

7. $\frac{2}{5}$ **8.** $\frac{3}{4}$

9. $\frac{2}{21}$ **10.** $\frac{2}{3}$

11. $\frac{1}{3}$ **12.** $\frac{4}{15}$

13. $\frac{1}{3}$ **14.** $\frac{1}{6}$

15. $\frac{3}{14}$ **16.** $\frac{1}{10}$

17. $\frac{5}{8}$ inch

$$\frac{\cancel{15}^{5}}{\cancel{16}_{8}} \times \frac{\cancel{2}^{1}}{\cancel{3}_{1}} = \frac{5}{8}$$

18. $\frac{1}{2}$ hour

$$\frac{\cancel{3}^{1}}{\cancel{4}_{2}} \times \frac{\cancel{2}^{1}}{\cancel{3}_{1}} = \frac{1}{2}$$

Page 115

1. $\frac{8}{75}$

2. $\frac{1}{9}$

Divide the numerator of the first fraction, 21, and the denominator of the third fraction, 9, by 3. Divide the new numerator of the first fraction, 7, and the denominator of the second fraction, 35, by 7. Cancel the numerator of the third fraction, 5, and the denominator of the second fraction, 5, by 5. Divide the numerator of the second fraction, 8, and the denominator of the first fraction, 24, by 8. Multiply the new numerators and denominators.

$$\frac{21}{24} \times \frac{8}{35} \times \frac{5}{9} = \frac{\cancel{21}}{\cancel{24}_{3}} \times \frac{\cancel{8}^{1}}{\cancel{35}_{\cancel{5}}} \times \frac{\cancel{5}^{1}}{\cancel{9}_{3}} = \frac{1}{9}$$

3. $\frac{3}{5}$ **4.** $\frac{1}{15}$

5. $\frac{5}{84}$ **6.** $\frac{5}{18}$

7. $\frac{3}{5}$ **8.** $\frac{3}{112}$

9. $\frac{1}{180}$ **10.** $\frac{1}{2}$

11. $\frac{2}{27}$ **12.** $\frac{4}{7}$

13. $\frac{1}{4}$ **14.** $\frac{1}{12}$

15. $\frac{2}{45}$ **16.** $\frac{1}{3}$

17. $\frac{1}{40}$ **18.** $\frac{6}{35}$

Page 116

1. $\frac{3}{8}$ **2.** $\frac{1}{3}$

3. 1   **4.** $\frac{1}{48}$

5. $\frac{1}{2}$ **6.** $\frac{1}{4}$

7. $1\frac{1}{7}$ **8.** $\frac{3}{32}$

9. $\frac{1}{2}$ **10.** $\frac{1}{4}$

11. $\frac{8}{21}$ **12.** $\frac{1}{3}$

13. $\frac{10}{13}$ **14.** $\frac{2}{7}$

15. $\frac{1}{5}$ **16.** $\frac{4}{27}$

17. $\frac{1}{8}$ **18.** $\frac{1}{2}$

19. $\frac{3}{5}$ **20.** $\frac{4}{15}$

21. $\frac{1}{12}$ **22.** $\frac{1}{6}$

23. $\frac{1}{18}$ **24.** $\frac{1}{12}$

25. $\frac{4}{15}$ **26.** $\frac{3}{28}$

27. $\frac{1}{60}$ **28.** $\frac{1}{60}$

29. $\frac{1}{3}$ **30.** $\frac{1}{10}$

31. $\frac{1}{90}$ **32.** $\frac{1}{2}$

33. $\frac{4}{7}$

34. $\frac{3}{8}$ pound   **35.** $\frac{1}{3}$ gallon

$$\begin{array}{r} \frac{13}{16} \\ -\ \frac{7}{16} \\ \hline \frac{6}{16} = \frac{3}{8} \end{array}$$

$$\frac{1}{\cancel{2}} \times \frac{\cancel{2}}{3} = \frac{1}{3}$$

Page 117

1. 18 inches

2. 12 inches

Set up the problem. Write 36 as an improper fraction with a denominator of 1. Cancel. Multiply the new fractions. The answer is an improper fraction. Change to a whole number by dividing the numerator by the denominator.

$$\frac{1}{3} \times 36 = \frac{1}{\cancel{3}} \times \frac{\cancel{36}}{1} = \frac{12}{1} = 12$$

3. 27 inches   **4.** 24 inches
5. 12 hours   **6.** 8 hours
7. 18 hours   **8.** 6 days
9. 13 weeks   **10.** 39 weeks

Page 118

1. 10

2. 5

Set up the problem. Write 10 as $\frac{10}{1}$. Cancel by dividing the numerator, 10, and the denominator, 2, by 2. Multiply the new numerators and denominators. The answer is an improper fraction. Change to a mixed number by dividing the numerator by the denominator.

$$10 \times \frac{1}{2} = \frac{\cancel{10}^{5}}{1} \times \frac{1}{\cancel{2}} = \frac{5}{1} = 5$$

3. 6   **4.** 3

5. 4   **6.** 6

7. 3   **8.** 16

9. $5\frac{1}{2}$ **10.** $3\frac{7}{9}$

11. $9\frac{3}{8}$ **12.** $6\frac{2}{3}$

13. $1\frac{2}{7}$ **14.** $16\frac{1}{5}$

15. $16\frac{2}{3}$ **16.** $9\frac{1}{2}$

17. 6   **18.** 6

19. $\frac{1}{2}$ **20.** $\frac{5}{6}$

Page 119

1. $9\frac{1}{3}$

2. 22

Write $4\frac{2}{5}$ as an improper fraction. Write 5 as an improper fraction. Cancel. Multiply. Write the answer as a whole number.

$$4\frac{2}{5} \times 5 = \frac{22}{\cancel{5}} \times \frac{\cancel{5}^{1}}{1} = \frac{22}{1} = 22$$

3. $11\frac{1}{4}$ **4.** 23

5. 20   **6.** 55

7. 51   **8.** $19\frac{1}{2}$

9. $17\frac{1}{2}$ **10.** $31\frac{1}{3}$

11. $24\frac{4}{5}$ **12.** 40

13. $3\frac{2}{5}$ **14.** $14\frac{1}{3}$

15. $15\frac{3}{4}$ **16.** $19\frac{3}{5}$

17. 54   **18.** 21

19. $34\frac{4}{5}$ **20.** 50

21. 25 orders

$$10 \times 2\frac{1}{2} = \frac{\overset{5}{\cancel{10}}}{1} \times \frac{5}{\underset{1}{\cancel{2}}} = \frac{25}{1} = 25$$

22. $13\frac{1}{2}$ miles

$$2\frac{7}{10} \times 5 = \frac{27}{\underset{2}{\cancel{10}}} \times \frac{\overset{1}{\cancel{5}}}{1} = \frac{27}{2} = 13\frac{1}{2}$$

Page 120

1. $12 per hour

Marina's regular pay rate is $8 per hour.
Multiply 8 by $1\frac{1}{2}$ to find her overtime rate.

$$8 \times 1\frac{1}{2} = \frac{\overset{4}{\cancel{8}}}{1} \times \frac{3}{\underset{1}{\cancel{2}}} = \frac{12}{1} = 12$$

2. $18 per hour

$$12 \times 1\frac{1}{2} = \frac{\overset{6}{\cancel{12}}}{1} \times \frac{3}{\underset{1}{\cancel{2}}} = \frac{18}{1} = 18$$

3. $15 per hour

$$10 \times 1\frac{1}{2} = \frac{\overset{5}{\cancel{10}}}{1} \times \frac{3}{\underset{1}{\cancel{2}}} = \frac{15}{1} = 15$$

4. $24 per hour

$$16 \times 1\frac{1}{2} = \frac{\overset{8}{\cancel{16}}}{1} \times \frac{3}{\underset{1}{\cancel{2}}} = \frac{24}{1} = 24$$

Marcy's Restaurant

Employee	Regular	Overtime
Kenichi	$ 6	$ 9
Marina	$ 8	$ 12
Nestor	$ 12	$ 18
Rita	$ 10	$ 15
Edward	$ 16	$ 24

Page 121

1. $21

Oscar's overtime pay rate is $6 per hour. Multiply 6 by $3\frac{1}{2}$ to find Oscar's overtime pay.

$$6 \times 3\frac{1}{2} = \frac{\overset{3}{\cancel{6}}}{1} \times \frac{7}{\underset{1}{\cancel{2}}} = \frac{21}{1} = 21$$

2. $51

$$9 \times 5\frac{2}{3} = \frac{\overset{3}{\cancel{9}}}{1} \times \frac{17}{\underset{1}{\cancel{3}}} = \frac{51}{1} = 51$$

3. $35

$$15 \times 2\frac{1}{3} = \frac{\overset{5}{\cancel{15}}}{1} \times \frac{7}{\underset{1}{\cancel{3}}} = \frac{35}{1} = 35$$

4. $153

$$18 \times 8\frac{1}{2} = \frac{\overset{9}{\cancel{18}}}{1} \times \frac{17}{\underset{1}{\cancel{2}}} = \frac{153}{1} = 153$$

EMPLOYEE	OVERTIME RATE	OVERTIME HOURS	OVERTIME PAY
Oscar	$ 6	$3\frac{1}{2}$	$ 21
Carl	$ 9	$5\frac{2}{3}$	$ 51
Ruthie	$ 15	$2\frac{1}{3}$	$ 35
James	$ 18	$8\frac{1}{2}$	$153
Mike	$ 12	$5\frac{3}{4}$	$ 69

Page 122

1. $2\frac{2}{5}$

2. $3\frac{1}{8}$

Write $4\frac{3}{8}$ as an improper fraction.
Cancel. Multiply the numerators. Multiply the denominators. Change the answer to a mixed number.

$$4\frac{3}{8} \times \frac{5}{7} = \frac{\overset{5}{\cancel{35}}}{8} \times \frac{5}{\underset{1}{\cancel{7}}} = \frac{25}{8} = 3\frac{1}{8}$$

3. $1\frac{7}{20}$ **4.** $5\frac{1}{3}$

5. $\frac{3}{4}$ **6.** $\frac{1}{4}$

7. $3\frac{4}{5}$ **8.** $\frac{23}{49}$

9. $1\frac{9}{16}$ **10.** $2\frac{5}{6}$

11. $5\frac{1}{10}$ **12.** $3\frac{12}{13}$

13. $4\frac{5}{6}$ **14.** $2\frac{11}{16}$

15. $4\frac{5}{24}$ **16.** $1\frac{14}{15}$

17. $1\frac{11}{27}$ **18.** $1\frac{9}{11}$

Page 123

1. $16\frac{1}{3}$

197

2. 35

Write the mixed numbers as improper fractions. Cancel. Multiply. Change the answer to a whole number.

$$9\frac{4}{5} \times 3\frac{4}{7} = \frac{\overset{7}{\cancel{49}}}{\underset{1}{\cancel{5}}} \times \frac{\overset{5}{\cancel{25}}}{\underset{1}{\cancel{7}}} = \frac{35}{1} = 35$$

3. $45\frac{1}{2}$
4. $6\frac{3}{4}$
5. 14
6. $3\frac{2}{5}$
7. $32\frac{2}{3}$
8. 11
9. $13\frac{2}{7}$
10. $4\frac{1}{9}$
11. $10\frac{4}{5}$
12. $3\frac{9}{10}$
13. $47\frac{1}{2}$
14. $22\frac{10}{11}$
15. 78

Page 124

1. $5\frac{1}{4}$ ounces

$$1\frac{1}{2} \times 3\frac{1}{2} = \frac{3}{2} \times \frac{7}{2} = \frac{21}{4} = 5\frac{1}{4}$$

2. $4\frac{3}{8}$ cups

$$1\frac{1}{4} \times 3\frac{1}{2} = \frac{5}{4} \times \frac{7}{2} = \frac{35}{8} = 4\frac{3}{8}$$

3. $2\frac{5}{8}$ cups

$$\frac{3}{4} \times 3\frac{1}{2} = \frac{3}{4} \times \frac{7}{2} = \frac{21}{8} = 2\frac{5}{8}$$

4. $\frac{7}{16}$ teaspoon

$$\frac{1}{8} \times 3\frac{1}{2} = \frac{1}{8} \times \frac{7}{2} = \frac{7}{16}$$

5. $2\frac{1}{2}$ cups

$$\frac{1}{2} \times 5 = \frac{1}{2} \times \frac{5}{1} = \frac{5}{2} = 2\frac{1}{2}$$

6. $3\frac{3}{4}$ cups

$$\frac{3}{4} \times 5 = \frac{3}{4} \times \frac{5}{1} = \frac{15}{4} = 3\frac{3}{4}$$

Unit 4 Review, page 125

1. $\frac{2}{9}$
2. $\frac{1}{6}$
3. $\frac{1}{12}$
4. $\frac{3}{10}$
5. $\frac{5}{36}$
6. $\frac{16}{25}$
7. $\frac{35}{48}$
8. $\frac{7}{20}$
9. $\frac{1}{24}$
10. $\frac{9}{140}$
11. $\frac{3}{80}$
12. $\frac{1}{4}$

13. $\frac{1}{42}$
14. $\frac{4}{45}$
15. $\frac{1}{7}$
16. $\frac{2}{3}$
17. $\frac{1}{6}$
18. $\frac{1}{9}$
19. $\frac{3}{20}$
20. $\frac{3}{35}$
21. $\frac{1}{4}$
22. $\frac{1}{7}$
23. $\frac{1}{10}$
24. $\frac{2}{9}$
25. $\frac{1}{6}$
26. $\frac{1}{9}$
27. $\frac{1}{5}$
28. $\frac{3}{10}$
29. $\frac{2}{45}$
30. $\frac{1}{15}$
31. $\frac{5}{84}$
32. $\frac{5}{18}$
33. $\frac{3}{32}$
34. $\frac{1}{9}$
35. $\frac{7}{60}$

Page 126

36. 5
37. 8
38. 15
39. 24
40. $3\frac{1}{3}$
41. $1\frac{3}{4}$
42. $3\frac{3}{5}$
43. $5\frac{1}{2}$
44. 8
45. $2\frac{2}{3}$
46. 7
47. 10
48. $4\frac{1}{2}$
49. 34
50. $9\frac{1}{2}$
51. $34\frac{5}{7}$
52. $1\frac{2}{5}$
53. $1\frac{8}{27}$
54. $2\frac{11}{30}$
55. $1\frac{3}{11}$
56. $3\frac{1}{6}$
57. 14
58. $11\frac{1}{7}$
59. 8

Unit 5

Page 127

1. $\frac{2}{9}$
2. $\frac{4}{7}$

$$\frac{2}{3} \times \frac{\overset{3}{\cancel{6}}}{7} = \frac{4}{7}$$

3. $\frac{1}{2}$
4. $\frac{2}{3}$

5. $\frac{1}{12}$ 6. $\frac{1}{14}$

7. $\frac{11}{36}$ 8. $\frac{3}{7}$

9. $\frac{4}{35}$ 10. $\frac{4}{7}$

Page 128

11. 6

12. $4\frac{1}{4}$

$17 \times \frac{1}{4} = \frac{17}{1} \times \frac{1}{4} = \frac{17}{4} = 4\frac{1}{4}$

13. 30   14. 4

15. 9   16. 2

17. $\frac{4}{5}$ 18. $3\frac{1}{9}$

19. $5\frac{1}{6}$ 20. $2\frac{13}{14}$

21. 5

22. $2\frac{3}{5}$

$$\begin{array}{r} 2\ \frac{3}{5} \\ 5\overline{)13} \\ -10 \\ \hline 3 \end{array}$$

23. $5\frac{2}{3}$ 24. $3\frac{3}{4}$

25. 4   26. $5\frac{1}{6}$

27. $2\frac{1}{4}$ 28. $1\frac{1}{2}$

29. 2   30. 4

31. $\frac{1}{2}$

32. LT
3 and 8 cannot be divided evenly by any other number but 1.

33. $\frac{1}{3}$ 34. $\frac{1}{2}$

35. LT   36. $\frac{2}{5}$

37. $\frac{2}{3}$ 38. $\frac{3}{4}$

39. $\frac{3}{7}$ 40. $\frac{2}{3}$

41. $\frac{3}{2}$

42. $\frac{8}{3}$

Multiply the denominator, 3, by the whole number, 2. $3 \times 2 = 6$. Add 6 to the numerator. $6 + 2 = 8$. Write 8 over the denominator, 3.

43. $\frac{17}{4}$ 44. $\frac{17}{5}$

45. $\frac{43}{8}$

Page 129

1. 5

2. 6
Invert the fraction to the right of the division sign. Change the division sign to a multiplication sign. Multiply by the new fraction. Cancel. Change the answer to a whole number.

$$\frac{3}{4} \div \frac{1}{8} = \frac{3}{\cancel{4}_1} \times \frac{\cancel{8}^2}{1} = \frac{6}{1} = 6$$

3. 4   4. 2

5. 6   6. 14

7. 6   8. 9

9. 10   10. 4

Page 130

1. $1\frac{1}{4}$

2. $2\frac{2}{9}$
Invert the fraction to the right of the division sign. Multiply. Change the answer to a mixed number.

$$\frac{5}{9} \div \frac{1}{4} = \frac{5}{9} \times \frac{4}{1} = \frac{20}{9} = 2\frac{2}{9}$$

3. $1\frac{11}{21}$ 4. $1\frac{1}{5}$

5. $\frac{1}{2}$

6. $\frac{18}{25}$
Invert the fraction to the right of the division sign. Multiply. The answer is a fraction in lowest terms.

$$\frac{2}{5} \div \frac{5}{9} = \frac{2}{5} \times \frac{9}{5} = \frac{18}{25}$$

7. $\frac{3}{4}$ 8. $\frac{5}{7}$

9. $\frac{8}{9}$ 10. $2\frac{1}{4}$

11. $\frac{5}{6}$ 12. $4\frac{2}{3}$

13. $1\frac{9}{16}$ 14. $\frac{22}{25}$

15. $2\frac{1}{2}$ 16. $\frac{1}{2}$

17. 2 pieces
Divide $\frac{1}{2}$ by $\frac{1}{4}$. Invert the fraction to the right of the division sign. Cancel and multiply. Change the answer to a whole number.

$$\frac{1}{2} \div \frac{1}{4} = \frac{1}{\cancel{2}_1} \times \frac{\cancel{4}^2}{1} = \frac{2}{1} = 2$$

18. 3 pieces

Divide $\frac{1}{2}$ by $\frac{1}{6}$.

$\frac{1}{2} \div \frac{1}{6} = \frac{1}{2} \times \overset{3}{\cancel{\frac{6}{1}}} = \frac{3}{1} = 3$

Page 131

1. 4

2. 3

Change 1 to $\frac{1}{1}$. Invert $\frac{1}{3}$. Multiply the new fractions. Change the answer to a whole number.

$1 \div \frac{1}{3} = \frac{1}{1} \times \frac{3}{1} = \frac{3}{1} = 3$

3. 8   **4.** 18

5. 16   **6.** 25

7. 20   **8.** 24

9. 54   **10.** 14

11. 45   **12.** 48

13. 100   **14.** 40

Page 132

1. $7\frac{1}{2}$

2. $6\frac{2}{3}$

Change 5 to $\frac{5}{1}$. Invert $\frac{3}{4}$. Multiply. Change to a mixed number.

$5 \div \frac{3}{4} = \frac{5}{1} \times \frac{4}{3} = \frac{20}{3} = 6\frac{2}{3}$

3. 15   **4.** $10\frac{4}{5}$

5. 28   **6.** $15\frac{3}{4}$

7. 25   **8.** $14\frac{6}{7}$

9. 20   **10.** 60

11. 81   **12.** 33

13. 21   **14.** $9\frac{3}{5}$

15. 50   **16.** $17\frac{1}{3}$

17. 24 pieces

Divide 2 by $\frac{1}{12}$.

$2 \div \frac{1}{12} = \frac{2}{1} \times \frac{12}{1} = \frac{24}{1} = 24$

18. 18 pieces

Divide 2 by $\frac{1}{9}$.

$2 \div \frac{1}{9} = \frac{2}{1} \times \frac{9}{1} = \frac{18}{1} = 18$

Page 133

1. 4

---

2. 10

Change the mixed number to an improper fraction. Invert and multiply. Cancel. Change the answer to a whole number.

$2\frac{1}{2} \div \frac{1}{4} = \frac{5}{2} \times \overset{2}{\cancel{\frac{4}{1}}} = \frac{10}{1} = 10$

3. 14   **4.** 15

5. 21   **6.** 10

7. 23   **8.** 68

9. 49   **10.** 126

11. 36

Page 134

1. $6\frac{3}{4}$

2. $43\frac{1}{5}$

Change $5\frac{2}{5}$ to an improper fraction. Invert $\frac{1}{8}$ and multiply. Change the answer to a mixed number.

$5\frac{2}{5} \div \frac{1}{8} = \frac{27}{5} \times \frac{8}{1} = \frac{216}{5} = 43\frac{1}{5}$

3. $3\frac{5}{6}$ **4.** $18\frac{1}{3}$

5. $46\frac{2}{7}$ **6.** $48\frac{3}{5}$

7. $17\frac{1}{2}$ **8.** $2\frac{1}{32}$

9. $5\frac{7}{22}$ **10.** $31\frac{3}{4}$

11. $46\frac{1}{5}$ **12.** $153\frac{1}{2}$

13. $4\frac{2}{3}$ **14.** $9\frac{1}{6}$

15. $7\frac{5}{6}$ **16.** $3\frac{1}{45}$

17. $4\frac{2}{3}$ loaves

Divide $3\frac{1}{2}$ by $\frac{3}{4}$.

$3\frac{1}{2} \div \frac{3}{4} = \frac{7}{2} \div \frac{3}{4} = \overset{}{\cancel{\frac{7}{2}}} \times \overset{2}{\cancel{\frac{4}{3}}} = \frac{14}{3} = 2\frac{2}{3}$

18. $10\frac{2}{3}$ dozen

Divide $5\frac{1}{3}$ by $\frac{1}{2}$.

$5\frac{1}{3} \div \frac{1}{2} = \frac{16}{3} \div \frac{1}{2} = \frac{16}{3} \times \frac{2}{1} = \frac{32}{3} = 10\frac{2}{3}$

Page 135

1. 20 pieces

$10 \div \frac{1}{2} = \frac{10}{1} \times \frac{2}{1} = \frac{20}{1} = 20$

2. 72 packages

$18 \div \frac{1}{4} = \frac{18}{1} \times \frac{4}{1} = \frac{72}{1} = 72$

3. 8 packages

$$\frac{1}{2} \div \frac{1}{16} = \frac{1}{\cancel{2}} \times \frac{\cancel{16}^{8}}{1} = \frac{8}{1} = 8$$

4. 8 packages

$$1 \div \frac{1}{8} = \frac{1}{1} \div \frac{1}{8} = \frac{1}{1} \times \frac{8}{1} = \frac{8}{1} = 8$$

5. 7 packages; $\frac{7}{20}$ pound is left.

$$4\frac{9}{10} \div \frac{2}{3} = \frac{49}{10} \div \frac{2}{3} = \frac{49}{10} \times \frac{3}{2} = \frac{147}{20} = 7\frac{7}{20}$$

6. 34 packages; $\frac{1}{3}$ pound is left.

$$25\frac{3}{4} \div \frac{3}{4} = \frac{103}{4} \div \frac{3}{4} = \frac{103}{\cancel{4}} \times \frac{\cancel{4}^{1}}{3} = \frac{103}{3} = 34\frac{1}{3}$$

Page 136

1. 4

2. $\frac{5}{6}$

3. $\frac{3}{20}$

4. 4

5. $1\frac{1}{2}$

6. $\frac{19}{56}$

7. $\frac{1}{12}$

8. $\frac{1}{3}$

9. $\frac{1}{9}$

10. 1

11. $\frac{53}{60}$

12. $\frac{3}{8}$

13. $2\frac{2}{3}$

14. 6

15. $2\frac{8}{9}$

16. 27

17. $6\frac{1}{5}$

18. $6\frac{3}{7}$

19. $6\frac{2}{5}$

20. $8\frac{1}{3}$

21. 32

22. $17\frac{1}{7}$

23. $5\frac{1}{2}$

24. 48

25. 21

26. 2

27. $1\frac{5}{9}$

28. 38

29. $2\frac{19}{32}$

30. $1\frac{5}{8}$

31. $12\frac{1}{3}$

32. $32\frac{8}{15}$

33. 12

34. $2\frac{2}{7}$

35. $27\frac{13}{15}$

36. $6\frac{7}{18}$

Page 137

1. $\frac{1}{8}$

2. $\frac{3}{10}$

Change 2 to an improper fraction. Invert. Multiply.

$$\frac{3}{5} \div 2 = \frac{3}{5} \div \frac{2}{1} = \frac{3}{5} \times \frac{1}{2} = \frac{3}{10}$$

3. $\frac{1}{6}$

4. $\frac{1}{10}$

5. $\frac{1}{14}$

6. $\frac{1}{48}$

7. $\frac{1}{10}$

8. $\frac{2}{63}$

9. $\frac{1}{8}$

10. $\frac{7}{30}$

11. $\frac{1}{18}$

12. $\frac{5}{18}$

13. $\frac{4}{25}$

14. $\frac{1}{36}$

Page 138

1. $\frac{1}{3}$

2. $\frac{1}{8}$

Change 6 to an improper fraction. Invert and multiply. Cancel.

$$\frac{3}{4} \div 6 = \frac{3}{4} \div \frac{6}{1} = \frac{\cancel{3}^{1}}{4} \times \frac{1}{\cancel{6}_{2}} = \frac{1}{8}$$

3. $\frac{7}{40}$

4. $\frac{1}{18}$

5. $\frac{1}{7}$

6. $\frac{9}{40}$

7. $\frac{1}{24}$

8. $\frac{3}{16}$

9. $\frac{1}{11}$

10. $\frac{1}{20}$

11. $\frac{1}{42}$

12. $\frac{1}{24}$

13. $\frac{3}{8}$ pound

$$\frac{3}{4} \div 2 = \frac{3}{4} \div \frac{2}{1} = \frac{3}{4} \times \frac{1}{2} = \frac{3}{8}$$

14. $\frac{7}{24}$ yard

$$\frac{7}{8} \div 3 = \frac{7}{8} \div \frac{3}{1} = \frac{7}{8} \times \frac{1}{3} = \frac{7}{24}$$

Page 139

1. $2\frac{5}{24}$

2. $2\frac{5}{6}$

Change $5\frac{2}{3}$ to an improper fraction.

Change 2 to an improper fraction. Invert and multiply. Change to a mixed number.

$$5\frac{2}{3} \div 2 = \frac{17}{3} \div \frac{2}{1} = \frac{17}{3} \times \frac{1}{2} = \frac{17}{6} = 2\frac{5}{6}$$

3. $1\frac{16}{25}$

4. $1\frac{5}{21}$

5. $\frac{7}{8}$ **6.** $\frac{17}{42}$

7. $\frac{11}{18}$ **8.** $\frac{23}{24}$

9. $2\frac{9}{55}$ **10.** $1\frac{29}{96}$

11. $5\frac{1}{4}$ weeks

$$10\frac{1}{2} \div 2 = \frac{21}{2} \div \frac{2}{1} = \frac{21}{2} \times \frac{1}{2} = \frac{21}{4} = 5\frac{1}{4}$$

12. $4\frac{1}{4}$ weeks

$$12\frac{3}{4} \div 3 = \frac{51}{4} \div \frac{3}{1} = \frac{\overset{17}{\cancel{51}}}{4} \times \frac{1}{\cancel{3}} = \frac{17}{4} = 4\frac{1}{4}$$

Page 140

1. $3\frac{5}{7}$

2. $1\frac{15}{31}$

Change both mixed numbers to improper fractions. Invert and multiply. Cancel. Change to a mixed number.

$$7\frac{2}{3} \div 5\frac{1}{6} =$$

$$\frac{23}{3} \div \frac{31}{6} = \frac{23}{\cancel{3}} \times \frac{\overset{2}{\cancel{6}}}{31} = \frac{46}{31} = 1\frac{5}{31}$$

3. $2\frac{20}{33}$ **4.** $4\frac{2}{9}$

5. $\frac{85}{93}$ **6.** $\frac{60}{71}$

7. $\frac{48}{55}$ **8.** $5\frac{19}{21}$

9. 1   **10.** $1\frac{34}{35}$

11. 5 windows

$$18\frac{3}{4} \div 3\frac{3}{4} =$$

$$\frac{75}{4} \div \frac{15}{4} = \frac{\overset{5}{\cancel{75}}}{\cancel{4}} \times \frac{\overset{1}{\cancel{4}}}{\cancel{15}} = \frac{5}{1} = 5$$

12. 3 laps

$$7\frac{1}{2} \div 2\frac{1}{2} = \frac{15}{2} \div \frac{5}{2} = \frac{\overset{3}{\cancel{15}}}{\cancel{2}} \times \frac{\overset{1}{\cancel{2}}}{\cancel{5}} = \frac{3}{1} = 3$$

Page 141

1. 4 shelves

48 inches $\div 11\frac{1}{2}$ inches $=$

$$\frac{48}{1} \div \frac{23}{2} = \frac{48}{1} \times \frac{2}{23} = \frac{96}{23} = 4\frac{2}{43}$$

Hector will be able to put 4 whole shelves in the bookcase.

2. $\frac{5}{6}$ foot apart

$$6\frac{2}{3} \text{ feet} \div 8 = \frac{20}{3} \div \frac{8}{1} = \frac{\overset{5}{\cancel{20}}}{3} \times \frac{1}{\cancel{8}} = \frac{5}{6}$$

Page 142

3. 3 tops

12 feet $\div 3\frac{1}{2}$ feet $=$

$$\frac{12}{1} \div \frac{7}{2} = \frac{12}{1} \times \frac{2}{7} = \frac{24}{7} = 3\frac{3}{7}$$

He can cut 3 whole bookcase tops from one 12-foot board.

4. 2 sides

14 feet $\div 6\frac{2}{3}$ feet $=$

$$\frac{14}{1} \div \frac{20}{3} = \frac{\overset{7}{\cancel{14}}}{1} \times \frac{3}{\underset{10}{\cancel{20}}} = \frac{21}{10} = 2\frac{1}{10}$$

He can cut 2 complete sides from one 14-foot board.

5. 7 shelves

24 feet $\div 3\frac{5}{12}$ feet $=$

$$\frac{24}{1} \div \frac{41}{12} = \frac{24}{1} \times \frac{12}{41} = \frac{288}{41} = 7\frac{1}{41}$$

He can cut 7 whole shelves from one 24-foot board.

6. $1\frac{3}{4}$ feet

$3\frac{1}{2}$ feet $\div 2 =$

$$\frac{7}{2} \div \frac{2}{1} = \frac{7}{2} \times \frac{1}{2} = \frac{7}{4} = 1\frac{3}{4}$$

Unit 5 Review, page 143

1. $1\frac{1}{3}$ **2.** $\frac{1}{2}$

3. $\frac{9}{14}$ **4.** $1\frac{1}{9}$

5. $1\frac{5}{22}$ **6.** $3\frac{3}{4}$

7. 4   **8.** $\frac{1}{2}$

9. 8   **10.** 27

11. $9\frac{1}{3}$ **12.** $12\frac{1}{2}$

13. $21\frac{1}{3}$ **14.** 21

15. $14\frac{2}{5}$ **16.** 12

17. 11   **18.** $17\frac{1}{2}$

19. $9\frac{5}{6}$ **20.** $5\frac{3}{5}$

21. $29\frac{1}{2}$ **22.** $17\frac{1}{2}$

23. 107   **24.** $9\frac{1}{5}$

25. $\frac{1}{27}$ **26.** $\frac{3}{8}$

27. $\frac{1}{8}$ **28.** $\frac{1}{9}$

29. $\frac{9}{100}$ **30.** $\frac{5}{24}$

31. $\frac{1}{24}$ **32.** $\frac{1}{14}$

33. $\frac{2}{25}$ **34.** $\frac{2}{27}$

35. $\frac{4}{19}$ **36.** $\frac{3}{32}$

Page 144

37. $1\frac{3}{8}$ **38.** $\frac{1}{5}$

39. $2\frac{23}{27}$ **40.** $\frac{11}{15}$

41. $3\frac{11}{16}$ **42.** $1\frac{1}{20}$

43. $\frac{39}{40}$ **44.** $\frac{25}{48}$

45. $\frac{62}{123}$ **46.** $2\frac{19}{39}$

47. $1\frac{88}{185}$ **48.** $2\frac{1}{3}$

49. $4\frac{1}{33}$ **50.** $6\frac{1}{15}$

51. $8\frac{13}{16}$ **52.** $4\frac{17}{30}$

53. $1\frac{9}{13}$

Unit 6

Page 145

1. $1\frac{5}{12}$

2. $2\frac{1}{8}$

$$1\frac{5}{8}$$
$$+ \quad \frac{4}{8}$$
$$\overline{1\frac{9}{8} = 2\frac{1}{8}}$$

3. $14\frac{1}{6}$ **4.** $1\frac{31}{40}$

5. 5 **6.** 1

7. $3\frac{7}{20}$ **8.** $3\frac{1}{3}$

9. $11\frac{1}{8}$ **10.** $3\frac{2}{9}$

Page 146

11. $\frac{1}{2}$

12. $1\frac{1}{2}$

$$1\frac{2}{3} = 1\frac{4}{6}$$
$$- \quad \frac{1}{6} = \frac{1}{6}$$
$$\overline{1\frac{3}{6} = 1\frac{1}{2}}$$

13. $2\frac{3}{10}$ **14.** $\frac{5}{8}$

15. $\frac{3}{14}$ **16.** $\frac{3}{4}$

17. $6\frac{7}{12}$ **18.** $5\frac{3}{10}$

19. $1\frac{4}{5}$ **20.** $\frac{7}{20}$

21. $\frac{3}{10}$

22. $1\frac{2}{9}$

$$1\frac{3}{8} \times \frac{8}{9} = \frac{11}{\overset{1}{\cancel{8}}} \times \frac{\overset{1}{\cancel{8}}}{9} = \frac{11}{9} = 1\frac{2}{9}$$

23. $9\frac{2}{3}$ **24.** 3

25. $\frac{1}{6}$ **26.** $3\frac{5}{12}$

27. $20\frac{1}{2}$ **28.** $\frac{5}{24}$

29. 5

30. 40

$$8 \div \frac{1}{5} = \frac{8}{1} \times \frac{5}{1} = \frac{40}{1} = 40$$

31. $2\frac{5}{11}$ **32.** $\frac{51}{104}$

33. $3\frac{3}{5}$ **34.** $\frac{8}{15}$

35. $4\frac{2}{3}$ **36.** $1\frac{49}{51}$

Page 147

1. 18 inches

$$1\frac{1}{2} \times 12 = \frac{3}{\underset{1}{\cancel{2}}} \times \frac{\overset{6}{\cancel{12}}}{1} = \frac{18}{1} = 18$$

2. 440 yards

$$\frac{1}{4} \times 1{,}760 = \frac{1}{\underset{1}{\cancel{4}}} \times \frac{\overset{440}{\cancel{1760}}}{1} = \frac{440}{1} = 440$$

3. c, 11,880 feet

$$2\frac{1}{4} \times 5{,}280 = \frac{9}{\underset{1}{\cancel{4}}} \times \frac{\overset{1320}{\cancel{5280}}}{1} = \frac{11880}{1} = 11{,}880$$

4. b, 3,960 yards

$$2\frac{1}{4} \times 1{,}760 = \frac{9}{\underset{1}{\cancel{4}}} \times \frac{\overset{440}{\cancel{1760}}}{1} = \frac{3960}{1} = 3{,}960$$

Page 148

1. Crispy Cherry Bites cost more.

   $\frac{79}{10} = 7\frac{9}{10}$ cents

   $\frac{89}{11} = 8\frac{1}{11}$ cents

   $8\frac{1}{11} > 7\frac{9}{10}$

2. Red apples cost less.

   $\frac{99}{4} = 24\frac{3}{4}$ cents

   $\frac{69}{3} = 23$ cents

   $23 < 24\frac{3}{4}$

3. Meaty hot dogs cost less.

   $\frac{6}{7} = \frac{36}{42}$

   $\frac{5}{6} = \frac{35}{42}$

   $\frac{35}{42} < \frac{36}{42}$

4. Squeezy costs more.

   $\frac{2}{3} = \frac{16}{24}$

   $\frac{6}{8} = \frac{18}{24}$

   $\frac{18}{24} > \frac{16}{24}$

Page 149

1. $1\frac{3}{4}$ points

$$13\frac{1}{4} = 13\frac{1}{4} = 12\frac{5}{4}$$
$$-11\frac{1}{2} = 11\frac{2}{4} = 11\frac{2}{4}$$
$$1\frac{3}{4}$$

2. $1\frac{1}{2}$ points

$$12\frac{3}{8} = 11\frac{11}{8}$$
$$-10\frac{7}{8} = 10\frac{7}{8}$$
$$1\frac{4}{8} = 1\frac{1}{2}$$

3. c, $265

$$20 \times 13\frac{1}{4} = \frac{\overset{5}{\cancel{20}}}{1} \times \frac{53}{\cancel{4}_1} = \$265$$

4. a, $15\frac{7}{8}$

$$14\frac{3}{4} = 14\frac{6}{8}$$
$$+ 1\frac{1}{8} = 1\frac{1}{8}$$
$$15\frac{7}{8}$$

Page 150

1. He needs 1 more quart.

   $\frac{1}{2} \times 4 = \frac{1}{\cancel{2}_1} \times \frac{\overset{2}{\cancel{4}}}{1} = \frac{2}{1} = 2$ quarts

   2 quarts − 1 quart = 1 quart

2. He needs 2 more quarts.

   $3\frac{1}{2} \times 4 = \frac{7}{\cancel{2}_1} \times \frac{\overset{2}{\cancel{4}}}{1} = \frac{14}{1} = 14$ quarts

   14 − 12 = 2 quarts

3. Dawn needs 2 more cups.

   $\frac{1}{2} \times 2 = \frac{1}{\cancel{2}_1} \times \frac{\overset{1}{\cancel{2}}}{1} = \frac{1}{1} = 1$ cup

   3 − 1 = 2 cups

4. 3 quarts

   $\frac{1}{2} \times 4 = \frac{1}{\cancel{2}_1} \times \frac{\overset{2}{\cancel{4}}}{1} = \frac{2}{1} = 2$ quarts

   2 + 1 = 3 quarts

Page 151

5. 22 pints

   $20 \times \frac{1}{2} = \frac{\overset{10}{\cancel{20}}}{1} \times \frac{1}{\cancel{2}_1} = \frac{10}{1} = 10$ pints

   12 + 10 = 22 pints

6. $1\frac{1}{2}$ cups

   $24 \div 8 = 3$ cups

$$3 = 2\frac{2}{2}$$
$$-1\frac{1}{2} = 1\frac{1}{2}$$
$$1\frac{1}{2} \text{ cups}$$

7. 36 ounces

   $3 \times 1\frac{1}{2} = \frac{3}{1} \times \frac{3}{2} = \frac{9}{2} = 4\frac{1}{2}$ cups

   $4\frac{1}{2} \times 8 = \frac{9}{\cancel{2}_1} \times \frac{\overset{4}{\cancel{8}}}{1} = \frac{36}{1} = 36$ ounces

8. $\frac{1}{4}$ cup or 2 ounces

$2 \times 8 = 16$ ounces

$16 \div 8 = 2$ cups

$\begin{aligned} 2 \quad &= 1\frac{4}{4} \\ -\ 1\frac{3}{4} &= 1\frac{3}{4} \\ \hline &\quad\ \frac{1}{4}\ \text{cup} \end{aligned}$

or

$1\frac{3}{4} \times 8 = \frac{7}{\cancel{4}} \times \frac{\overset{2}{\cancel{8}}}{1} = \frac{14}{1} = 14$ ounces

$16 - 14 = 2$ ounces

9. 8 servings

$32 \div 8 = 4$ cups

$4 \div \frac{1}{2} = \frac{4}{1} \div \frac{1}{2} = \frac{4}{1} \times \frac{2}{1} = \frac{8}{1} = 8$

10. 6 rooms

$2\frac{1}{2} \times 4 = \frac{5}{\cancel{2}} \times \frac{\overset{2}{\cancel{4}}}{1} = \frac{10}{1} = 10$ quarts

$10 \div 1\frac{2}{3} = \frac{10}{1} \div \frac{5}{3} = \frac{\overset{2}{\cancel{10}}}{1} \times \frac{3}{\cancel{5}} = \frac{6}{1} = 6$

11. 11 pots of coffee

$22 \div 8 = \frac{22}{1} \div \frac{8}{1} = \frac{\overset{11}{\cancel{22}}}{1} \times \frac{1}{\underset{4}{\cancel{8}}} = \frac{11}{4} =$

$2\frac{3}{4}$ cups

$2\frac{3}{4} \div \frac{1}{4} = \frac{11}{\cancel{4}} \times \frac{\overset{1}{\cancel{4}}}{1} = \frac{11}{1} = 11$

12. 12 servings

$1\frac{1}{2}$ quarts $\times 2 = \frac{3}{\cancel{2}} \times \frac{\overset{1}{\cancel{2}}}{1} = 3$ pints

3 pints $\times 2$ cups $= 6$ cups

$6 \div \frac{1}{2} = \frac{6}{1} \times \frac{2}{1} = \frac{12}{1} = 12$

Page 153

1. 10 pounds

$\frac{20}{4} = \frac{?}{2}$

$\frac{20}{4} = \frac{20 \div 2}{4 \div 2} = \frac{10}{2}$

2. 2 pounds

$\frac{4}{2} = \frac{?}{1}$

$\frac{4}{2} = \frac{4 \div 2}{2 \div 2} = \frac{2}{1}$

3. $6

$\frac{2}{3} = \frac{4}{?}$

$\frac{2}{3} = \frac{2 \times 2}{3 \times 2} = \frac{4}{6}$

4. $15

$\frac{2}{5} = \frac{6}{?}$

$\frac{2}{5} = \frac{2 \times 3}{5 \times 3} = \frac{6}{15}$

5. $12

$\frac{5}{4} = \frac{15}{?}$

$\frac{5}{4} = \frac{5 \times 3}{4 \times 3} = \frac{15}{12}$

6. 6 pies

$\frac{3}{10} = \frac{?}{20}$

$\frac{3}{10} = \frac{3 \times 2}{10 \times 2} = \frac{6}{20}$

7. 4 pounds

$\frac{1}{2} = \frac{8}{?}$

$\frac{1}{2} = \frac{1 \times 4}{2 \times 4} = \frac{4}{8}$

8. $10

$\frac{3}{5} = \frac{6}{?}$

$\frac{3}{5} = \frac{3 \times 2}{5 \times 2} = \frac{6}{10}$

9. $2

$\frac{6}{4} = \frac{3}{?}$

$\frac{6}{4} = \frac{6 \times 2}{4 \times 2} = \frac{2}{1}$

10. 9 pints

$\frac{3}{4} = \frac{?}{13}$

$\frac{3}{4} = \frac{3 \div 3}{4 \div 3} = \frac{9}{12}$

11. $2

$\frac{3}{1} = \frac{6}{?}$

$\frac{3}{1} = \frac{3 \times 2}{1 \times 2} = \frac{6}{2}$

12. $6

$3 \times 12 = 36$

$\frac{6}{1} = \frac{36}{?}$

$\frac{6}{1} = \frac{6 \times 6}{1 \times 6} = \frac{36}{6}$

1. $3\frac{1}{2}$ hours

11 hours 30 minutes
− 8 hours 0 minutes
3 hours 30 minutes $= 3\frac{30}{60} = 3\frac{1}{2}$

2. $4\frac{1}{2}$ hours

12 hours 30 minutes
− 8 hours 0 minutes
4 hours 30 minutes $= 4\frac{30}{60} = 4\frac{1}{2}$

3. $2\frac{1}{4}$ hours

3 hours 45 minutes
− 1 hour 30 minutes
2 hours 15 minutes $= 2\frac{15}{60} = 2\frac{1}{4}$

4. $5\frac{1}{2}$ hours

11 hours 30 minutes
− 6 hours 0 minutes
5 hours 30 minutes $= 5\frac{30}{60} = 5\frac{1}{2}$

5. $3\frac{1}{2}$ hours

6 hours 45 minutes
− 3 hours 15 minutes
3 hours 30 minutes $= 3\frac{30}{60} = 3\frac{1}{2}$

6. 3 hours

6 hours 30 minutes
− 3 hours 30 minutes
3 hours 0 minutes

7. $17

$4 \times 4\frac{1}{4} = \frac{\cancel{4}^{1}}{1} \times \frac{17}{\cancel{4}_{1}} = \frac{17}{1} = 17

8. $2\frac{3}{4}$ hours, $11

3 hours 45 minutes
− 1 hour 0 minutes
2 hours 45 minutes $= 2\frac{45}{60} = 2\frac{3}{4}$

$4 \times 2\frac{3}{4} = \frac{\cancel{4}^{1}}{1} \times \frac{11}{\cancel{4}_{1}} = \frac{11}{1} = 11

Child	Mon.	Tues.	Wed.	Thurs.	Fri.
Teddy	7:30-11:45	8-11:30	Sick	Sick	8-12:30
Peter H.	1-3:45	12:30-6:30	1:15-5:30	2-6:30	—
Susie	5:30-10:45	—	6-11:30	—	5:45-10:45
Peter W.	—	—	—	1:30-3:45	—
Hannah	3:15-6:45	—	—	—	3:30-6:30

Page 156

1. $\frac{1}{2}$ **2.** $\frac{1}{4}$

3. LT   **4.** $\frac{3}{4}$

5. $\frac{2}{3}$ **6.** $\frac{4}{12}$

7. $\frac{6}{21}$ **8.** $\frac{5}{10}$

9. $\frac{16}{20}$ **10.** $\frac{20}{32}$

11. $1\frac{1}{4}$ **12.** 2

13. $2\frac{1}{7}$ **14.** 4

15. $2\frac{1}{10}$ **16.** $\frac{12}{5}$

17. $\frac{10}{3}$ **18.** $\frac{23}{4}$

19. $\frac{11}{9}$ **20.** $\frac{97}{12}$

21. $\frac{1}{2}$ **22.** 1

23. $1\frac{1}{2}$ **24.** $1\frac{1}{8}$

25. $4\frac{6}{7}$ **26.** $10\frac{2}{5}$

27. $13\frac{1}{3}$ **28.** 6

29. $7\frac{3}{4}$ **30.** $\frac{1}{2}$

31. $\frac{17}{20}$ **32.** $\frac{5}{7}$

33. $\frac{37}{40}$ **34.** $1\frac{11}{36}$

Page 157

35. $8\frac{1}{21}$ **36.** $10\frac{3}{8}$

37. $14\frac{1}{7}$ **38.** $15\frac{19}{20}$

39. $5\frac{23}{24}$ **40.** $\frac{1}{2}$

41. $\frac{4}{9}$ **42.** 0

43. $\frac{3}{5}$ **44.** $6\frac{2}{3}$

45. $6\frac{2}{5}$ **46.** $4\frac{1}{2}$

47. $2\frac{2}{5}$ **48.** $6\frac{10}{21}$

49. $\frac{5}{7}$ **50.** $4\frac{7}{9}$

51. $6\frac{2}{5}$ **52.** $1\frac{3}{4}$

53. $\frac{5}{6}$ **54.** $\frac{1}{2}$

55. $\frac{1}{6}$ **56.** $\frac{23}{40}$

57. $\frac{17}{28}$ **58.** $\frac{2}{15}$

59. $3\frac{1}{9}$ **60.** $8\frac{31}{35}$

61. $3\frac{9}{16}$ **62.** $\frac{11}{12}$

Page 158

63. $\frac{1}{5}$ **64.** $\frac{1}{4}$

65. $\frac{3}{14}$ **66.** $\frac{2}{15}$

67. 2   **68.** $2\frac{2}{3}$

69. 32   **70.** $6\frac{3}{7}$

71. $3\frac{1}{2}$ **72.** $2\frac{1}{4}$

73. 13   **74.** $7\frac{4}{5}$

75. 3   **76.** $1\frac{1}{3}$

77. $\frac{50}{81}$ **78.** $2\frac{1}{3}$

79. 16   **80.** 42

81. $12\frac{2}{5}$ **82.** $8\frac{1}{2}$

83. $\frac{1}{3}$ **84.** $\frac{1}{25}$

85. $\frac{17}{27}$ **86.** $2\frac{1}{12}$

87. $2\frac{1}{10}$ **88.** 2

89. $\frac{3}{7}$ **90.** $7\frac{11}{13}$